A sociology of the mentally disordered offender

Tom Mason and Dave Mercer

LONGMAN
London and New York

Pearson Education Limited
Edinburgh Gate
Harlow
Essex CM20 2JE
England
and Associated Companies throughout the world

Published in the United States of America
by Pearson Education Inc., New York

Visit us on the world wide web at:
http://www.awl-he.com

First published 1999

ISBN 0 582 31741 X

British Library Cataloguing-in-Publication Data

A catalogue record for this book is available from the British Library

Library of Congress Cataloging-in-Publication Data

Mason, Tom, 1950–
    A sociology of the mentally disordered offender / Tom Mason and
Dave Mercer.
        p.   cm.
    Includes bibliographical references and index.
    ISBN 0–582–31741–X   (pbk.)
        1. Mentally handicapped offenders—United States—Psychology.
2. Mentally handicapped offenders—Services for—United States.
3. Mentally handicapped and crime—United States.   I. Mercer,
Dave, 1957– . II. Title.
HV6791.M365   1999
364.3—dc21   98–51542
                                                                         CIP

Typeset by 35 in 10/12pt New Baskerville
Printed in Malaysia, PP

A sociology of the mentally disordered offender

We would like to dedicate this book to our good friend and mentor Professor Joel Richman. Not that this book is worthy of him but that he taught us not to be afraid of our own ideas and to fight every inch of the way. Surrender is not an option.

Contents

Preface

Having worked in clinical practice, education and research for a quarter of a century with mentally disordered offenders we have come to realise that traditional perspectives in psychiatry and psychology are but attempts to understand difficult issues in this highly complex field of practice. Whilst not dismissing the role that these approaches offer we now conclude that they are both limited, and limiting, unless we have the courage to break out of their bondage and search for differing realities. This current project was born in the dark tunnel between Moorfields and Sandhills whilst travelling on the underground train in Liverpool, UK when bursting into the daylight the idea came to us. The mentally disordered offender is socially constructed from a fusion of psychiatry and criminality, from a merging of mental disorder and crime, and from a melding of the pathology of the monstrous with the symbolics of the soul. We cannot explain the extremes of human behaviour without using as a reference point, or anchorage, other human spirits, and only when we achieve this relational perspective can we hope to fathom the depths of depravity to which a few plummet. This sociological view allows us to glimpse into our own psyche and create meaning through its association with the social body.

Not being sociologists, in an academic sense, we do not claim the grand mastery of their professional conceptual frameworks, but having long been keen students of sociology we have learnt to scratch beneath the veneer and to penetrate the masks of pretence to search for differing levels of meaning. We are aware that the acquisition, and exercise, of power lies at the core of the 'forensic' enterprise by all professional groups (but not necessarily to the same extent by all individuals within them) and that the mentally disordered offender is used as a pawn in their game. In this current project we have attempted to reveal some, but by no means all, of the contradictions, tensions, and dilemmas that litter the conflict zone between forensic psychiatry and society. In this we have probably done sociology a disservice and for that we apologise; we may have done psychology some mischief but that is not deliberate; and we hope that we have done psychiatry a favour but expect that they will miss the point.

Chapter 1

Introduction

In attempting to establish a sociological understanding of the mentally disordered offender, contextualised within society, we need to investigate three fundamental areas of our social fabric. Firstly, we need to analyse crime. We need to know as much of our fascination for it as our fear of it. We need to be equally aware of our attempts to control it, as we are regarding our role in producing it. And, whilst we will concentrate on our abhorrence of crime, we must not forget our desire to be a part of it. Secondly, it will be required of us to address the nature of mental abnormality, its construction and function. We will need to assess our perceptions, beliefs, and prejudices in relation to its uses and abuses in social terms. It will be required of us to understand the vested interests in relation to the sphere of mental disorder and analyse the affiliations of power that are constructed to manage it. Thirdly, we must attempt to penetrate that, as yet, veiled area that lies between crime and mental disorder, the social domain in which resides the mentally disordered offender. There are few signposts in this area and so we must navigate carefully.

Furthermore, we will need to draw on the relations between all three provinces and meticulously analyse the structural processes that draw them together. It will be our task to identify the sources and mechanics of these arrangements and to build our thesis carefully, step by analytical step. We will need to understand the processes by which the mentally disordered offender is constructed from the domains of law and psychiatry and also to investigate the social structures by which the mechanics effect this construction, and derive their driving force. There is little doubt at the outset of this project that we will need to employ different strategies and focus on novel aspects of our social lives in order to make visible a sociology of the mentally disordered offender.

What becomes apparent in building this thesis is the extent of binary opposition usage. The discourse of opposites, conflicts, contradictions, tensions, and dilemmas, are strewn throughout the text. Words such as paradoxes, solutions, and dialectics are peppered within the manuscript, just as phrases such as 'on the other hand', 'alternatively', and 'so too' appear to counter balance every argument. This is significant because the very nature of the mentally disordered offender lies *between*; namely, the law and psychiatry. The nature of our work is, thus, to draw from these two domains and create a third arena, the middle-ground, which inevitably must be qualified with counter proposals.

Setting the scene

Mankind has always found crime a fascinating topic, and in both primeval and mythological terms it has lain at the heart and soul of generic man. We are, both, intrigued and horrified by heinous offenses and, both, attracted and repulsed by them. Severe criminal acts are often termed 'sick' and sometimes 'evil' with calls for their perpetrators to be incarcerated, or in some countries to be put to death. Crime features large, to one degree or another, in the vast majority of news broadcasts as well as newspaper reports. Succeeding generations of adults testify to the passing of safer bygone days when one could leave one's back door open, or allow children to play in the street with relative impunity. Yet, historical analysis reveals a different story.

Crime is both popular and popularised. There are many examples in folklore, on television, and in the cinema regarding the hero villain. For example, Robin Hood, Dick Turpin, The Godfather, Butch Cassidy, Smith and Jones, to name but a few of the fashionable lawbreakers that inverse our repulsion of offenders to become the likeable rogue. These offenders receive a social legitimation by targeting their malfeasance against institutions or organisations rather than becoming a direct threat to the individual within the social realm. What each of these hero villains have in common is a focus on the social. By this, it is meant that they each aspire to succumb to, and reinforce the values of the society in which they are located. They are somewhat marginalised but appear to manifest a motivation to be a part of that family, community, and society that they are at odds with. Their transgressions are mitigated by a process of locating their offenses into picayune proportions by the use of 'charitable status' (robbing from the rich to give to the poor), 'peer target specificity' (crimes committed only against other criminals or the rich), or 'penance' (amnesty following a period of atonement). These states have their counterparts in contemporary criminal times in the many burglars who claim only to steal from 'wealthy' houses, and such as the Kray twins who reportedly only targeted their violence on their own criminal fraternity, and Myra Hindley who returned to the Catholic faith in imprisonment and now claims she was led astray by her lover, Brady.

There are also hero detectives that battle against the criminal on the side of righteous law and order, for example, Sherlock Holmes, Columbo, Hawaii Five O, Starsky and Hutch, Kojak, and the more recent Power Rangers. These heroes do battle against the bad and the mad, usually in the arena of crimes against individuals: murder, sex offenses, drug abuse, and so on. Rarely, if at all, does white-collar crime feature on the screen. Dirty Harry does not track down a Nick Leeson, the British Baring Bank employee who lost millions on the stock market causing the collapse of the Bank and losing vast sums of money for individual stock holders. Nor does Bruce Willis investigate a Robert Maxwell fraudulently mis-managing pension funds. The story of these hero-cops are against the crazed psychopathic type or the professional gang of criminals. In both, there is a direct threat of harm to innocent others which must be rescued by the police. The crimes of Nick Leeson and Robert Maxwell were not of this ilk.

Mental disorder, too, is part of the social. In that, insanity requires the plurality of sanity by which it can be judged. When the 'abnormality' is clearly perceived as stark madness, or profound intellectual incapacity evinced by irrationality, or grotesque deformity as manifest incoherence, then the person thus afflicted is not held responsible for his or her actions. The explicit social value is compassion albeit that the implicit motivation may well be institutionalisation, incarceration, marginalisation, and separation. However, when that 'abnormality' is comprehended within a framework of rational action as in psychopathic disorder, personality defects, or merely neurotic, then the person is generally perceived as culpable and responsible for their actions. The location of this responsibility is a central issue within the social construction of the mentally disordered offender.

Now, when the two, the lawbreaker and the mentally disordered, are drawn together in the event of a crime, *the mentally disordered offender* becomes the epitome of social dangerousness, on both counts. The offence and the mental aberration become the focus of one narrative. A complex interplay of social forces are mobilised to account for the Act, and its consequences. These can range from the use of descriptors such as 'sick' or 'evil' with their concomitants of disgust and dismissal which socially allow for any form of disposal, and the use of prescriptors such as 'throw away the key' or 'hang them'. Furthermore, this social dispute is carried over into the professional domains of law and medicine with both groups claiming the criminal as their territory.

Breaking norms – making crime

Hobbes (1968) informs us that if man (generic) is left in a natural uncontrolled state, life would be 'nasty, brutish, and short'. By this he was arguing that individuals tend to bond together to form groups, clans, tribes, and societies, which is a natural process by which social controls are introduced in order for protection and survival. This is a trade off of freedom for longevity. Such rule formation is seen in many groups of people, sometimes formalised but often merely implicitly held. In any event, they are espoused and legitimated by members of that group. This rule formation can be said to fall into three general areas; laws, norms, and values. Laws are commonly interpreted as formal rules of a society and are usually written down as statute. They can differ from society to society and change and adapt within groups. An example of such a law is bigamy, which in some countries is illegal but expected in others. Norms, on the other hand, are largely informal rules, unwritten, and serve to represent a good standard for the particular group establishing them. Examples of this can range from behaviours concerned with table manners to behaviours concerned with gang membership. Values relate to what a society, or group, considers to be worthwhile, good, desirable, and important. Again, this can range from eating with the right soup spoon to not 'grassing' on fellow gang members.

The transgression of a formal rule, known as a law, is a crime and at this level is relatively easily defined. However, it is not always as simple as this. Crime is a dynamic concept and not a static one. Laws are constantly changing, evolving, being formed, and being abolished; and they are always relative to the particular society that upholds them. What is a crime in one society is not necessarily a crime in another (Marsh, 1986). The breaking of a law may or may not lead to prosecution as there are many factors that converge to uphold a decision one way or the other. These factors include the severity of the offence, the previous record of the perpetrator, the producibility of reliable evidence at the trial, the chances of a conviction, the public response, media attention, and so on. The convergence of these factors can be summarised as a social tension. That is, the extent to which the crime committed has damaged the social cohesion, the fabric, of that society. The outrage of the public, the media, and sometimes the judge in his sentencing speech are representative of the social abomination of the crime.

Before moving on to those offenders who are deemed mentally aberrant we should mention that social intermediary between the 'straight' criminal and the mentally disordered offender, namely the deviant. Deviancy can mean anything akin to eccentricity or merely behaviour that differs from the norm and is unusual (Marsh, 1986). It can mean bizarre or unconventional, or perverse and perverted. However, more commonly, deviancy is understood as rule breaking behaviour which is sanctionable as it transgresses the law, the social code, or moral sensitivities. Again, it is the social reaction that gives deviancy its defining quality. As Marsh (1986) puts it: 'for an action to be deviant it has to cause some form of critical reaction and disapproval from others . . . no action is deviant in itself: it has to excite some reaction from others' (p. 4). Therefore, deviancy must be understood, in part, as a social phenomenon rather than a psychological or biological one. One cannot be deviant alone on an island.

Mental abnormality often receives a reductionist approach in attempting to classify it. For example, the Mental Health Act (HMSO, 1983) identifies the four categories of (a) mental illness, (b) psychopathic disorder, (c) mental impairment, and (d) severe mental impairment. The Diagnostic and Statistical Manual, fourth edition (DSM IV) is an extensive classificatory system based on the work of the American Psychiatric Association (APA, 1994) and involves a multiaxial assessment on five axes. These axes refer to a sphere of data which contribute to an overall plan of treatment. Axes four and five begin to explore the nature of the patients' problem in relation to the social domain but there is little conceptual development regarding social theory. The ICD 10 is another classificatory system based on the work of the World Health Organisation (WHO, 1992) and is equally sparse on social dimensions although it provides a detailed breakdown of mental and behavioural disorders.

These classificatory systems are merely lego-nosological and are relatively meaningless in sociological terms. Society, generally, is concerned with those people who are considered irrational, uncontrolled, irresponsible, and dangerous. It is the extent to which their mental aberration is a danger to other members of that society that defines their categorisation. Furthermore, this defining quality has a prescriptive element based on the extent to which the person is considered to 'know what they are doing'. This then, in lay terms, establishes culpability outside of the legal constraints and provides, as a corollary, a 'sentence'. For example, the psychopathic teenager sex offender in society's eyes is viewed very different from the mentally impaired adolescent who cannot control his sexual urges. What now comes into view is the many 'shades of grey' in between these extreme cases that causes such social upheaval when the criminal becomes the mentally disordered offender, and society is looking where to attach the blame.

Harm and the social

Typically, the standard texts on harm and injury caused by psychiatric populations are divided into (a) the harm to self and (b) the harm to others, with scant reference paid to the social impact of such harm. Whilst not wishing to dilute the individual and personalised pain and tragedy that both these foci of harm can engender there is the added dimension of the social to consider. Harm to the self creates a different social tension to the harm caused to others. Furthermore, we can delineate a direct harm to the social by the actions of mentally disordered offenders at large in the community. Although qualitatively different there is the harm to the social whilst the offender is engaged in criminal acts and there is the harm created whilst the offender is being managed in the community but is criminally dormant (note, for example, the release of the convicted sex offender, Sidney Cook, in the South West of England in 1998).

Harming oneself is a personal prerogative of us all. Those who choose to smoke and drink alcohol are clearly putting themselves at risk to one degree or another. Yet, this is socially acceptable when it is perceived that it is not taken to excess. However, deliberate self-harm in the form of direct injury, such as cutting and stabbing oneself, disturbs the social by breaking the body imagery of completeness and wholeness. A tension is created by such harm loosening the bond between that individual and the community. The damage to self equates with damage to the group. It appears that the visibility of the harm disturbs our sensibilities more so than the hidden dangers of, say, someone poisoning themselves from the inside. The disfigurement becomes an increased stigma (Goffman, 1963). The ultimate harm to the self, suicide, which has only relatively recently shed its illegal status, is closely related to social disorganisation. The suicide represents a statement regarding the lack of social community and suggests a lack of group belongingness. It is, perhaps, not surprising that high suicide rates are correlated with areas of high crime and unemployment, both being strong social arenas loaded with expectations of status and acquisition.

Harm to others can be sub-categorised into psychological or emotional trauma, physical or biological damage, and financial or economic injury. Possibly, there is no other sphere of human operations that has exercised ingenuity to the same degree than man's inhumanity to man. The ways in which harm can be inflicted on another knows no limitations and can be both direct as in face-to-face encounters or indirect as in arson attacks. Such reductionist approaches are unhelpful to us in developing a sociology of the mentally disordered offender as there are, clearly, considerable areas of overlap that affect not only the victims themselves but also their family, friends, and community. The physical harm to one person can create emotional trauma in a related other, and, perhaps, a financial burden in, say, the direct family through loss of earnings.

The mentally disordered offender causes harm to the social through the perception of threat and the construction of dangerousness. By galvanising fear the social order is disturbed to the extent that its operational functions are altered. An example of this is when a society is terrorised by serial offenders such as the 'Yorkshire Ripper' or the 'Black Panther' in which communities were forced to change their behaviours to safeguard against the threat of attack.

Although, as we will see, certain sociologies, such as functionalism, suggest that crime fulfils a role in society, or at least can be understood in terms of the part it plays, the offender who is also mentally disordered disrupts this state. Crime usually has a logic of acquisition and gain, of *something* which non-criminal members of society can understand. Mentally disordered offenders evoke the perception of irrationality in their criminal activity and produce a belief in a twisted logic which defies 'normal' comprehension. This is fear provoking to a society that relies on order, even within its criminal activity, rather than disorder.

Vulnerability

Vulnerability is a broad conceptual area that is highly relevant for a sociology of the mentally disordered offender. In understanding this importance it is necessary to focus on its opposite relation, *imperviousness*, which suggests an element of safety. In this latter mode any disaster to befall an individual is unlikely whereas in relation to the notion of vulnerability we can see that an individual or group becomes more at risk than others. A further dimension is located between those vulnerable individuals or groups who are at greater risk because they place themselves, for whatever reason, in areas of increased danger (for example, prostitutes) and those whose inherent individual state puts them at risk (for example, children). Vulnerability, therefore, has several dimensions.

There are individuals who are vulnerable. These may be young children and babies who can be harmed by mentally disordered offenders through abuse or neglect, or they may be young girls and boys snatched by sex offenders. This vulnerable group cause great social disquiet when a victim is created through the actions of a mentally disordered person. Other groups include the elderly who are often the victim of burglary, muggings, and even rape. They evoke a strong public reaction when victimised by offenders. Women, too, are seen as vulnerable with an increased reporting of sex attacks and stalking. An ethnic minority in a larger racial density are vulnerable to discrimination both in terms of covert prejudice against them and overt physical attack. Other groups deemed vulnerable would include ministers of religion and voluntary workers operating in the community as well as famous personalities who become the target of fixated individuals. All these groups are considered susceptible to harm, to one degree or another, with a social understanding that their vulnerability is in no way their fault. However, there are some individuals and groups in society who are considered to be exposed but also largely to be blamed for this state of affairs.

An obvious group of vulnerable people are prostitutes, but they are often trivialised when they are recipients of violent action being referred to as *only* prostitutes or not *decent girls* (Beattie, 1981). The reasons for their resorting to prostitution are often overlooked and the focus is usually centred on questions of morality, the prostitutes morality that is, and not the morality of their customers. By the nature of their job the police, too, are a vulnerable group who are considered to be, in part, responsible for their susceptibility. As upholders of the law they inevitably face the dangers of criminal activity and frequently come under attack from many sources. However, as most police choose their occupation they are considered responsible for putting themselves at risk, although, there is usually considerable social outrage when a police officer is harmed in the course of their duty. A similar situation is when health professionals, for example social workers, G.P.s, psychiatrists, psychologists, and nurses, who are also vulnerable groups, are injured or killed by mentally disordered offenders.

The mentally disordered themselves are also vulnerable (Gudjonsson, 1994; 1995). It is clear that many individuals with varying degrees of mental disorder can become offenders as well as victims. Those with mental illnesses and learning disabilities, who become caught up in the criminal justice system are often at risk because of their impaired functioning (Bull and Cullen, 1992). Subject to intense police interrogation they can be the victim of leading questions, be easily led, be highly suggestible, and provide false confessions (Gudjonsson, 1992). Their vulnerability can also extend to issues regarding their credibility in providing testimony or even as witnesses themselves in court (Gudjonsson, 1995).

Vulnerability, therefore, has serious social ramifications for the mentally disordered offender. Although individuals or groups can be identified as at risk, it is the individual or group *within* a wider community that provides the social relations of fear and outrage when the vulnerable are offended against.

The structure of the book

Chapter 2 presents a theoretical overview of the sociology of crime, deviance, and difference. It is argued that the rise, and subsequent fall, of deviance as an academic subject paved the way for the emergence of the mentally disordered offender as an intellectual field of study. The notion of difference inverted following the post-second world war years with the revelations of the holocaust and the dropping of the atom bomb by the allies. Right and wrong became twisted ideologies in which 'them' and 'us' became blurred concepts, the postmodern inversions allowing for all manner of alternative interpretations. Thus, as deviance died, the mentally disordered offender was born. The relationship between crime and mental disorder is the focus of chapter 3 in which we deal with the traditional approaches attempting to understand this phenomenon. The search for mental disorder in criminal populations, and the search for criminal behaviour in psychiatric populations are laid bare and the argument is posed that the true nature of this relationship is social. Through the medicalisation process we note how the mentally disordered offender has been brought under the psychiatric rubric through what Foucault (1978) termed the 'pathology of the monstrous'. In chapter 4 we discuss how the social impact of crimes can impinge on professional practice and cause pressures to respond in different ways, to different offenders, and in different times. We will set out a number of sensational cases of recent years that have contributed in shaping public reaction, and professional response, to such heinous crimes resulting in a contentious debate regarding the status of the offender's mental health and their culpability.

Chapters 5 and 6 will deal with the developing system of forensic services that have resulted from the massive expansion in this sapling discipline. The penetration of psychiatry into the domain of the court and prison has incorporated the criminal ever more under the influence of medicine. The major thrust of risk assessment is discussed in chapter 5 which lies at the heart of forensic services, and which is also its achilles heal should things go wrong. Chapter 6 augments the service development with the notion of institutional arrangements for policing the social body with the growth in role functions of mental health workers. Contemporary issues are discussed and the service development is seen in relation to the wider national frameworks such as the move towards Trust status. In chapter 7 we deal with the second most important aspect of the medicalisation process, the application of treatment to this difficult group of patients. For psychiatry to succeed in its quest to maintain the mentally disordered offender as a focus of its operation it must provide effective therapeutic interventions. We will argue in this chapter that traditional treatment modalities are found wanting whilst the contemporary thrust is towards treatment and management from a social perspective. In chapter 8 we will deal with the most significant issue of re-offending. If patients who receive treatment at the hands of forensic psychiatry go on to recidivate then the public will ultimately conclude that the professional endeavour is ineffective. If this occurs the forensic enterprise will collapse. In this chapter we will outline some recent studies of re-offence and recidivism of mentally disordered offenders and the public response to such events. In our concluding chapter we will draw the main themes of our thesis together and offer some signposts for the future development.

Summary

In summary we have set out a skeletal framework for a sociology of the mentally disordered offender. This is based on certain social elements that must be understood in relation to each other and how they interact to form the dynamic state that underpins the emergence of the mentally disordered offender in our society. These elements involve the nature of crime and its relationship to mental disorder, the social construction of dangerousness through the production of fear, the notions of harm and vulnerability, and the capture, containment, and treatment of the offender within the discursive practice of forensic psychiatry. The binding element in all this is the media which functions to organise and reinforce our social responses to mentally disordered offenders. The remainder of the book broadens and deepens this analysis.

Thus, we have our sphere of enquiry. The sociology of the mentally disordered offender incorporates the areas outlined above but *within* an overall conceptual framework that cradles a number of philosophical issues. The ideology of degeneration, in which individual weakness accounted for the condition, gave way to the notion of social deviancy in which society constructed its mutant progeny. This sociology of separateness and difference became the academic genre fixed within the emerging theory of legalism. These two structures provided the means to create the mentally disordered offender. The ever increasing medicalisation of life led to, and continues to lead us toward, ever more sophisticated mechanisms of social regulation. Ridden throughout the ordering of society is the philosophy of punishment, that most complex of issues which bristles with legal and moral difficulties. Moreover, there is the development of political hegemony with increasing liberalism and social democracy that requires a finely tuned political awareness of the mentally disordered offender in our society and a clear set of responses to their offences to keep the public satisfied. There is a political balance to be maintained by on the one hand ensuring psychiatric power is gratified and on the other public danger circumscribed. In the formation of modern societies the boundaries between the norm and the deviant become obscure and, thus, it becomes necessary to identify a distinguishing group. The group that now gives society its Other is the mentally disordered offender.

Chapter 2

Theoretical overview

Introduction

To develop a sociology of the mentally disordered offender it is inevitable that we must deal with the sociologies of both mental disorder and crime. However, the sociology of the mentally disordered offender is more than a mere amalgam of the latter two, and represents a fusion in which the process of synthesis creates a new field of study. Furthermore, it is the social processes of this fusion, and the forces that effect it, that constitutes our starting point. We cannot begin to understand the social creation of the mentally disordered offender unless we grapple with the wider issues that not only allow, but also provide, the motivational drive for this emergent field. Whether we trace back through literary documents for factual statements, or archaeologically 'dig' for contemporary ideas, matters little as historical tracings must be arbitrarily anchored in time and subjectively interpretational. Our mapping of this field of study is no different in this respect, and we begin our analysis in the years between the world wars with the sociology of deviance.

The sociology of the mentally disordered offender is based on the notion of difference, but it is well recognised that this difference is both complex and chaotic. In the inter-war years the sociology of deviance was created through the pathologisation of society and the sociological rooting of psychiatry. One should remember here that Freud, whose theories were dominant at the time, was also a keen anthropologist and very much aware of cultural differences and totems. During the thirties there was a growing awareness of psychiatry and sociology, particularly in relation to the concept of deviance, which very quickly became territory to which both disciplines staked claim. As deviance can mean a defect within the individual's psyche or personality, or equally, refer to social action in which rules or norms are broken, both disciplines considered this notion as ripe for their attention and viewed each other with some degree of suspicion. This awareness of each other – it cannot as yet be viewed as a conjoining, fusion, or amalgam merely an *awareness* – led to shifts in how deviance could be perceived. At the psychiatric level the individual could be seen as deviant or ill whilst at the sociological level society itself could be viewed as sick. This eruption of so many deviances, both, within the individual, throughout society, and even within the social system itself, caused a profound loss of normality which was to have serious ramifications. As Frank (1948) put it: 'today we have so many deviations and maladjustments that the term "normal" has lost all significance. Indeed, we see efforts being made to erect many of the previously considered abnormalities into cultural patterns for general social adoption' (p. 1). Clearly, the difference between normal and abnormal was beginning to become blurred. Social structures could now be perceived as signs of degeneracy. Crime, unemployment, prostitution etc., were the signs of a 'sick' society.

Furthermore, in 'medicalisation' terms, if society was sick then it could also be treated: 'the disintegration of our traditional culture, with the decay of those ideas, conceptions, and beliefs upon which our social and individual lives were organized, brings us face to face with the problem of treating society, since individual therapy or punishment no longer has any value beyond mere alleviation of our symptoms' (Frank, 1948, p. 1). Class division, poverty, the economy, could now receive therapy and if individuals could be cured of their deviancy then there was some hope that this curative function was transmittable to society.

Difference

At one level there has always been a clear moral distinction between those who are insane and those who are not, and between those who are criminal and those who are law-abiding. However, at another level the distinctive qualities evaporate and leave an amorphous interface without clear boundaries between operating within the law and, say, feeling depressed. For some degree of sense to be made we need to turn to notions of degree or extremes of difference between 'them' and 'us'. The creation of this 'them' and 'us' position is said to safeguard and reassure ourselves that we are firmly established on the right side; that is, sane and law-abiding (Foucault, 1973). This social positioning legitimates any number of strategies to identify those of the Other and to employ any number of tactics to maintain and enhance that difference. Perhaps, the reason for creating this difference is the fact that, in reality, there is no difference. Insanity lies within us all, dormant for most of us, most of the time. And criminal? What dark secrets could be unlocked from the psyche; from the destructive forces in the name of revenge or protection, to the pool of power in the name of sex. Perhaps, just perhaps, this difference is that very mirror which reflects the hidden soul of the Other within us all. A glimpse of the reflection which terrifies us (George, 1998).

It seems to us that establishing a difference between groups of people is a social process having a psychological motivation. There seems to be a strong association between this need to establish a difference and the notion of 'fallen from grace' (Foucault, 1973). It no longer seems surprising that this 'fallen from grace' situation formed the motivation for the first murder, in biblical terms, as Cain killed Abel for this very reason. To this day it continues to be an aspect of human behaviour which seeks ever more subtle ways of identifying differences as stigma, and then making those differences obvious. Speaking of Tannenbaum's work Sumner (1994) observed 'Tannenbaum's basic standpoint was that modern societies shared the same Manichean vision of good and evil as archaic ones and that they too needed their devils or scapegoats: people who could be portrayed as qualitatively different from the rest of the community, then blamed and punished for their difference' (p. 124).

Blamed and punished is one thing, pathologised and treated is another. Once the difference can be identified in medical terms, it can also be objectified and become the focus of psychiatric intervention. This objectification may include the academic encirclement of science upon it or the focusing of the medical 'gaze' and its application of power. Often both occur. Once objectified it may become pathologised with the imputation of labels such as sickness, illness, disease, and disorder, following which, a process is applied and includes diagnosis, treatment, and prognosis. As Sumner (1990) put it 'once divorced from the normative and political conjuncture that give it meaning, "deviant behaviour" was ready as an apparently neutral object of knowledge to serve in the power-laden practices of policing, tutelage and discipline, as an agency in the processes of domination and social regulation . . . The deviant was now identifiable directly, as an "inadequate", "undersocialised", or "inappropriately" socialised cultural rebel: as a rebel without a cause' (pp. 18–19). Thus, as we approached the second world war, the boundaries between deviancy and normal, if a little blurred, were at least discernible for most people, both scientific and lay.

Two Hs

The mass slaughter of soldiers in the first world war stunned and shocked those that were aware of the extent of fallen and wounded. However, the astonishment was more concerned with the quantity of men that were needlessly killed rather than with the type of death they faced. In one sense the Armageddon was quite normal, in that they were soldiers within armies that fought on battlefields with contemporary weapons of destruction. Nothing new here, except the vast numbers of lost lives. The difference between the armies was clearly delineated by the uniforms of their soldiers. The 'them' and 'us' was explicitly marked by the term enemy. After this war 'to end all wars' which 'must never be allowed to happen again', the two cliches usually heard following most wars, the majority in society returned to the more routine activities of life, hunger, and poverty.

Although for different reasons, during the inter-war years, Britain, Germany, France, and the USA all went through long periods of depressed economies. However, the differences in societies were still quite usual in terms of the rich and the poor, the haves and the have nots, the employed and the unemployed, and so on. This was a *rational* situation, if grossly unfair. Furthermore, in our social disciplines, psychiatry, criminology, sociology, etc., the stress was upon the rationalisation of theory pertaining to the criminal, the mentally ill, the deviant, and the disordered. This rationalising took the form of suggesting that the criminal was a progeny of society (Tannenbaum, 1938), or that the class structures produce criminal activity (Merton, 1939), or that those legislators and scientists who label a criminal, merely produce those types (Sellin, 1938). The thrust of the inter-war science of deviancy located the cause in terms of the proximity of the criminal to society. Just as the deviant could be the pathology, society could also be pathologised. From the sick individual to the sick society, and, as we mention above, if the person could be cured then so too could society. A mental hygiene as well as a public one. The difference was between the criminal and the law-abiding, the deviant and the normal, the sick and the well, with few shades of grey between 'them' and 'us'.

The second world war arrived and took our minds off hunger and poverty as the war machine filled pockets and bellies. Another war 'to end all wars' but this one was not the same as previously. The difference was that not only were soldiers and armies targeted and killed, but also civilians. Men, women, and children were all killed as bombs dropped on all sides – indeed, a 'hard-rain' (Dylan, 1967). However, notwithstanding the claims, by all parties, that military establishments were the target and that men women and children who got in the way were just unfortunate, it was not this difference that eradicated all difference. Nor was it, in academic explanatory frameworks the traditional three Ds, defective, dependent, and delinquent; nor the seven Devils of Giddens, depraved, deficient, deranged, deformed, disorderly, dirty, and devitalised, that destroyed difference. It was, in fact, two Hs that annihilated distinction between 'them and us'.

The first H belongs to the Holocaust. In its entirety this is commonly held to be the mass destruction of six million Jews by the end of the war; in reality, the systematic slaughter by the German death machine probably claimed nearer twenty million people, including the mentally ill, the mentally impaired, soviet prisoners of war, and Gypsies. These concentration camps, in the main kept secret from the outside world, reduced the human being to living skeletons through work and starvation prior to their extermination and then reduced the remnants to mere piles of hair, glasses, gold teeth, and ash. Products to be recycled to service the machine of their destruction. All went into the furnace, men, women, and children, merely because they were Jews, Handicapped or Gypsies. Differences so different as to cause them to be exterminated. At the end of the war the world was shocked. Could this really have happened whilst a world war raged on all around? Could the enemy, the 'them' really have gone that far with innocent victims? It was as if even 'they' had gone *too* far, beyond the pale, the deviants deviated beyond known parameters. 'They' were now unrecognisable and 'it', the Holocaust, was unfathomable. Zygmunt

Bauman (1991) argued that the Holocaust was a phenomenon of inversion and was 'born and executed in our modern rational society, at the high stage of our civilization and at the peak of human cultural achievement, and for this reason it is a problem of that society, civilization and culture' (p. x). That its perpetrators were all considered 'normal' – concentration camp guards who showed a liking for their brutality were quickly transferred elsewhere – makes the problem all the more difficult to understand. In fact, if it had been carried out by the deranged it would have a certain rationality and the fact that it was undertaken by the ordinary obscures its sense. The unfathomability of the Holocaust, in its immediate aftermath, produced a numbness, not an outrage, but a silence. Those involved denied any wrongdoing, the victim survivors could not tell their stories, and the experience was beyond recollection. It has been described as the end of experience in the following terms 'he remains suspicious of an "experience" of the end of "experience"; of any narrative that purports to be the narrative of the subject subjected to "Auschwitz", where subjects were destroyed and where the destruction of subjectivity necessarily led to an ideological renaissance of the subject in extremis' (Hewitt, 1996, p. 75).

The second H stands for Hiroshima (not to forget Nagasaki). When Truman gave the go-ahead for the dropping of the atomic bombs he was giving permission for the obliteration of difference. Tens of thousands of innocent men, women, and children vaporised, fragmented, or melted in one single action. The total destruction of two cities, by two bombs, on the 6 and 9 August 1945, following which survivors suffered horrendous burns and continued to die the slow radiation death. The fact that it was not necessary to drop the bomb to end the war was overlooked. It was a political decision, as much to prevent Russia from being seen as peacemaker as it was for America to be seen as all-powerful. The decision was made by 'good men'

> I wish to stress that term: 'good men'. None of the officials
> involved in this tale had evil intentions. What can be said of them,
> I believe, is that some became so taken by the power that the
> atomic bomb seemed to give them to do good (as they defined it)
> that they seem to have gotten carried away. Stimson put his finger
> on a key point when he observed privately to his colleague Joseph
> Grew that they were 'very fine men' – but also that they 'should
> have known better . . .
>
> (Alperovitz, 1996, p. 13)

The similarities between the normality of the guards of Nazi death camp, who ought to have known better, and the American politicians emphasises the distortion of the rational. Again, the world was shocked and stunned by such destruction, but this time it was 'us'. We were now beyond the pale. We had become like 'them' as 'they' had become like 'us'. The difference had been shattered.

In this early post-war phase the bounds of normality had disappeared, rationality was inverted, and 'we' (there were no 'them' and 'us' now) were beyond belief. How could it have happened? What forces drove such action to the surface? From what depths of depravity had these behaviours emanated in what was now the universal 'us'. The search was now on for a demarcation line, a parameter that could distinguish, once again, some boundary of difference. In this phase of disorganisation, irrationality, and illogicality society was deemed out of control. What was now needed was the creation of another form of deviance focusing upon the disorder of society. Fifty years of psychoanalysis had failed to avoid the Holocaust and Hiroshima and could not adequately explain such action, nor help the survivors with their emotional trauma. Social disorder was up-for-grabs and social control was the hunting ground.

Social control

Prior to the war the pathologisation of society, generally, referred to economic conditions in which poverty, social deprivation, and class divisions were seen as contributing factors in the development of deviancy. Merton's (1939) analysis of social structures and anomie was a classic example which saw non-conformist behaviour as a result of pressures and stresses emanating from the thwarting of goals and personal achievements through class inequalities. Writing at the same time Kingsley Davis (1938) noted that 'bad mental hygiene' was closely associated with class structure and that cultures and institutions which fostered 'bad mental hygiene' should be 'treated'. The popular belief, of this pre-war period, was that if society was sick it was sick because macro-structures, such as economics, class, and morality, made it so. Therefore, 'treat' the underlying causes and society will get 'better'. Unfortunately, this was a simple naivete which was to founder in the post-war years.

Following the war, deviancy in society became a moral question, as had become the Holocaust and Hiroshima. Strenuous efforts were made to give society a cohesive structure which could harness the drives and motivations of aberrant members. Parsons' (1951) analysis of the social system was but one attempt. For Parsons, deviancy was a problem for the social system and needed to be controlled as 'rationalisation is an adjunct and instrument of repression in that cognitively it denies the existence of conflict and attempts to present a consistent picture in accord with approved normative standards of proper motivational orientation' (Parsons, 1951, p. 266). Who decided what the 'proper motivational orientation' was, were the moral middle class.

Society in the post-war years was also seen as 'sick' but on a different level. Whereas prior to the war it was sick because of macro-structures affecting it, in the post-war era it was sick at a micro-level. Its internal structures were the focus of attention; there were delinquent boys, deviant sub-cultures, and suburban youth in cultural crisis. The problem of deviancy lay *within* society not above it as previously believed. The sociopath was not far away. 'Streetcleaning' ideology became more focused on deviants and drug addicts, and on prostitutes and destitutes; policing, regulation, and ordering became the focus of specialist attention by a number of theorists in a vain attempt to re-establish the shattered difference. However, we suggest that it was the mentally disordered offender that provided the fertile ground to re-institute the difference.

Overview of offender theories and mental disorder

There are many theories of both criminality and psychiatric disorder, which are too numerous to deal with fully in this chapter. However, a brief overview will suffice before focusing more specifically on the theorists who we believe are more closely related in their professional studies to the development of the mentally disordered offender. This extremely brief overview will attempt to draw on the three areas of criminality, mental disorder, and the mentally disordered offender.

Criminality

The tendency towards a criminal career has been the subject of much research. Some have focused on variables that are considered internal to the individual, for example, low intelligence quotients are said to be good predictors of self-reported crime (Farrington, 1992). Others have concluded that cognitive and neuropsychological deficits may account for delinquency (Moffit and Silva, 1988), with still others suggesting the 'executive' functioning of the frontal lobe as being related to criminal behaviour (Moffit, 1990). Altering the physical composition of body chemicals by illicit drugs or alcohol are also said to be related to criminal activity (Collins, 1989). Within this debate there are issues pertaining to whether people ingest drugs or alcohol and then commit crime or commit crime to support the supply of these substances (South, 1995).

Other theories of criminality refer to relationships with gender (Heidensohn, 1995), age (Cohen and Land, 1987), and race (Smith, 1995). However, more psychological constructs have been studied, such as, attention spans, reading ability, abstract reasoning, concept formation, inhibition, and impulsivity (Moffit, 1990). Deficits in these areas are said to be related to criminal behaviour. Moving to a more social domain Loeber and Stouthamer-Loeber (1986) analysed family factors in relation to criminal activity, whilst Agnew (1991) found that peer influence was closely related to crime. Socioeconomic factors have also received close scrutiny (Cloward and Ohlin, 1960) as have school factors and educational performance (Rutter *et al.*, 1979). Widening the net, community influences have been studied (Reiss, 1986) and found to correlate with high crime rates, whilst situational factors in relation to the environment have also been examined (Clarke and Cornish, 1985). Thus, criminality duly received academic attention as a distinct area of study, but alone does not convey sufficient difference between 'them' and 'us' because much crime is perceived as rationally motivated.

Mental disorder

There are four main categories that fall under the rubric of mental disorder, (a) psychoses, (b) neuroses, (c) personality disorders, and (d) mental impairment. However, there are many sub-types of these categories. There are far too many theories offered to account for these disorders so some broad conceptual areas will suffice. The psychoses, in particular the schizophrenias and manic-depressive conditions are the type that are popularly known as insanity. Theories attempting to explain these conditions can be grouped into biochemical, psychophysiological, and psycho-social.

...es can be understood in psychodynamic terms as well
...ural nomenclature, whilst personality disorders are ex-
...by developmental, environmental, and social learning the-
...The mental impairment disabilities are usually located as
or... ...nic deficits, genetic, or brain dysfunctions. Notwithstanding
the foregoing it must be emphasised that there is a considerable
overlap of all these explanatory theories and the sub-types within
the four broad categories. In nosological terms, mental disorder
has grown steadily in true reductionist fashion and it was not until
the academic fusion of both crime and mental disorder exploded
on the intellectual scene that the social vacuum of difference was
filled.

Mentally disordered offender

The mentally disordered offender is, thus, conceptually an amal-
gamation of theories pertaining to offending and theories pertaining to mental disorder. This clearly suggests a relationship between
the two. No theory, to our knowledge, exists to explain the mentally disordered offender independent of this amalgam and it is
this relationship between a mental disorder and a criminal action
that is the focus of sociological enquiry in the next chapter.

The mentally disordered offender is constructed from psychiatric
terminology and a criminal act but it is the power of this compound
that produces the social construction of dangerousness.

The mentally disordered offender is first and foremost based
on a 'pathology of the monstrous' (Foucault, 1978) and it is this
monstrousness that provides the leverage for psychiatry to penetrate
criminology. Although many crimes committed by mentally disordered offenders are of a relatively minor nature it is the outrageous, bizarre, and extreme cases that give forensic psychiatry
its power over the criminal. Without this extreme the mundane
would prevail, which would result in the neutralisation of this disciplinary power as it would deal with the lower echelons of dangerousness, leaving the social fear at the hands of the prison to
contain it.

The creation of the mentally disordered offender occurs in the
professional domain in which the psychiatric 'expert' ensnares the
offender in the web of medicalised explanation. However, in terms
of the social the creation of the mentally disordered offender is
subject to a different legitimation. Although, as was mentioned,
certain serious crimes are perceived as 'sick' their perpetrators are

often viewed as lying beyond 'illness' and residing in the area of 'evil'. This legitimates a punitive response rather than a therapeutic one. An example of this is the Moors Murderer, Ian Brady, who is now a patient in a special hospital, and quite clearly categorised as a mentally disordered offender, but is unlikely ever to be perceived as such by society. The relationship between Brady's crimes and his mental state lies outside of the realms of 'illness' from the public's point of view.

Post-war theorists

In choosing to highlight the following post-war theorists we would make two points. Firstly, the lack of space dictates that we cannot deal in total with the numerous pre-war writers that contributed so significantly to the theories of deviancy, crime, and mental disorder, and therefore we restrict ourselves to those whose work has central tenets which are relevant for the development of our ideas relating to the mentally disordered offender. Secondly, whilst some of the post-war authors we refer to are central theoretical frameworks others represent exemplars within a general school of thought, and in no way do we wish to do any author a disservice by their omission. The following influential works are chronologically ordered in illustration 2:1, and although most of the authors' work spans many years we have arranged them in this manner in relation to the major impact that their work achieved.

Reckless

In choosing the work of Walter Reckless as our first author we ground our project firmly within the realm of understanding the development of mentally disordered offenders in terms of the intermeshing of social forces. As we mentioned above, like many authors the work of Reckless and his associates was developmental and refined over many years. However, the central tenets of his perspective are pivotal in comprehending the post-war shift in criminological theory. Walter Reckless studied at the Chicago School at the height of their sociological prowess and, like many others from the Chicagoan perspective, believed that contemporary social problems could be understood in relation to the transformation of societies from simple integrated rural communities

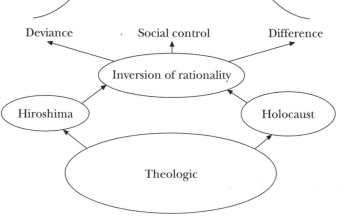

Laing 1982

1978 Foucault

Laing 1976

1973 Foucault

1972 Lemert

1968 Goffman

1967 Garfinkel/Foucault

Scheff 1966

1963 Becker/Goffman

Szasz 1963

1962 Goffman

Jones 1962

Szasz 1961

1960 Cloward *et al.*

1950 Reckless

Deviance   ·   Social control   Difference

Inversion of rationality

Hiroshima   Holocaust

Theologic

Figure 2.1

to more complex industrialised environments where the division of labour was more complicated. This Reckless argued, following in the Durkheimian tradition, brought with it a completely different set of pressures, contradictions, and tensions to modern social life. Historically, such stresses and strains created the need for societies to control and regulate individual members via social mechanisms, such as integrating norms and values of conformity. This being achieved by subtle means such as creating expectations of marriage, employment, class divisions, etc., and not so subtle means as policing, surveillance, and correction of aberrant members. Institutions were developed to contain and control such non-conformists, for example, prisons and mental hospitals, legitimated through the social forces of law and psychiatry.

It is often difficult, and sometimes dangerous, to attempt to classify theorists into neat categories, however, it is fair to say that Reckless worked in the field of criminology which is now termed the containment theory. Reckless's containment theory focused attention in the area between, or beyond, the 'pulls' and 'pushes' theories that existed at that time. Various theories of offending appeared to suggest that social forces 'pulled' individuals into criminal activity, for example, imitation–suggestion theory, differential association theory, companionship theory, delinquency sub-culture theory, and class structure theory. The 'pull' being that: 'individuals embrace certain patterns or models of behaviour. They reach out for them. They follow them. They are pulled toward them' (Reckless, 1950, p. 335). On the other hand, the 'push' theories would include those perspectives which argue that, rather than the individual *needing* to reach out to criminal activity, they are *compelled* to embrace crime. These would include the biophysical and psychological causations of offending behaviour, which argue that inherent structures of the human body, organic and psychic, force the person to engage in criminal activity. However, we can see that within certain 'pull' theories there is clearly an inner 'push'. For example, Cohens sub-culture theory in which the cultural forces not only 'pull' the individual in making him *want* to engage in crime but also there is an element of peer pressure which forces this engagement. Reckless's work attempted to go beyond these 'inner' and 'outer' pressures, to explain why despite these 'pulls' and 'pushes' some individuals turn to crime whilst some do not (Lilly, Cullen, and Ball, 1989).

The importance of Reckless's theory for our project is that it operated *between* the two central perspectives of criminological theory at that period in time, and attempted to synthesise theory from both camps in providing a new thesis. Reckless drew on 'pulls' and 'pushes' theories, inner and outer containments, and from psycho-social motivations. Although working in the USA, Reckless's theory showed that the combination of social forces contributed to individuals offending and that an 'inner drive' was motivated by 'outer factors'. Both the USA and the UK were progressing to that social phase characterised by the term 'you've never had it so good', in which material possessions through technological advances were providing a greater degree of comfort, for the majority of people, than previous generations had ever witnessed. These social forces were changing the dynamic between deviancy and normal. Our project is similar in that we draw from law and psychiatry, crime and mental disorder, and from lay and professional understandings to attempt to build a sociology of the mentally disordered offender.

Cloward and Ohlin

Again, Richard Cloward and Lloyd Ohlin's work is representative of a school of thought and is presented here as it is an excellent example of developmental work which drew upon several theories from which their own perspective emerged. Richard Cloward had been a student of Robert Merton and was later to become a working colleague of his. Lloyd Ohlin, on the other hand, studied under Edwin Sutherland at the University of Chicago. Both Merton and Sutherland were influential theorists in deviancy and criminal behaviour in the 1930s and 1940s and had a big impact on Cloward and Ohlin respectively. They drew heavily on Merton's idea that structures of society create the pressures that move people to deviancy. Merton's argument, simply stated, was that when there was a breakdown in the relationship between the achievement of goals in society and the legitimate avenues of access to them, a tension was created. This situation was adapted to by individuals in several ways, through innovation, ritualism, retreatism, or rebellion. However, Merton laid only the bare bones of this theory and it fell to Cloward and Ohlin to furnish an answer as to why one individual would choose one particular adaptation over another (Lilly, Cullen, and Ball, 1989). In developing their theory Cloward and Ohlin drew not only from strain theory and Merton's structural tradition, but also from the Chicago school of criminology which had focused on the social environment as causative elements in crime.

Turning their attention to delinquent sub-cultures they attempted to show that the type of neighbourhood that a person was located in would govern the particular adaptation through values and norms which were acceptable to that group. They argued: 'delinquent subcultures, we believe, represent specialised modes of adaptation to this problem of adjustment. Two of these sub-cultures – the criminal and the conflict – provide illegal avenues to success-goals' (Cloward and Ohlin, 1960, p. 107). The evolution of these delinquent sub-cultures occurred when processes of alienation from dominant norms of a social group transpired which causes failure, or the anticipation of failure. The way in which a person views this failure will determine what he will do about it. If he ascribes his failure to injustices in the social order he may criticise the system, make efforts to reform it, or retreat from it. On the other hand, if he locates the source of the failure within himself he may develop mechanisms to protect his damaged self-esteem or develop better personal skills. In any event what these adaptations achieve is a group cohesiveness towards the expected deviant behaviour or criminal conduct.

The work of Cloward and Ohlin focused upon the notion of opportunity in society to achieve goals and suggested that criminal conduct could occur in response to the thwarting of these goals. Moreover, they believed that they had explained how individuals adapted to this frustration and although not specifically referring to mentally disordered offenders their work has insights for this group. Within Cloward's and Ohlin's work there is a tension created between the society and the individual who then appears frustrated by the social system in which he is locked. Writing in 1960 their ideas were to be ominously accurate for the decade that was about to unfold. They appear to have glimpsed into the future which would see opportunity, achievement, and acquisition as central drives to be inverted by the hippie, drop-out, and the drug addict.

Szasz

There is often great dispute between professionals, with regard to specific aspects of their professions. For example, mechanistic surgeons, in private, may deride holistic physicians, and vice versa, but in public will appear to respect, or at least tolerate them. The important point being that these antithetical views, although expressed privately, are rarely voiced publicly, let alone published in print. Thomas Szasz is an exception to this rule. Having strong views regarding what he termed the myth of mental illness he has argued consistently and vociferously for over thirty years through numerous published books and many articles. As a psychiatrist his opinions represent the extremes of protest against many central aspects of his own profession – in many thousands of words. As always it is difficult to summarise such prolific writings in the space of a few pages, therefore, as with the other authors that we are reviewing we must restrict ourselves to the general principles of their work in relation to their impact for the development of the mentally disordered offender, as we see them.

In two books, the *Myth of Mental Illness* (1961) and *Law, Liberty and Psychiatry*, (1963) Szasz lays down his general thesis regarding his views on psychiatry and the role of psychiatrists. In the many other publications that followed he expanded and emphasised the groundwork that he laid in these two earlier books. The first point to be made is regarding mental illness as a myth. There are two popular interpretations to Szasz's myth, firstly, that he is claiming that the condition of mental illness does not exist in reality and that it is fictitious – a story being told. Or, secondly, that some psychopathology does exist but that it is not an illness as we know it. Szasz himself uses both meanings within, and between, his writings which suggests that either he himself is unclear as to the meaning or, perhaps, that it does not really matter. A myth in anthropological terms refers to an allegorical narrative whose facts cannot be corroborated but the communicative meaning relays important messages regarding social or cultural values. In this sense, then, mental illness is seen as a social communication concerning problems or statements of life. The important point being that mental illness is very much socially constructed. As is the mentally disordered offender.

If Szasz is correct, in that mental illness does not exist as an entity, then people presenting with certain 'problems' have every right to be helped, according to Szasz. This is useful, considering that he holds a Chair of Psychiatry and has practised psycho-analysis for most of his working career. However, he draws the line very clearly between a person wishing to be helped voluntarily and a person being compulsorily detained and forced to have treatment that he would otherwise not wish to have. This Szasz believes to be a discriminatory sanction and a crime, as, if mental illness does not exist, compulsory detention for psychiatric treatment is clearly erroneous. In *Law, Liberty and Psychiatry* (1963) Szasz draws parallels between those committed for treatment against their will and criminals in a rather trenchant way. He states: 'the similarities between committable mental illness and crime . . . emerge. In both, the person "offends" society, and is therefore restrained. The motives for restraining the mentally ill person are ostensibly thera-peutic, whereas for the criminal they are allegedly punitive. This distinction, however, cannot be defended satisfactorily' (Szasz, 1963, p. 47). In considering that the majority of mentally disordered offenders are compulsorily detained, against their wishes, for psy-chiatric treatment, these sentiments hold a chilling authenticity.

Another view of Thomas Szasz was that institutional psychiatry was a form of social control. Following on from the arguments above he claimed that, if mental illness was fictitious and merely socially constructed and that hospitals existed in which patients were coerced into treatment, then this form of psychiatry oper-ated as a means of social control. However, institutional psychiatry for Szasz not only meant forced involuntary treatment but all psy-chiatric practice which was not contractual. In short, contractual psychiatry was private practice, and this led to charges of him being an unabashed capitalist (Jones and Fowles, 1984).

Notwithstanding this, Szasz's work is clearly important for the sociology of the mentally disordered offender as he locates men-tal illness within the realms of society and claims that compulsory detention exists as those deemed mentally ill, also, offend society. However, it is his more subtle parallels between mental illness and crime, treatment, and punishment, and psychiatry and social con-trol which give us an anchorage point in time. In the topsy turvey world of the 1960s Szasz unleashed a protest against psychiatry which was so powerful that it would later need to be dismissed by the establishment as mere nihilism. However, with the rise of the mentally disordered offender as a focus of psychiatry this nihilism takes on a greater acuity than does its antithetical proponents.

Jones

Maxwell Jones, a psychiatrist and Director of Education and Research working out of the University of Oregon, USA, published a book on social psychiatry in 1962. Although, as we pointed out earlier in the chapter the concept of sociology and psychiatry as complimentary to each other had, by then, a relatively long his-tory. What was different in Jones's ideas was that whereas previ-ously there may well have been a sociological understanding of psychiatry or a psychiatrisation of sociology we now saw social psychiatry as a proposed conjoint entity. The difference being that with the former two intermeshings the theoretical application conceptually took place within the structures of society whereas Jones's idea focused upon social psychiatry not only within the community but also, more significantly, within the institutions of hospitals and prisons. This moved the theoretical construction to a more practically focused endeavour. Prior to Jones there may well have been a sociology *of* psychiatry now there was, purportedly, a sociology *in* psychiatry. This suggested that the creation of a social psychiatry could now claim to have identifiable constructs, an analytical model, a set of interventions, and clear modes of evaluation. Furthermore, this theoretical framework was applied not only to the psychotic groups of patients but also to that more difficult group to manage, the maladjusted individuals with personality disorders. In fact it was to become the latter groups' main therapeutic intervention.

Jones was very much aware that psychiatric assumptions regarding this patient population were particularly prone to overlook the cultural factors that contributed to their production, maintenance, and reinforcement. He argued for an increase in training in sociology for psychiatrists and centred his ideas on understanding group dynamics. These groups not only consisted of the patient group but also their family members, the dynamics of cultural ward formation, and both, staff–staff interactions and staff–patient interactions. Jones believed that psychiatry must develop to understand the roles and work of the multi-professions. However, this may be seen as a laudable enterprise at one level but a domineering expansion of psychiatry into others' domains at another. Notwithstanding this, we could, perhaps, give Jones the benefit of the doubt and assume that his intentions were honourable.

The nature of his social therapy is less clearly defined, and we are only given glimpses into his ideas. He proclaims that 'one of our goals in social psychiatry is to change community attitudes in the direction of greater acceptance and familiarity with mental illness on the part of the general public, then desirable change will be in the direction of increased public responsibility for the mentally ill' (Jones, 1962, p. 7). This is hardly new, not even in 1962, and is laden with paternalistic, and idealistic, aspiration rather than practical suggestions. One has to proceed to Jones' ideas of a 'therapeutic community' before we begin to see some of the constructs of his social psychiatry. He highlights improvement of communications between the smaller units he envisaged and outside agencies, and closer ties between patients, staff, and relatives. He suggested that smaller units aided a closer examination and modification of roles, role-relationships, and the over-all culture on the unit. He further claims that 'socio-cultural process becomes an integral part of treatment' (Jones, 1962, p. 53). Unfortunately, he failed to say how exactly this process occurs, but evidently believed that some psychological benefits were gained from the patient having a closer involvement in the unit into which he was admitted. He mentions, loosely, a 'therapeutic attitude' as against custodialism and segregation and for democratisation and permissiveness in contrast to stereotyped behaviour. Furthermore, he was in favour of 'communalism as opposed to highly specialised therapeutic roles often limited to the doctor' (Jones, 1962, p. 55). It is difficult to read the passages now, some thirty five years later, without them striking chords of liberal ideology and the self-indulgent 1960s flower-power ethos sweeping through California at that time.

That said, from a psychiatrists' point of view, Jones opened the way, in the post-war years, for a greater appreciation of socio-cultural dimensions in the treatment of maladjusted persons and later the mentally disordered offender. He was aware of this in 1962: 'so far we have talked more in terms of deviant behaviour than of concepts of overt crime or illness. There would appear to be an analogy between the two latter concepts' (Jones, 1962, p. 19). Moreover, it was not by coincidence that he called his book social psychiatry in the community, in hospitals, and in prisons. The mentally disordered offender role was clearly indicated if not explicitly stated. Jones may well have had a greater impact if it had not been for the anti-psychiatry movement which had begun its campaign.

Becker

Howard Becker (1963) produced his seminal work on the sociology of deviance by incorporating certain social elements into the concept. He put to one side the simplistic definitions of deviance which involved essentially statistical approaches as anything that deviates from the norm or average. He also shelved the pathological notion of deviance as correlating with 'disease' in relation to 'healthy', both in terms of medical metaphors as well as individual physical characteristics. Furthermore, he was rather dismissive of the sociological model of deviance which saw some parts of society as promoting stability (functional) and others as disrupting stability (dysfunctional). He saw this mainly as a political issue.

Finally, he believed that societies have many groups, each with their own set of rules, and individuals could belong to many different sub-groups. Group members who break the rules of these groups are not a homogenous category but merely deviant within that specific group.

We can see that Becker defined deviance in terms of it being constructed by the social groups forming the rules whose infraction constituted the deviance. As Becker adds: 'from this point of view, deviance is *not* a quality of the act that a person commits, but rather a consequence of the application by others of rules and sanctions to an "offender". The deviant is one to whom that label has successfully been applied; deviant behaviour is behaviour that people so label' (Becker, 1963, p. 9). He summarised the position: 'whether an act is deviant, then, depends on how other people react to it' (p. 11).

Setting out four categories of deviant behaviour Becker illustrated this in the following manner:

Becker's types of deviant behaviour

	Obedient behaviour	Rule-breaking behaviour
Perceived as deviant	Falsely accused	Pure deviant
Perceived as not deviant	Conforming	Secret deviant

At one end of this spectrum conforming behaviour is known as such and is simply seen as obeying rules. Similarly, at the other extreme, pure deviant, is disobeying rules and is also seen as such. It is the other two categories that are of more direct interest to us. Obedient behaviour may be perceived, wrongly, as deviant and thus the person is falsely accused. Ascribing this deviance to someone may well stigmatise the person as in labelling someone mentally disordered. At the other extreme the secret deviant may evade being found out and enact his deviant behaviour without notice. In this category there may well be a large 'pool' of deviance remaining hidden, as Becker suggests, such as sado-masochism.

Becker draws a major distinction between simultaneous and sequential models of deviance. In the former the focus is upon establishing variables purportedly accounting for deviant behaviour that are apparent at the time of the deviant action. For example, the person's IQ, housing conditions, family factors, etc., may be established. In the latter model it is argued that causes do not all operate at the same time and that deviant behaviour is formed through a sequential order of behavioural patterns. These steps towards deviancy may be viewed as a 'career'. The first step on this career may be intentional or unintentional and we must differentiate between those who commit a deviant act once and then cease, and those who develop a pattern of deviance.

Becker believed that deviant motivations had a social character despite their actions being predominantly secretive. Part of this social character were various media communications and the expectancy of being caught and labelled as deviant. He then went on to show how members of organised deviant groups also had mechanisms of a social character to reinforce and maintain their status. These included such concepts as a common fate, rationalising their position, self-justifying strategies, and a history on which to pin the experience.

The importance of Becker's work for our project is that although he used the deviant behaviour of marijuana use as an example of deviancy one can substitute any of the socially recognised deviant behaviours. He identified stages in the deviant career which were: learning the technique, learning to perceive the effects, and learning to enjoy the effects. This appears much the same for using marijuana as it does for serial killing.

Scheff

In developing a sociological theory of mental illness Scheff (1966) concentrated on the concept of the adoption of a social role and its reinforcement through the mechanism of the societal response to the manifestation of that role. His emphasis was upon perceiving the symptoms of mental illness, at least in part, as violations of residual social rules, and which, therefore, could be viewed as a type of deviance. The response of other members of the society in which this deviance occurs is seen as crucial in determining entry into the role and the 'career' of the rule-breaker. This theory locks the deviant into a system which acts as a self-reinforcing circuit, as the society responds to the deviant who, in turn, reacts to the response, and so on. This circularity is similar to that seen in labelling theory in which a person operates according to the role expectations of a particular label (Becker, 1963).

Scheff's approach was to focus on the signs and symptoms of mental illness and perceive them to be an extension of social

rule-breaking in terms of behaviour which was ill-mannered or
ignorant, but involved an element of 'unnatural'. He located his
theory in sociological terms as behaviour that was, to one degree
or another, understood in relation to the extent of involvement a
person had with their society. Thus, the more a person withdrew,
or dis-engaged, from their cultural norm the more they could be
viewed as mentally ill. Scheff set out a sociological theory of the
causation and stabilisation of mental disorder which involved complex social processes which reinforced the mentally ill person's role
as someone who was insane. Through nine hypotheses Scheff
argued that the social system operated to enclose the person into
a cycle of reinforcement that maintained the person in that role
through a positive feedback mechanism of a deviance amplifying
system. This included the mental health profession's constant requirement for the person to accept that they are ill, and the social
system of relatives and friends who provide an entire network of
suggestibility of deviance. Scheff claims that society learns this
stereotyping of insanity in early childhood, in all societies, through
the social medium of jokes, books, comics, films, T.V. news, and
newspapers. Furthermore, in adult life, the role imagery of this
prejudiced system is maintained through the same media.

The nine hypotheses are:

1 Residual rule-breaking arises from fundamentally diverse
  sources.
2 Relative to the rate of treated mental illness, the rate of
  unrecorded residual rule-breaking is extremely high.
3 Most residual rule-breaking is 'denied' and is of transitory
  significance.
4 Stereotyped imagery of mental disorder is learned in early
  childhood.
5 The stereotypes of insanity are continually reaffirmed,
  inadvertently, in ordinary social interaction.
6 Labelled deviants may be rewarded for playing the
  stereotyped deviant role.
7 Labelled deviants are punished when they attempt the
  return to conventional roles.
8 In the crisis occurring when a residual rule-breaker is
  publicly labelled, the deviant is highly suggestible and may
  accept the proffered role of the insane as the only
  alternative.
9 Among residual rule-breakers, labelling is the single most
  important cause of careers of residual deviance.

Scheff then set out a structure of decision-making, in varying fields of medicine, including psychiatry, and showed that there were strong similarities with decision-making in law and in science. This is based on justifying the rejection of hypotheses (type 1 and type 2 errors) in relation to the consequences of a wrong decision, both for the patient and the professional. This, then, paves the way for the mental illness to be socially constructed.

The importance of Scheff's sociological theory of mental illness for our understanding of the mentally disordered offender in society is that, along with other studies, Scheff shows how the idea that a mental illness, and by implication the motivation for a criminal offence, could only exist independently within the human body is fallacious. Those who believe that a mental illness is contained within the human mind, in its genesis, its career, and its outcome, are as misled as those who would have us believe that an offence by a mentally disordered person can locate its structures only within the human psyche. On the contrary, a mental illness, like a criminal offence, only 'exists' in the sense that they are created by the society in which they are located.

Garfinkel

Another writer, perhaps not commonly associated with the pre-conditional sociology that set the scene for the rise of the mentally disordered offender, is Harold Garfinkel. Garfinkel is recognised as the founding father of ethnomethodology, however, before this development he was publishing work that was later to become accepted as the early formulations to his central method. As a sociologist working at the University of California, in Los Angeles, Garfinkel published an article on the 'conditions of successful degradation ceremonies'. The article is generally concerned with how shame is induced, how this is achieved, and what it means for the society in which it is occurring. Its concern was for members in everyday life and not especially for the mentally ill or for criminals. However, we can now clearly see its importance in understanding the stigmatisation and degradation that occurs in relation to the mentally disordered offenders in our society. The contention is propounded in the axiom that there is no organised society that does not have in the social structures of its organisation the features of identity degradation. Garfinkel (1956) claims that, based on shame and guilt, the social mechanisms for removing, or being removed from, the source of the shame is found in everyday statements such as 'I could have sunk through the floor' and 'I wanted the earth to open up and swallow me'. The removal of oneself, or another, from the source of shame has parallels with the *distancing* noted in chapter 1, for when one is removing oneself from shame one is actually engaged in removing oneself from *public view*. As Garfinkel (1956) incisively remarks: 'the paradigm of moral indignation is *public* denunciation' (p. 421) (italics in the original). This is yet another example of the 'them' and 'us' principle outlined earlier. A singular difference in terms of group solidarity is that whereas shame does not bind groups together, moral indignation has a tendency to do so.

The person thus denounced (in our case the mentally disordered offender) is not so much changed, but reconstituted. The thing that is being blamed on the person is called the event, and these events are not merely added on to the 'old' character as in claiming that he 'is basically a good person except for this one objectionable trait'. Rather, he is reconstituted into a new identity as in 'he must have been like that all along'. Society now dismissed him from all former constructions of his character: 'in the social calculus of reality representations and test, the former identity stands as accidental; the new identity is the "basic reality"' (Garfinkel, 1956, p. 422).

The second half of the article concerns itself more with those involved in the denouncing, rather than those degradated. Garfinkel shows how the person is transformed, which involves the denouncer, the perpetrator (the person being denounced), and the event (thing being blamed on the perpetrator). He achieves this by setting out certain principles of which only a few will be mentioned here. Firstly, the perpetrator and the event must be made to 'stand out' from the realm of everyday normality. Second, the denouncer's identify themselves during the denunciation, and regard him not as a private person but as one who is publicly known. The denouncers are *bona fide* members of society, speaking for that society. Third, the denouncer must establish the dignity of the opposite behaviour from that of the perpetrator and the event. He does this in the name of the society. Fourth, those doing the denouncing must be invested with the right to speak on behalf of that society and bear witness to being a supporter of those values. Fifth, the denouncer not only must fix his distance from the perpetrator but must also make the perpetrator experience this. Finally, the perpetrator must be 'ritually separated from a place in the legitimate order, i.e., he must be defined as standing at a place opposed to it. He must be placed "outside", he must be made "strange"' (Garfinkel, 1956, p. 423). Seen in relation to the mentally disordered offender of today we can see that the achievements of the degradation ceremonies are accomplished; these include the police interviewing suspects, psychiatric assessments, court appearances, commitment to institutions, media coverage, public outrage, coercive therapy, Mental Health Review Tribunals, etc. However, criticisms followed in the wake of Garfinkel's article as Sumner (1994) points out: 'the essay was a contender for the Orwell prize for amoral, authoritarian, technocratic discourses of the 1950s' (p. 183) but that is only relevant to when it was written. At the turn of the century, on reflection over the post-war years, we see many social structures, the police, the law, psychiatry, and much of forensic mental health practice, as amoral, authoritarian, technocratic discourses.

An emphasis on a paper that did not have much impact for a further ten years may seem out of place in Garfinkel's chronology. However, its importance was crucial to the developmental work leading to the blossoming of ethnomethodology. If there was any doubt about the macro- versus micro-structures of society Garfinkel exploded such debate by demonstrating not only micro-analyses but with microscopic vision. His work developed into the most intricate social analysis, able to tease out 'the most intimate assumptions about normality which undoubtedly help to structure an otherwise fast-changing amorphous and bewildering social world' (Sumner, 1994, p. 239). Through a series of works in the 1960s and beyond Garfinkel shows how people make sense of their world through detailed use of norms and rules that structure everyday activity, from queuing at a supermarket check-out to organising judgements at trials by juries (Garfinkel, 1964; 1967; 1986).

Lemert

Edwin Lemert's work spans a quarter of a century and was predominantly rooted in deviance as a formative result of the intermeshing of power relations through the agency of social control (Lemert, 1942). He had transcended the notion that society was 'sick' (Lemert, 1951) and refused to believe that there was a clear distinction between abnormal and normal human behaviour. Claiming, instead, that deviation was socially constructed out of societal reaction. This social response not only included the expressive reactions of others, as in moral outrage, but also involved the social action governing its control. He gives as examples of socially constructed deviants as the physically handicapped, stutterers, homosexuals, drug addicts, alcoholics, mental patients, delinquents, and criminals. Lemert (1967) showed how the stigmatisation process and the creation of a sense of injustice could contribute towards reinforcing the deviant behaviour. Picking up on themes of taboo he notes: 'the general principle at work is a simple one: when others decide that a person is *non grata*, dangerous, untrustworthy, or morally repugnant, they do something to him, often unpleasant, which is not done to other people' (Lemert, 1967, p. 44). The strength of Lemert's work is that it was ahead of its time and particularly contemporary, in that, he absorbed the themes of his peers into his overall thesis, in dealing with labelling, stigma and the issue of terminology in the study of deviance.

In attempting to dismiss the idea that deviance was somehow psycho-pathological, and that it all really depended upon the cultural context in which it is set, at one level it would appear strange that Lemert's earlier book was entitled *Social Pathology* (Lemert, 1951). However, at another level, he was about to sound the death knell of the pathologification of deviancy and move into more closely related areas. These areas were chiefly two concepts which formed the basis of his thesis. The first refers to the social construction of difference whilst the second relates to the societal reaction to this difference in the form of a social construction of deviance. What Lemert had, in effect, achieved was a convincing repudiation of any notion of individual difference between conforming people and deviant ones, with the inevitable conclusion that any differences belonged merely to the attachment of the social label of deviancy by others.

In Lemert's (1967) book on *Human Deviance, Social Problems and Social Control* we witness further the splitting of the concept of deviancy into primary and secondary types. He does this to show the importance of the societal response to the formation of deviancy. Primary deviancy refers to those deviations that arise from social, cultural, psychological, and physiological causations. These may include the physical as well as mental disorders in which no blame is attached. The afflicted person is a primary deviant through no fault of their own. Secondary deviation, on the other hand, is concerned with a special class of socially constructed responses which are made as reactions to problems encountered by the social construction of deviance. These problems, Lemert ascertains, 'are essentially moral problems which revolve around stigmatization, punishments, segregation, and social control' (p. 40). In this sense, it is the social response to the person considered deviant which is central in terms of how he is ultimately treated. As much for the deviant when he was the focus of social control as for the mentally disordered offender who now occupies that space.

Lemert appeared to know that deviancy as a sociological concept was dying but was not brave enough, or ready to, issue the death blow – this was left to Goffman.

Goffman

Colin Sumner (1994) claims that Goffman killed off the concept of deviancy as a psychiatrised phenomena in that: 'Goffman summed it all up in one devastating indictment of the moral pretensions of the fifties, a nice ending to a book which effectively demolished the legitimacy of sociology's dalliance with psychiatry' (p. 222). If Sumner is correct, and we have little reason to doubt him, Goffman achieved this with three central works spanning almost fifteen years. Taken overall, these works represent an analysis of the power relations between individuals and institutions in which the vested interests of powerful professions are protected and fulfilled through regulatory agency.

The first work referred to is 'on cooling the mark out' (1952) in which Goffman claims that the con (confidence trickster) undertakes strategies of 'cooling' (accepting the loss) the 'mark' (victim) as he is 'stung' (separated from his money). The victim is expected to go on his way after being 'stung', not particularly happy, but at least quietly. However, some 'marks' do not accept this and report it to the police or pursue the operators of the 'sting'. To counteract this the 'cooling' is undertaken very subtly and usually by third parties rather than by those directly involved in the 'sting'. Goffman mentions several areas of social life in which 'cooling the mark out' is undertaken, including admitting mental patients to hospital. In this scenario the 'mark' is the patient, the 'sting' is the loss of freedom, and the 'cooling' is undertaken, usually, by family and friends. Goffman (1952) put it this way: 'in some cases . . . the task of cooling the mark out is given to a friend and peer of the mark, on the assumption that such a person will know best how to hit upon a suitable rationalization for the mark and will know best how to control the mark should the need for this arise' (p. 492). Strategies of 'cooling the mark out' in relation to the mentally disordered offender remains to be undertaken.

Goffman's (1962) *Asylums* is now considered a classic. This work showed how a mental hospital could become a total institution in which the authority of the organisation was in complete control of the individual. He explained how the techniques and rituals of incorporating the patient into the domain of the organisation, such as stripping, bathing, and shaving, were equated with other totalising institutions such as prisons and the most complete, thorough, and permanent of all total institutions the concentration camp. He told the 'sad-tale' of the patient whose resistance to this became the very proof of his symptomatology, and highlighted the vested interests of asylum workers in fulfilling their regulatory role. *Asylums* jarred on many sensibilities as it revealed the awesome nature of institutional power which rather than being exercised to counter the very problems that patients evidently presented actually contributed to creating the problems. Little wonder, then, that Sumner concludes that Goffman 'effectively demolished the legitimacy of sociology's dalliance with psychiatry' (p. 222).

In his thesis on spoiled identity Goffman (1963) set out the concept of stigma in relation to the social identity of the person so stigmatised and the social network to which he belonged. Although Goffman is concerned with the three types of spoiled identity – (a) abominations of the body, (b) blemishes of individual character, and (c) tribal stigma of race, nation and religion – we can use the thesis to focus on the mentally disordered offender more specifically. According to Goffman (1963) the mental patient is stigmatised through a process of known-about-ness, that is, the knowledge of his being a mental patient is known by his social network. Although, largely, the signs of his stigma are not visible the mental patient knows that he is a mental patient. The mental patient now finds himself in 'the infinite regress of mutual consideration that Meadian social psychology tells us how to begin but not how to terminate' (p. 30). This has serious implications for those that constitute the social group to which he belongs. The discrepancy between his virtual social identity, i.e. those traits that are attributed to him, and his actual social identity, i.e. those traits that he actually possesses, is wide. Whatever personal attributes he may have in reality are subjugated to the characteristics that are attributed to him. Therefore, the sex offender may well have certain endearing personal qualities but these are dismissed by our imputing negative attributes that emanate from our abhorrence of his crimes. However, Goffman also noted that the stigmatised person may well have a group of social friends or family that remain in sympathy with him. They become what Goffman termed the 'wise', that is, a group who are knowledgeable about the stigma and the stigmatised. The other group to which Goffman refers is the 'own', i.e. other similarly stigmatised persons.

From these three central works we can see that Goffman had turned the concept of deviance upside down. What was a clear deviance before now became normalcy and what was legitimate previously now became illegitimate. Not only had Goffman killed off deviancy as a psychiatric phenomena he, unknowingly, paved the way for the gaze of psychiatric attention to shift to the mentally disordered offender.

Foucault

Michel Foucault is possibly the single most influential writer to aid us in developing a sociology of the mentally disordered offender. A prolific, and profound, philosopher, whose work spans many areas of social life, he is often summarised as concentrating on power, knowledge, and sexuality. However, this does not do him justice, as he uses these 'fields' to offer penetrating analyses of many aspects of human society and its organisation. Of particular relevance to our work on mentally disordered offenders are the material he wrote on madness, prisons, psychiatry, dangerousness, and the postmodern 'normal'. Moreover, much of his work deals with the relationship between reason and unreason in which he explores those tenuous bonds that, at one level link the two and draw them together, whilst at another level appear to force them apart. Spanning just over twenty years work, cut short by his early death in 1984, Foucault's brilliance not only witnessed the end of deviancy but was also a major influence in the portentous analysis of the dangerous individual. His work is likely to be hugely influential for at least the next generation of mental health professionals if not for many generations to come.

In 1961 Foucault published *Madness and Civilisation*, which was his doctoral thesis entitled in the original Folie et deraison: histoire de la folie a lage. The book is focused not upon madness, but upon the difference between 'them' and 'us', through pages of semi-poetic prose he gives us glowing insights into the abyss of human behaviour that encompasses this most primitive of all divisions. In pre-medieval times the leper stood for the damned in a colony of lazar houses, they could be seen for what they were considered to be, outcasts and symbols of those who had fallen from

God's grace. When leprosy died out in Europe this void was filled by the mad, who previously were encompassed *within* the village concept, now distanced as strange and unacceptable. Using allegorical imagery Foucault regales us with an apparently apocryphal tale of the Ship of Fools which kept the mad on the move along the waterways of Europe. Later they were to be contained in the Hospitals that sprung up in the seventeenth century, in a movement he calls the Great Confinement. He goes on to invert our common appreciation of the psychiatric libertarians such as Tuke and Pinel, who are now considered by Foucault to be patriarchal ideologues who may have freed the patients from chains but who manacled them with Quaker morality. Through many twists and turns Foucault dazzles us with the images of his interpretations, often subliminal, and not noted for factual accuracy, he attacks the very sources of professional power and appeals to the emotions of the reader with painful allusions and metaphors.

Twelve years later Foucault (1973) extended his critique of the power of medicine in the *Birth of the Clinic* in which he deals with his, now famous, medical gaze. Medical perception is seen as a tangible power through which many aspects of the human being can become medicalised. This has as much to do with body parts such as the heart and the brain as it does with the emotions and the mind. Little is sacred from the ever-encroaching medical gaze, human behaviour, mental aberration, sexuality, and crime, all become psychiatrised into an ordered system of judgements. This is the domain of the deviants and the deranged.

What he had done in 1961 with institutional madness he did in 1977 with institutional criminality. In his book *Discipline and Punish* Foucault argues that the spectacle of punishment in the long drawn out tortures and executions were replaced by another Great Confinement, this time by incarcerating the criminal. Whereas the body of the offender had been the focus of attention in terms of pain and punishment, now the convergence was upon his soul, through warders, doctors, chaplains, psychiatrists, psychologists, and educationalists. The boundaries between the madman and the criminal were now very blurred indeed and in the following year, 1978, the Foucauldian mentally disordered offender, in the form of the dangerous individual, burst upon the scene.

It no longer seems surprising, or even coincidental, that the first pages, of the first volume, of the new *International Journal of Law and Psychiatry* were 'about the concept of the dangerous individual in 19th century legal psychiatry', and that the author was Michel

Foucault. The journal that draws law and psychiatry together launched itself with a seminal paper that, very cleverly, achieved three fundamental objectives. Firstly, it located the penetration of psychiatry into the court of law as an accomplished act, second, it gave birth to the dangerous individual as a social being in the form of the relations it drew between the offenses and the reactions that they cause, and, third, it married the rise of professional power with the system of knowledge pertaining to the field of study that the dangerous individual represents. The paper analyses and discusses the rise of the dangerous individual as a legal psychiatric focus during a period between 1800 and 1835, yet in a strange way, its publication in 1978, through the power of Foucault's interpretations, roots the sociology of the mentally disordered offender in that year.

Laing

R.D. Laing said that: 'psychiatrists have been among the severest critics of psychiatry' (Laing, 1982, p. 45). They would need to be, as any other critic would be dismissed as insignificant. Although Laing said little, directly, about crime, mentally disordered offenders or even punishment, his work is important because he was concerned with how psychiatry could be used and abused, both, knowingly and unknowingly. The one single theme that emerges from Laing's philosophy of psychiatry is the notion of schism or caesura. He was singularly concerned with rupture and break in many different forms and settings. In *The Divided Self* (1960) he was interested in the idea of the self in relation to others, in *The Facts of Life* (1976) he focused upon the separation of birth and the severing of the umbilical cord, and in *The Voice of Experience* (1982) he dealt with objective science and its application to the subjective self. He was a writer who was attentive to isolated individuals who had somehow been split off from reality, somehow cast off from the community, and somehow shunned into a desolate existence.

Laing saw psychiatry as a machine that owed its existence to drawing ever-more aspects of human behaviour under its scrutiny and control. Through its ability to label and diagnose what it cannot understand psychiatry operates as a mechanism of control: 'it is a ceremonial of control, control of mind, body and conduct, and always whatever else, control for the sake of sheer control, of more control, of perfect, complete control. Total control would presumably be reached when nothing happens except what we allow' (Laing, 1982, p. 36). He argued that once this extent of scrutiny and control was complete there are fundamental questions as to who owns it, who makes the decisions, and who decides to do what to whom. Although not specifically referring to the mentally disordered offender it is not difficult to adapt his ideas on general psychiatry and apply them to the role and function of the forensic patient. He clearly saw the power that was located at the root of the psychiatric label and realised that the exercise of this power had not always had a benign protective function. He argued that: '[the diagnostic decision] . . . is a very political decision. People declared "mentally ill" on expert opinion, and accepted as such by administrative authorities in the context of civil or criminal law, have to have decisions taken about them over their heads' (Laing, 1982, p. 47).

Again, the problematic of psychiatry, for Laing, was a social one. It is within the social that breaks and splits occur and it is from the social that 'offenders' must be removed. Laing completes the circle for the mentally disordered offender. He noted the rupture between 'them' and 'us', and the impact that an established *difference* could mean. He saw the power of psychiatry to separate, isolate, and incarcerate.

The end of deviance and the rise of the MDO

The sociology of deviance has grown steadily over the century with numerous professional disciplines involved in its exploration. These sciences would include sociologists, anthropologists, criminologists, social psychologists, and psychiatrists. However, despite the plethora of interpretation and causal theory of deviancy, the main pivot on which it balances is the manner of its control. If the economy is considered to be the cause of deviancy, changing the structure of the economy may be considered a simplistic necessity. Similarly, if class division is seen to be causally related to deviant conduct then deconstructing class inequality would possibly regulate such deviancy. However, not only are the theories of deviant behaviour numerous, with each one arguing for causative relations, its control, or cure, is highly complex with many interrelated variables meshing with sub-cultural, national, and often global factors. It is the expansiveness of its aetiology, the extent of its inter-penetration with many aspects of social life, and the universal nature of its occurrence which have contributed to its demise as a social science (Sumner, 1994). However, deviancy has long had a close relationship with 'sickness' and 'health', usually in the form of a partnership between the sociology of psychiatry and the psychiatrisation of society. The beginning of the century saw a close affinity between psychoanalysis and anthropology with a focus on deviant behaviour. Based on the naive assumption relating to the benevolence of psychiatry, the relationship waxed and waned over the century until its severance, and death, during the sixties and seventies (Sumner, 1994).

Summary

We have seen in this chapter that since the second world war, which inverted our understanding of rational thought, scientific disciplines have transposed our beliefs in deviancy as a distinction from normality, reversed our understanding of psychiatry as a benevolent function, and shattered the dream of a curative public hygiene. Authors on both sides of the divide, crime and mental disorder, destroyed their own myths which was profoundly felt just because they did it to their own professions rather than against each other. The 'them' and 'us' dissipated, as did difference and deviancy. The power of micro-analyses, the self-analysis of anti-psychiatry, and the analytic imagery of postmodernism created the conditions, not only for the demise of deviancy but also ripe for the rise of the mentally disordered offender from its ashes, or, rather, from the void left by the absence of difference. This primitive division would inevitably need to be re-established, yet again, the void would be filled by the mentally disordered offender through the relationship between crime and mental disorder.

Chapter 3

The relationship between criminal behaviour and mental disorder

Introduction

In chapter 2 we argued that rational society saw itself inverted in the post-second world war era as the boundaries between good and bad, right and wrong, them and us, became nebulous. The distinctions of logical binary oppositions blurred so that in both science and society anchorages slipped and polarities became a matter of relativity. The search for the difference between the 'abnormal' and the 'normal' was fundamentally cradled in the idea of deviancy. Grounded in the sciences of sociology, psychiatry, and criminology, deviance was at one time considered in terms of individual traits versus societal norms; at another it became an inquiry into 'madness' or 'badness'; and, at still another, it was formed in the relationship between criminal behaviour and mental disorder. Laid to rest somewhere between the macro- and micro-analyses of the sociologists, and the transformations of the anti-psychiatry lobby, the deviant disappeared as *different* and made way for the emergence of the modern day mentally disordered offender as a field of study.

The relationship between mental disorder and crime has long been the focus of scientific and philosophical inquiry which involves several dimensions. The first dimension involves two social processes: namely, the psychiatrisation of crime and the criminalisation of mental disorder. In the former process, professional power fuses with social values to legitimise the application of a medical model on offenders. This involves a complex interplay of analytical proceedings, theoretical applications, and the construction of medical discourse pertaining to 'health careers' of criminalised conduct.

It, thus, locates offending within psychiatric perception and objectifies the Act, or Event, of crime as the subject of psychiatric manipulation. Socially, this is legitimated if it is seen to be effective or compassionate to *some* degree. In the second process, the criminalisation of mental disorder, we are faced with the social forces of lay understandings of the dangerousness of the insane brought into scientific credibility by researchers providing evidence to support this view. Society has long viewed the mentally ill as being, stereotypically, dangerous and violent with a self-reinforcing circularity of argument that suggests those who are mentally ill are violent and therefore those who are violent must be 'mad'.

The second dimension in the relationship between mental disorder and crime refers to the cause and effect issue. Axiomatically, it is well understood that a particular act can only be socially understood if it can be caused by a mental aberration. Operationally rational minds produce 'normal' behaviour, thus, one needs to be deranged to act in certain ways. *A priori* we believe that the mind of sentient beings produces, or causes, their behaviour, therefore, the mind that is malfunctioning must produce abnormal behaviour. However, in terms of the specific abnormal behaviour of a criminal act being produced by a specific abnormality of mind it is much more difficult for professionals to accept although society appears to be more at ease with this. There are as many criminals who are not mentally disordered as there are insane people who are not criminal. The central issue appears to be how these terms are socially defined and constructed. Cause and effect, sometimes referred to as causation, is fundamentally a philosophical question concerned with one event occurring which then necessitates the occurrence of another event. We can see this in the physical world, from grand cosmological events to sub-atomic happenings, as particles collide and trigger other reactions. However, many theorists point out that these are purely random occurrences with no causal necessity, other than action and motion, reflecting a universal dynamism. An example of this could be an asteroid travelling through the cosmos for millennia, which then strikes the earth and causes the destruction of life on the planet. At one level we understand it as merely a random collision in the negentropy of space and matter – and in terms of the cosmos a minor event at that. At another level we may desire to understand the end of the human species as having meaning in itself, in that, the asteroid is sent on a specific course, with a specific destiny, and a specific purpose at the volition of a vengeful divinity. Causal relationships are, thus, problematic even in the physical world. When extended to the realms of the human psyche, human nature, and human relations, causation is fraught with conceptual difficulties; namely, cause and effect are difficult to observe independent of the many other variables that accompany such actions. Furthermore, human beings are unique, and to assume that they will behave akin to natural objects is riven with contradictions. Human actors respond according to the meaning that they give to their world, and searching for a causal relationship between mental disorder and crime may well be a quest for the Holy Grail; that is, the searching being more significant than the finding.

The third dimension is the location and direction of the search for the relationship between crime and mental disorder. One approach is to examine criminals for signs of mental disorder. There are many studies that have focused their attention on the mental state of criminals. John Gunn, a British forensic psychiatrist, is one of the country's principal investigators of mental disorder in prison populations. In 1978 Gunn *et al.* found 31 per cent of a prison population to have met psychiatric diagnostic criteria and thirteen years later this had risen to 37 per cent (Gunn *et al.*, 1991). However, this still leaves two thirds of the prisons' inmates quite sane. Another approach is to search the mentally ill population for signs of criminal activity. Again, many studies have focused on this approach. Henry Steadman, in the USA, has produced extensive research in this area but the relationship remains elusive as there are more mentally ill people who do not engage in criminal activity than do. We will expand on these approaches later in the chapter.

So, the quest to establish a relationship between criminal behaviour and mental disorder is a complex undertaking which has centred on research that either establishes criminal activity in mentally ill persons or identifies mental abnormality in criminals. We are, thus, at an impasse unless we can change this narrow polar view. It will be a central tenet of our thesis that there is, indeed, a relationship between mental disorder and crime but that this relationship is not a biological, or even a psychological, one. It is our contention that the relationship is of a sociological nature. A relationship between crime and mental disorder has long been identified, at least popularly, by the general public and also apparently by those charged with the management of the criminally insane (Partridge, 1953). Early institutions to cater for such individuals clearly indicated both a client group, and specific function, in naming the organisation a 'criminal lunatic asylum'. Whether the category of 'criminally insane' refers to a person who is mentally ill and therefore engages in crime, or pertains to a criminal who then becomes insane, reflects the contemporary dilemma discussed below. Briefly, this is concerned with the study of mental disorder in offender populations and the study of criminal action in the mentally ill. The ultimate problem is the relationship between the two independent states of criminality and insanity, the conjoining of which suggests that one *causes* the other. The question is how tenable, or tenuous, is this relationship in empirical terms?; or, does it really matter?

Traditional approaches

As we pointed out above one traditional approach in searching for a causal relationship between mental disorder and crime is to look for criminal behaviour in psychiatric populations.

Criminal behaviour in psychiatric populations

It has long been held that those suffering from mental disorder are more likely to act violently and to break the law. Certainly, newspaper reports, television, documentaries, and fictional accounts frequently depict the mentally disordered as more violent or threatening than the remainder of the population. Not surprisingly, many studies have been conducted on mentally disordered groups to attempt to establish the extent of their violence or criminal activity. However, to date, the results have been varied and inconclusive.

Early studies reported that mental patients who were released from hospital were, in fact, less likely to engage in criminal activity than the general population (Rabkin, 1979). However, later studies have, generally, shown that mentally disordered persons are more likely to be arrested for criminal activity or re-hospitalised for violent behaviour (Blackburn, 1993). What seems to have occurred over the years is not so much the establishment of conclusions concerning the relationship between criminal behaviour and mental disorder, but a greater sophistication in the search strategies; otherwise known as 'methodological advances', it relates to developments in the way we look for supposed answers. For example, studies that report on research in this area offer differing assessment instruments for measuring both mental disorder and criminal behaviour, different data gathering procedures, as well as differing analyses of data (Palmero, Gumz, and Liska, 1992). Furthermore, there are also differing assumptions regarding psychiatric status and demographic comparability (Blackburn, 1993).

However, what is difficult to delineate from research reports regarding the relationship between mental disorder and criminal behaviour is the multi-factorial aspect of changing socio-cultural contexts over time. Although there are some indications of these dimensions in later studies, they tend not to emphasise the point nor appreciate the importance of their findings to the social dynamic. Steadman *et al.* (1985), for example, found that the number of mental patients with prior arrests had increased substantially over a number of years, and argued that this higher arrest rate among former mental patients reflected a change in the 'type' of patients in the American State Hospitals. This 'type' appears to be a qualitative change in relation to the extent of criminality in the hospital population. Such, leads to a suggestion that admission criteria may well have changed; that court decisions may have been influential in determining a qualitative shift; or that police arresting patterns could also have changed as a result of altered attitudes towards mentally disordered people.

Whatever constitutes the factors that affect the 'type' of patients in which criminality is observed, it is misleading to suggest that a static, independent, link exists between criminal behaviour and mental disorder. Rather, if anything, it is a state of affairs that dynamically shifts over time.

Mental disorder in criminals

Another popular approach in establishing a relationship between mental disorder and criminal behaviour is to examine criminal populations and investigate for mental disorder. However, these approaches share the same fate as those previously stated, in that, there is little agreement in diagnostic criteria. The reliability of diagnosis is often neither tested nor reported, the samples are often small and biased, and comparable rates are not offered for the general population (Hodgins, 1993). The arbitrariness of researchers investigating prison populations is such that it is not surprising that the results reported are wide and varied. For example, Guze

(1976), in the USA, reports that all females and 90 per cent of male offenders received a psychiatric diagnosis in their study, contrasted with Gunn *et al.* (1978) finding only 31 per cent of a British prison population to have met their psychiatric case criteria. However, with the passing of time, later studies showed fewer methodological weaknesses but continued to report diverse findings. For example, Hodgins (1993) in the USA found rates of mental disorder in their prison population almost four times higher, whilst in Britain Gunn *et al.* (1991) found only a small increase of 6 per cent between the 1978 study and this latter one.

Again, inconsistencies abound in these studies which makes interpretation of findings tenuous. For example, what constitutes a psychiatric condition often varies, with some studies including alcohol and drug abuse as criteria and other studies omitting these. Again, court decisions at the time of trial may influence the prevalence of mental disorder in prisons as the defendants' mental state may have been overlooked or hidden during court proceedings. Court pleas often influence a person's disposal either to the criminal justice system or the mental health system, which is a complex area often manipulated to secure a particular route. There is also the suggestion of a link between the number of psychiatric beds available in a community and the number of mentally disordered persons in the prison population. Furthermore, the conditions of prison life itself may increase the extent of mental disorder in those who had not previously experienced a psychiatric illness. These, and others, are social forces that influence the prevalence of mental disorder in prison populations, and, again, are not static entities but constantly changing according to social influences such as prison conditions, availability of resources, and political influences.

Clearly, a person may well be a criminal and become mentally ill whilst in prison, and, similarly, a person may be mentally disordered and commit an offence whilst ill. In the former there is apparently no case for a causal relationship between mental disorder and crime, whilst in the latter case there may well be so. However, the majority of studies merely report prevalence of these states and argue, rather unconvincingly, that because of this prevalence there is *a priori* causation. We can conclude, thus far, that the states of criminality and mental disorder are certainly not mutually exclusive and quite clearly can co-exist in the same person, at the same time. However, whether one can affect the other, or not, remains speculative.

Criminal behaviour and mental disorder in the 'mad' and the 'bad'

The relationship between mental disorder and criminal behaviour can be viewed at a number of levels. Mentally ill people are often viewed as dangerous or violent, rather than criminal, by the general population. This is associated with the long-standing image of the 'mad' being tormented by voices, out of control, or indiscriminately attacking others. Often the obviously mentally ill person in society is shunned and avoided where possible, with children brought out of the way and others crossing the street to avoid a perceived problem. It is the popularly held view that their irrationality and unreason equates with impulsivity, which causes them to be discerned as dangerous. Although many people are considered mentally ill, only a few act dangerously. However, it is the few sensational cases that attract media attention, which then fuels the opinion that all mentally ill persons are dangerous.

The relationship between criminal behaviour and mental disorder has received much attention over the past two decades. In reviewing the literature Spry (1984) found that the incidence of schizophrenia in the general population was 1 per cent whilst in those who had committed a serious offence it was much higher. Earlier, Hafner and Boker (1982) claimed that schizophrenics were arrested more often for crimes of violence than were other categories of mental illness. In non-offender studies associations have been found between acts of violence and specific symptoms of psychosis, with some claiming a higher risk of violence with the presence of delusions (Taylor, 1993). Possibly the latest major collection of studies to explore this association is gathered in Hodgins (1993); with statistical relations reported between schizophrenia and crime, violence and substance abuse, and psychopathy and mental disorder. Although actuarial relationships can be spurious what is important in this volume is that it breaks with the traditional 'scientific' view that no relationship between mental disorder and dangerousness exists. On the back cover it is claimed that 'while the public has always believed that the mentally disordered were more violent than others, these and other leading researchers in the field, until now, argued that the public's fear was unwarranted. Now, they have changed their mind' (Hodgins, 1993).

This last sociological point is possibly the most central issue pertaining to the relationship, real or imagined, between mental disorder and crime. That is, the general public *believe*, almost emphatically, that there is a relationship and that mentally ill people are dangerous. When they *act* according to this axiom, they create the tension which *is* the relationship. Therefore this relationship is real because it is imagined.

Another dimension to this relationship concerns the notion of psychopathy. The term 'psychopath' has become popularly synonymous with evil, representing depths of abhorrence and symbolising the dark side of the human psyche. In the public's mind the 'psychopath' is a cold, ruthless, killer, usually preying on vulnerable groups such as children, women, and the elderly; driven without compassion, and merely serving their own personal gratification. They occupy the nether regions of mental aberration in which they maintain responsibility for their actions, unlike those considered mentally ill. They *are* their behaviour. As far as society is concerned their 'badness' is a madness but qualitatively different from the common understanding of mental illness. In lay terms, 'psychopath' is a pejorative label.

From the professional's perspective the term 'psychopath' is more of a legal entity than a clinical one, with mental health workers preferring to consider psychopathy as a cluster of personality traits and socially deviant behaviours. From Hare's psychopathy checklist we observe such aspects as 'a glib and superficial charm; egocentricity; selfishness; lack of empathy, guilt and remorse; deceitfulness and manipulativeness; lack of enduring attachments to people, principles or goals; impulsive and irresponsible behaviour; and a tendency to violate explicit social norms' (Hare, 1980, p. 118). While these traits can be seen to construct what is understood to be 'psychopathy', such aspects are shared by what is considered to be the normal population. What is more difficult to locate is some form of *degree* to which these traits exist in the construction of a diagnosis. Viewing psychopathy in terms of categorised personality disorders, Blackburn (1993) differentiates between primary and secondary types, and stakes a claim for understanding these disorders in terms of binary dispositions; for example, hostile–friendly, sociable–withdrawn, compliant–coercive, and submissive–dominant. As a leading academic in this field, Blackburn (1993) concludes 'the categorical concept of psychopath is, in these terms, merely a convenient fiction, and improved classification of personality disorders will probably render it redundant' (p. 86).

It may well be that the term 'psychopath' falls into professional disuse, however, what will maintain its popular usage is its function as a signifier. It connotes the association between mental disorder and criminal behaviour in their most extreme forms. They become one unified entity in the social domain.

Social relationship

In charting the insertion of psychiatric power into the criminal justice domain, and pin-pointing in time the birth of the mentally disordered offender, Foucault's (1978) sociological analysis commences with a contemporary exchange between trial judge and accused man. The latter, charged with multiple rape, in refusing to answer a series of questions causes the gears of the French legal system to grind to a halt. Yet, the silence here is not about the facts of the case, for details of the crime have been established; rather, the individual is reticent to provide an answer to a central concern of the modern tribunal: 'Who are you?' If this dialogue is part of a familiar scenario in contemporary judicial arrangements, it both obscures and illuminates the medico-legal battle for the 'soul' of the deviant. The point which Foucault makes is that just one hundred and fifty years ago this discourse would be incomprehensible, where an admission of guilt would be sufficient to pass sentence. Now that has changed, and the criminal has a new responsibility: 'Much more is expected of him. Beyond admission, there must be a confession, self-examination, explanation of oneself, revelation of what one is' (Foucault, 1978, p. 2). Since the middle of the nineteenth century, the *criminal* has come to overshadow the *crime* in the business of the court-room; and from the monstrous to the mundane, forensic psychiatry has expanded its influence in the description and disposal of the offender. Exploration of the relationship between law and psychiatry must recognise that it 'was not only complex but inextricably bound up with developments in the behavioural sciences, in philosophy and politics' (Prins, 1980).

Bluglass (1980) notes that the shift in emphasis toward the criminal, as opposed to his deeds, heralded the first phase in the emergence of forensic psychiatry. A concern with the mental state of the offender, paralleled the objectives of a positivist, scientific, criminology most notably associated with Cesare Lombroso; the identification of a 'criminal type' characterised by measurable, physical, 'stigmata'. In claiming a biological base for deviance, criminality became an innate trait capable of being transmitted from one generation to another. At the same time as Lombroso was conducting his anthropometric studies on prison and asylum populations, leading psychiatrists in France and England began to consider criminality as a form of mental illness; initiating a search for developmental explanations, and possible treatments (Sapsford, 1981). It is of little surprise, then, that this conjoint focus witnessed the genesis of the 'criminal lunatic' in the works of physicians like James Bruce Thompson (1867): 'Wondering where actually "badness ended and madness began", he concludes that "the inmates of the asylum and the prison are so allied that thin partitions do their bounds divide"' (Jayewardene, 1963, p. 165).

By 1863, Broadmoor, the first English institution for the containment of the criminally insane furnished a home for this exclusive category of offender, and a power-base for modern forensic medicine. In reviewing the legislative apparatus which accommodated this psychiatric incursion, it is important to contextualise the changes within wider political and social upheavals. The rapid expansion of an industrial economy and a new urban landscape, where the threat of madness merged with the contagion of disease epidemics, gave rise to increased state control over the individual exercised through an ideology of public hygiene; psychiatry situated social danger in the 'micro-physics' of the 'societal body' and the 'individual body' (Foucault, 1978). Indeed, a new form of 'body-punishment' relations emerged, a mental discipline rather than a physical pain, a private penance rather than a public spectacle, and the morality of cure rather than the shame of condemnation: 'As a result of this new restraint, a whole army of technicians took over from the executioner, the immediate anatomist of pain: warders, doctors, chaplains, psychiatrists, psychologists, educationalists; by their very presence near the prisoner, they sing the praises that the law needs: they reassure it that the body and pain are not the ultimate objects of its punitive action' (Foucault, 1977, p. 11).

Standard histories documenting developments in the legal status of the insane typically present a series of reforms as the, intellectual and institutional, markers of an advancing humanitarianism. Too often, a modern frame of reference in constructing the questions posed, shrinking the distance between past and present, overlooks the uniqueness of those day-to-day discourses which evidenced a medical–legal conjecture. It has been suggested, therefore, that: 'Even if inchoate, the social field was thus a necessary substratum for loftier discourses on political society and civil society. Reconstructing medical psychology makes at least a start in laying out the wider outlines of contemporary discourses on "the social"' (Donnelly, 1983, p. xii). From this position, critical accounts have begun to excavate, as an archaeology of ideas, those links between the advent of a carceral system and broader social trends (Scull, 1985; Ignatieff, 1985).

This 'shadow side of modernity' suggests that an understanding of decision-making in relation to the mentally disordered needs to focus on the 'trivial circumstances in which experts operate' (Smith, 1989), as much as the structural framework of policy. Thus, in proffering a comparative history of nineteenth-century forensic psychiatry, and the insanity defence in particular, this author highlights a controversy which has persisted to the present; a conflict, or more precisely an inter-relationship, between 'voluntarism' and 'determinism' or 'theory' and 'practice'. The faith of an embryonic psychiatry, in offering solutions to the problem of 'dangerous lunatics', was not uncontested in the courtroom: 'Contemporary commentators on this situation explained it by reference either to the inappropriateness and inadequacy of medical argument to assist the court's decision-making or to legal and public resistance to scientific thinking' (Smith, 1989, p. 292). If the occupational and institutional procedures evolved in different ways, these same tensions manifested themselves on the opposite side of the Atlantic. In the USA the origins of legislative provision for mentally disordered offenders became embroiled in conflicting definitions of mental disease, expressed in psychological and neurological discourse; a distinction between the 'insane criminal' and the 'criminally insane' (Quen, 1994).

Medicalising the relationship

We tend to accept that the domain of the body is the territory of doctors, that is, physicians and surgeons. In Western society should the body become diseased or disordered in its functioning the usual source of referral is to a (wo)man of medicine, and the reasons for this are said to lie within the relationship between medicine and religion (Turner, 1987). Medicine is concerned with the relief of pain, and pain is the pathway to death. Most humans fear pain above all else, even more than our own extinction; fully understanding those unfortunates who, in suffering for protracted periods, crave the release of death. Therefore, it is not surprising that the principle in the Hippocratic oath sets the relief of pain as a priority over the extension of life. At the same time, we long for good health and an extended life, and should we become diseased we naturally turn to those we believe have the power to relieve any discomfort and deter the end for as long as possible. Within most religions there are two central concepts which tie in to these human desires. The first relates to the notion of heaven which is a place, such as Elysium or Valhalla, where those in God's favour dwell after death in a state of supreme happiness. This is the state of perfect health, physical, psychological, emotional, and spiritual. The second concept concerns the notion of eternity, a state of endless, or infinite, time which manifests itself as the human urge for longevity and procreation, that is, eternal genetic life. Both religion and medicine, then, offer the promise of a state of health and happiness for as long as possible, with those providing the keys to such gateways, ministers and medics, being held in high esteem.

The medicalisation process

When a specific aspect of the body becomes the focus of medical attention there is a process by which it is claimed, controlled, and brought within medical ideology. This process involves five central stages; identification, classification, diagnosis, treatment, and prognosis. The first stage, identification, is concerned with how a certain element of the body is considered abnormal, and for this to occur there must be some understanding of what is judged to be normal. For example, cancerous cells are viewed as being different from normal ones only because we have some understanding of what normal cells should look like and how they ought to behave. The important point of this identification stage is the medical surveillance that accompanies the process; without this constant observation, and mapping of normality, any identification of the abnormal could not be achieved. The second stage refers to classification, in which diseases and disorders are categorised, designated and related, through a specific branch of medical science known as nosology. This ordering of disorders develops the illusion that diseases can be known, in the sense that those who claim such knowledge also claim the power that accompanies it. The third stage is diagnosis in which the knowledge concerning a disorder suggests that the aetiology is understood through a series of causes and effects. By asserting a knowledge of a course of events concerning a disease, through its history, there is an implicit assumption that it can, thus, be controlled. The fourth stage, treatment, is concerned with the application of interventions to correct the disease. These are often considered new, pioneering, traditional, heroic, or alternative, but all must claim some justification for their application, and some degree of expertise by the applicator; there must be the suggestion of an effective therapy. Finally, the process requires some predictive element that can establish the probability of success, or otherwise, referred to as prognosis. In this final stage, as in all the others, there is an implicit message concerning the power to control disease and disorder.

Seen in relation to the body, this process of medicalisation appears as a logical function of Western health care, though various groups, such as midwifery, do offer challenges from time to time. However, when the medical 'gaze' falls on less-certain territory, such as the psychiatrisation of the criminal, there is often a hotly contested dispute over the subject area. We have noted this battle for the criminal in the preceding section of this chapter, and now proceed to briefly discuss the relationship between mental disorder and crime in terms of pathologising offending behaviour.

Pathology of the monstrous

With the expansion of technology, and increasing speed of communication, the globe is said, in postmodern terms, to be shrinking in time and space (Giddens, 1990). By this it is meant that through the medium of technology, international events are brought under scrutiny and transmitted into homes around the world. Journalists are jetted to the scene of newsworthy incidents within a few hours, and televise their analyses through a plethora of media outlets. The event, say a sensational criminal act, receives, in the first instance, a macro-analysis of its occurrence which entails regaling the listener with the known facts of the case as a form of story to be told. As the commercialised account is re-told new slants and pitches are searched for, and a micro-analysis undertaken, often relying heavily on interpretive licence and intrusive investigative journalism. The perpetrator, the victim, and their respective families, are scrutinised ever more closely for 'facts' pertinent to the telling of the story.

Great crimes and criminals, first and foremost, are attributed with the labels of 'sick', 'mad', and 'evil' by members of society, communicated through the media. Later, these labels are manipulated by courts of law and the profession of psychiatry, with the process of medicalisation endowing a notion of scientificity. If Foucault (1978) is correct in claiming that criminal psychiatry first proclaimed itself a 'pathology of the monstrous', it would appear that contemporary forensic psychiatry merely perpetuates this function. If society creates, and then reveals, the monster, forensic psychiatry medicalises them and professes a knowledge of their actions through purported expertise.

In the mind of the public the heinous crime and the monstrous criminal are clearly related to the 'evil madman', and there can be little doubt as to the social importance of this relationship. It is not surprising, therefore, that considerable effort is exerted by researchers in investigating the nature of this affiliation. Despite claims that forensic psychiatry merely treats clinical conditions, apart from their offending behaviour, they are inextricably embroiled in addressing the relations between the two. The monster belongs to society, and that some become the subjects of psychiatry is tolerated only so long as they are not permitted to re-offend. The pathologisation of the monstrous, therefore, engages forensic mental health workers to deal with the relationship between mental disorder and criminal behaviour irrespective of their desire to do so, or their success in this undertaking.

Index offence and scene of crime

The relationship between criminal behaviour and mental disorder involves further medicalisation, with the shifting focus of the medical 'gaze' penetrating the index offence and scene of crime. Typically, there is a focus upon ever more minutia, dividing cells and structures through microscopic vision. However, this mode of reduction also allows the medicalisation of large-scale social systems and grand schemata, for example public hygiene, health education, and mass inoculations. Through this two-way focus it 'gazes' on micro units and constructs large-scale epidemiological theories inductively. For example, the medical microscope may 'gaze' on minute water-borne organisms, but draws conclusions that a particular village is at risk through drinking from an infected supply. In terms of the mentally disordered offender a similar system is in place, which operates from capture and captivity to case management following release. Here, we outline two aspects which relate to the capture of the offender.

The first concerns a medical policing of the victim, from an examination of someone who has been assaulted to the post-mortem examination of a corpse. In all these forensic examinations the minutia of the event are collected as specimens, as units of analysis, and as signifiers of meaning; for example fibres, hairs, blood, scrapings from nails, or semen, represent the signposts of interpretation. Wounds are counted and measured, angles of assault carefully calculated, and traumatised areas of the body observed with a qualitative assessment of types of injuries sustained. All of this provides, cumulative, meanings for subjective interpretation concerning the perpetrators age, weight, height, strength and dominant handedness. There will be theories of emotional state at the time of the attack, and questions raised as to whether it was frenzied, with multiple stab wounds, or calmly callous with deliberate cutting patterns of the skin. Other investigations might focus on the disfigurement of body parts such as the eyes, genitals, or hands, with meanings deduced from any systematic, sexual, or ritualistic patterning. From these static points of the victim a dynamic picture emerges, which however accurate or inaccurate, then informs police investigations. This relationship between the pathologist's account and the investigative strategy has been romanticised on T.V. in the role of Quinsey, a police pathologist who from post-mortem findings is able to deduce the culprit and solve the crime.

The second, related, aspect of capture concerns policing the scene of crime. Investigative psychology, otherwise known as offender profiling or crime scene analysis, is concerned with establishing certain personal attributes of the offender from particular aspects of the scene of crime. For example, the placement and positioning of the victim, or the extent of disturbance to surrounding areas, may indicate that a struggle took place, or that certain items were used in the attack. Other variables would include the clothing of the victim, the neighbourhood in which the crime scene is set, and the timing of the assault; inferences are then drawn as to the sequence of events and possible motivations. Submitted to the police, these variables narrow the focus of an investigation to certain personal and social typologies. This, again, has been fictionalised in the role of 'Cracker' in which Fitz, the investigative psychologist, describes an offender from the scene of crime analysis. The description usually involves not only personality structures but also psycho-dynamic states, and social functioning. Although purely entertaining drama, the popularity of the programme clearly indicates, in the public mind if nowhere else, a connection between criminal behaviour and mental disorder.

Bad men make good news

Perhaps nowhere is the horror and fear of the disordered offender more dramatically captured, and exploited, than in the uncompromising headlines of tabloid journalism. Routine reports of mental illness are, not untypically, linked to pejorative stereotypes which emphasise threat and danger (Lehane and Rees, 1996; Linehan, 1996). However, when offenders, or their trials, are of such a nature as to attract a degree of notoriety the language shifts from venal to vitriolic, often as sustained campaigns against individuals over many years: 'These immediate reactions of revulsion and anger are reflected in the rhetoric of the popular press. On the whole, the more populist and popular the paper, the more it expresses the traditional reaction of hatred and vindictiveness' (Bavidge, 1989, p. 3). The extent to which sensationalist storylines describe, or actually incite, angry public protest within and without the courtroom is certainly linked to circulation rates and profit. The effect that the media has on the public was graphically portrayed by Greg Philo reporting on the Glasgow Media Group's recent research in which the notion of psychiatric patients were thematically depicted as 'freed to kill'. The Glasgow group show how the linking of the community care programme of decanting large numbers of psychiatric patients from institutional care to care in the community with the notion of 'freed to kill' distorted the public's perception of sufferers with mental illness (Philo, 1996). If sexual violence against women is an endemic feature of contemporary culture, it is the most disturbed and disturbing attacks which are selected as the most newsworthy (Soothill and Walby, 1991). Sadistic assailants and 'gang rapists' are easily constructed into the loathed and fearsome figure of 'beast' and 'monster'; as something sub-human and animalistic, a species apart from the rest of humanity. The debate about madness and badness, though, cannot be restricted to media representations; it is part of a philosophical discourse about wickedness and symbolises the fundamental contradiction of forensic practice. Punishment or treatment hinge on an understanding and demonstration of criminal responsibility, and medicine, no less than the law, is muddled up with morality.

Concepts of badness and madness are usually presented as polarised opposites, regardless of the possibility, or desirability, that is suggested (Bowden, 1983). In terms of societal responses to individual offenders, this 'irresistable phrase' reflects a distinction between the dual camps of 'traditionalists' and 'progressives' (Bavidge, 1989). The former directing attacks upon the perceived liberalism of a growing army of therapists, whose shared psychospeak underpins the medicalisation of wickedness; an over concern with the interests of the criminal at the expense of the victim. In retort, the progressives condemn an antiquated system where revenge masquerades as justice; that psychiatry, apart from its developmental state, is compromised in its dealings with the legal mentality. Again, we are reminded of the Szaszian (1961; 1970) argument that ideologically exclusive cosmologies determine human difference and its management, where the Age of Faith has been superseded by the Age of Therapy. The on-going expansion of psychiatric classification to embrace a wider range of deviant activities, testifies to the claims of science to control non-conformity. Increasingly, issues of guilt and responsibility are subsumed by a monolithic medical standard, mental health (good) and mental illness (bad). Here, the focus shifts from what the offender has *done* to what the offender *is*.

While psychiatric and psychological assessments permit internal dissent about whether or not individual offenders warrant differential treatment on the basis of a diminished responsibility for their actions, moral responses are much less flexible (Bavidge, 1989). The psychopathic offender is a case in point, where professional judgements are eclipsed by personal feelings; in particular cases diagnosis and classification may be commonly agreed, while the value of therapeutic intervention remains a source of conflict. As one forensic psychiatrist has recently remarked: 'A total self-absorption and disregard for others is the sign of the psychopath, and, in my opinion, the origin of what much of the world calls evil' (Simon, 1996, p. 317). It is this 'psychopathology of evil', of crimes which lie beyond ordinary human comprehension, which links together madness, medicine, and the media in a reflexive and rhetorical dialogue. Top selling novels like American Psycho (Ellis, 1991) and their movie/video adaptations such as *Cape Fear*, purvey serial killers in a serial format for home entertainment. Fiction becomes faction in a postmodern reality, as Plummer (1995, p. 137) illustrates with reference to one survivor narrative: 'Nancy Ziegenmeyer's rape becomes a story told on chat shows, paperbacks, serialised newspaper columns and a docudrama. Hence the boundaries between her life and the multiple media events blurs.' Highstreet newsagents and stores stock an ever increasing number of books and magazines which focus on the gruesome details of 'true-crime'. Alongside these are titles which offer a populist version of 'the world of forensic psychiatry' (Miller, 1994), so it is of little surprise that *Criminal Shadows* (Canter, 1995) should enter the best-seller lists. The consumption of sexual violence for sexual pleasure is central to the feminist assault on pornography in the widest sense: detective magazines which eroticise the suffering of victims, and mainstream material that extols praise for the multiple killers of women (Caputi, 1988). It is the cultural capital of mass-murder and marketability which has elevated Jack the Ripper to the status of 'folk hero', an icon for T-shirts, key rings, and day trips. How apposite that a recent addition to the literature exploring the darker dimensions of human nature should be titled *Bad men do what good men dream* (Simon, 1996).

The attribution of evil as popular currency is a regular feature of newspaper descriptions of psychiatric inmates in maximum secure settings, akin to the broadsheets which celebrated the public execution of condemned criminals. Indeed, if morality once crystallised at the foot of the scaffold (Box, 1981), a little imagination might suggest that the walls of the prison and asylum have assumed this ideological boundary. In this sense the structural and symbolic imagery of the special hospitals edify the 'bastion of society's nightmares'; a configuration of madness, dangerousness, and evil into a 'nineteenth-century trinity' (Richman and Mason, 1992). Pathology has replaced theology in the creation of a stigmatised and marginalised 'other'. The infamy and interest generated by the most sinister denizens of these institutions seem to purge, if not always purify, the collective conscience. Crimes of wickedness perpetrated by one man are sufficient to contaminate both the 'guests' and 'guards' of 'Brady Hospital'; while postal sacks of fan mail and Valentine cards add a medieval twist to any 'glamour' or 'charm' associated with Britain's most reviled child killer.

To date, debates about the concept of evil have remained the province of theologians (James, 1960), anthropology (Parkin ed., 1985), and moral philosophy (Midgley, 1985); with minor exceptions (Tannenbaum, 1973), the topic has failed to excite a sociological imagination (Wolff, 1969). Pioneering accounts have been offered of this elusive and intangible quality in relation to the discipline of psychiatry (Prins, 1994); premised upon a recognition that forensic science, in confronting the bizzare extremes of human behaviour, can usefully embrace the subject matter of mythology, folklore, demonology (Prins, 1992; 1984; Fahy *et al.*, 1988). Less attention, though, has been directed at the everyday experience of caring for that group of mentally disordered offenders whose actions have transgressed the threshold of conventional morality; accommodating them within a clinical model of aetiology and intervention (Mercer, 1998). The role and function of 'gallows humour' in forensic settings has been noted (Kuhlman, 1988), yet to relegate cultural totemics to a macabre form of stress management misses an important point. It is suggested that the use of evil in a 'strong' sense is obsolete in contemporary society, with the possible exception of specific exemplars such as sadistic crime, torture, and genocide (Macfarlane, 1985). If the medicalisation of deviant behaviour has been central to an overt exclusion of evil from any vocabulary of intent (Conrad and Schneider, 1980), tensions emerge within the psychopathology model; for the paradox of evil is the idea that certain individuals are responsible for their deeds, yet somehow driven by uncontrollable forces (Babuta and Bragard, 1988). One study (Richman *et al.*, 1998), attempting to understand how forensic nursing staff conceptualise offending behaviour, has reported the construction of a taxonomy of evil, strongly related to diagnostic type. Thus, deviance perpetrated by those with a psychotic symptamotology are typically accorded a primordial contract of innocence. In contrast, extreme offences committed by those with a psychopathic disorder are considered to be evil; engaging in behaviour which purposefully transgresses natural boundaries, where moral bonding is extinct. This interplay between the socially sanctioned and the socially sacrificed is vital to an understanding of the lives of those women who enter the forensic network; who, if small in number, are statistically overrepresented in the total patient population.

Woman as deviant

In the 'rogues gallery' of tabloid journalism discussed above, there can be no more enduring, or haunting, image than the figure of Myra Hindley. Thousands of words, over thirty years, have promoted a cult of mass hatred; yet in a sense the print is wasted, for a single, grainy, black and white photograph from the 1960s indelibly fixes this woman in the collective mind as an icon of evil

(Birch, 1993). In narrowly escaping the death sentence, she has become larger than life. Unlike her lover, Brady, she has resisted the comforts of madness and relentlessly campaigned for freedom. Those brave enough to suggest that punishment can exceed justice, face contamination by association. Her story is a paradox for feminist criminology; for in her crimes, and her refusal to be silenced, Myra Hindley affronts the rules which govern her gender: 'Such a woman is beyond understanding, hardly human at all. We must place her as far as possible away from all other women, from all of us' (Lloyd, 1995, p. 49). Indeed, the case of Myra Hindley demonstrates, in its extremest form, the sex-specific discourse which constructs the female offender; innocent or wicked, mad or bad, there are no grey areas (Cameron and Frazer, 1987).

In contrast, many of the women who enter the forensic services present a greater risk to themselves than to others, often sharing horrific histories of childhood abuse (Potier, 1993). Their offences, if there are criminal convictions, are generally of a lesser order of severity than their male counterparts (Adshead and Morris, 1995). It is ironic that while the discipline of criminology should express little interest in the criminality of women (Gelsthorpe and Morris, 1988), they should find themselves at the 'centre of the professional gaze' (Sim, 1990). For the medical men of the nineteenth century, deviant women represented a threat to the stability of family life, and ultimately the social order. As objects of power and knowledge, they were to become a 'species' apart, like the insane and the sexually perverse (Faith, 1994). Within institutions designed for men, female offenders found themselves subjected to a specific form of rehabilitation; one guided by an ideology of domesticity and motherhood, and aimed at returning them to their natural role (Rowatt and Vaughn, 1981).

Criminal activity *per se* is predominantly a male activity with an increased ratio over female crime in the region of 3.1 for petty offences and 7.1 for violent crimes, both in the USA and the UK (Blackburn, 1993). However, that women who break the law, or act in a violent way, are more likely to receive psychiatric treatment than punishment cannot be explained by mental health differences between the sexes. Rather, their psychiatrisation is a complex interaction of discursive structures and gendered understandings of the world (Allen, 1987). In this sense, the relationship between mental disorder and criminality is sociologically fashioned; where the 'normal' is affirmed by the 'deviant', and a moral code outlined for all women (Hutter and Williams, 1981).

Summary

An attempt has been made to explore the relationship between mental disorder and crime; two distinct spheres of human experience, conjoined in the mentally disordered offender. Traditional research approaches, focusing on the populations of prisons and asylums, remain inconclusive about this marriage of badness and madness. More significantly, from a sociological perspective the equation is framed by the dominant discourses and institutional power of law and medicine. The genesis, and growth, of forensic science symbolises a one hundred and fifty year struggle for the 'soul' of the deviant. It is contended, here, that the relationship between criminality and madness is socially constructed, and mediated by social class, race, and gender.

Chapter 4

The social construction of the dangerous offender

Introduction

The mentally disordered offender is an amalgam of conceptualisations from various sources, including legal, psychiatric, criminal, and social. However, the social construction of the mentally disordered offender requires a central focal point which can galvanise the issues of danger, threat, harm, etc. This focal point is the crime itself.

Crimes and the social impact

When we believe that we can understand crime we also believe that we are more in control, and when we can apply reason to an unreasonable event we feel that we have, both, mastered it and fathomed its depths. However, when we cannot penetrate its mystery, and in our final analysis we are left facing the abyss of Unreason, then, we catch a glimpse of the Other in all of us. It is this relational position, between a person suffering from a mental disorder and the remaining members of society, that, for us, makes it necessary to adopt a sociological perspective. Furthermore, when this relationship is anchored in a criminal offence it provides an agency for the forces of threat, danger, and power to become central issues in the sociology of the mentally disordered offender.

The criminal act brings into stark relief certain features pertaining to, both, the mentally disordered person and the society that produces them. This was noted in a seminal paper by Michel Foucault (1978) which was 'About the Concept of the Dangerous Individual in Nineteenth Century Legal Psychiatry'. In this paper Foucault argues that six serious crimes occurring in a period spanning approximately thirty five years between 1799 and 1835 provided the basis of the medicalisation of the criminal. Although psychiatrists had given evidence in legal proceedings prior to this time it was over this period, according to Foucault, that judges and jurors began to take note of the crimes and the psychiatric explanation of 'homicidal monomania'.

Briefly, the cases were that of a retired officer who became attached to his landlady's child and without motive or emotion attacks the child with a hammer, though not fatally. In the second case, during a famine, a peasant woman kills her daughter and cooks one of her legs in the soup. A servant girl, in the third case, insists on looking after her neighbour's daughter, who is hesitant about this, but the servant girl convinces her neighbour, subsequently kills the child, cuts off her head, and throws it out of the window. In the fourth case a woman kills her illegitimate child, is acquitted on the grounds of insanity but declares that she will do it again. She becomes pregnant and murders the baby at birth claiming at the trial that she became pregnant for the sole purpose of killing the baby. She is executed. In the fifth case a man kills a woman in her house for no apparent motive whatsoever and is executed. Finally, a man kills his foster mother, whom he got on well with, and after initially confessing to the murder he remembers nothing. He is executed.

Foucault (1978) observes that these cases, and the judges' responses to them, differed from other cases in this period on several counts. Firstly, they were committed without passion, or fury, without any obvious sign of dementia or intellectual impairment, and were inexplicable by traditional definitions of insanity. Thus, whatever had 'caused' the crimes was an invisible threat. Secondly, they were all serious and strangely cruel. Thirdly, they all took place in a domestic setting which involved family or neighbours. They were also cross generational, usually adult–child or adolescent–adult. These were the sacred domains of relationships, place, and kinship which had been transgressed by these most heinous of crimes. Although, the crimes were not directed at society at large by, for example an attack on a stranger, they went to the very heart of the social unit, i.e. the family, the family home, and the familial relationships.

For psychiatry to successfully penetrate the courts, and form what would later become forensic psychiatry, it required a pathology to provide explanatory power. The pathology it used was the fictitious *homicidal monomania*. This became the explanation for these entirely insane crimes. This not only provided the 'scientific' account but also furnished the leverage for psychiatry to intervene in the process of law. This powerful Foucauldian analysis clearly shows the power of the crime in that social sphere which embroils the madman and society's fears.

Foucault's analysis

Foucault's analysis is concerned with these six cases stretched across Europe over a thirty five year period at the turn of the nineteenth century in relation to the discursive practices of the knowledge-system pertaining to the influential developments forging the concept of the 'dangerous individual'. The power of Foucault's analytic synthesis is that it does not attempt to separate out, in any clearly delineated manner, the causal forces and resultant effects of this development from either the pragmatics or the epistemology of crime. That is, his thesis does not isolate single entities that drive the development forwards in a linear fashion whether these entities are professional advances from scientific disciplines, changes in semantics on related conceptual areas of risk assessment, alterations in perceptual frameworks of the judiciary, or shifts in societal understanding of insanity and its relationship to crime. Rather than offer these forces as a nexus of causal drives Foucault's penetrating expose locks each of these forces into each other in one dynamic epistemic movement that manufactures the 'dangerous individual' as an emergent and mutant progeny. Interlinked, inter-penetrated, embedded, and embodied the pathologification of social danger is born. Not from an organised, structured, planned, and co-ordinated motivation, but from a cornucopia of criminal imagery, symbolic explanation, and scientific persuasion.

How does Foucault achieve this? In his paper (Foucault, 1978) he begins by inserting the right of silence in relation to medical or judicial testimony. This transgression of the moral imperative to defend oneself against accusers, by refusing to confess either to the events of the crime or the secrets of his own being not only ensures that 'the judicial machine ceases to function' but that also psychiatry becomes paralysed (p. 18). The claim is that the criminal must reveal himself, make visible the inner motivator of actions, and produce a revelatory confession. This opening up of himself allows for the insertion of psychiatric explanation or judicial punishment. The quest is more than knowing the facts of the crime, which can be ascertained from the evidence of the scene, it is to know him – the criminal – that was now sought. Prior to this, a criminal act informed 'what must be punished and how', however, what now developed was the question 'whom do you think you are punishing?' (p. 3).

The cases that Foucault presents in brief (see above) are merely examples of an interpretive typology of crimes committed over the period (episteme) of his analysis. We cannot say that similar cases did not exist before, nor do we say that they did not occur after this epoch. It is that, for Foucault, the nature of European thought at this time created the conditions enabling this thematic appraisal. The cases, or more accurately the Foucauldian analysis, reveals five main themes that underscore the penetration of psychiatry into the court of law at that time. The first theme was the focus away from the criminal act *per se*, to the criminal himself. This required a need to understand the nature of the person and the extent to which they posed a dangerous element in the social body. Previously, the crime was understandable, in terms of it being an act, i.e., a murder is a murder, and thus punishable by a set code. Once the criminal's motivations and intentions became the focus of investigation this need to understand became all important. However, understanding the criminal will could not be achieved in such cases as Foucault highlights as they were deemed beyond reason. This, then, allowed the intervention of supposed 'experts' in criminal intention. Such expertise demanded a 'scientific' explanation which came in the form of *homicidal monomania*, a derangement which only occurs within the context of the criminal act, or more accurately, a 'zero degree of insanity' that is the crime itself. The psychiatrists of this period used this conceptual, and fictitious, entity to intervene in the process of law for approximately a hundred years before it fell into disrepute. This *homicidal monomania* 'explained' the inexplicable criminal being and the criminal act. As Foucault puts it, it allowed the pathologification of the monstrous.

Once medicine had penetrated the court with the birth of forensic psychiatry there was a need for it to secure a foothold and increase its power base. Therefore, the gaze widened from the 'scientific rationality' of psychiatric explanation within the legal process to secure a modality of power that existed in criminality within the community. Forensic psychiatry, thus, conquered a field of knowledge that was located in the concern with the dangerous offender in the social body. There was a growing concern with the extent of crime in society and this alarm permitted forensic psychiatry to produce interventions in order to reduce this growing dangerousness. Therefore, forensic psychiatry functioned as a form of public hygiene. It followed that society became viewed as a biological entity for medical scrutiny which could *produce* more crime through increased specialists identifying dangerous individuals in terms of such categorisations as *homicidal monomania*. A criminal could be crystallised into a madman whose only insanity was to commit a criminal act. Thus, from then on, the criminally insane, the mentally disordered offender, became one single object – the dangerous individual. The two concepts, insanity and crime, fused into one; cause and effect melded into the same thing; and the criminal act became integrated into the total behaviour of the subject. In science, psychiatric or legal, the relationship between these entities needed to be identified which required a separation. This was achieved through the mechanics of punishment.

As Foucault put it 'among all the new techniques for controlling and transforming individuals, punishment had become a system of procedures designed to reform lawbreakers' (Foucault, 1978). The crime was not punished, instead the criminal was. The sanctions brought to bear were designed to affect his motivations, his intentions, and his will to criminality. However, these are the very foci of the psychiatrist's expertise and thus punishment mutated into treatment. One could not punish what one could not make sense of. Whereas, previously, punishment fitted the crime in a reasoned sort of way, now the crime was without reason and could no longer be punished. Thus, the search began in earnest for an 'intelligible link between the act and the author' (Foucault, 1978, p. 10).

Finally, Foucault locates a second period between 1885 and 1910 during which time Criminal Anthropology emerged and a transformation in civil law occurred, both being influential in the abandonment of the notion of *homicidal monomania*. The idea that a condition could exist which unleashed itself on the individual causing him to commit monstrous crimes, affecting his emotions and motivations whilst leaving intact his thought processes both before the act and after the event, fell outside of contemporary scientific understanding of the nature of insanity. The great crimes as a focus of scrutiny were replaced by the degeneration of morality (for example, deviations is sexual conduct) across a wide range of transgressions. From the depth of the inexplicable monster to the breadth of minor infractions the psychiatric gaze absorbed new categories. This allowed for a clearer causal analysis of the motivations and intentions across a wide range of human behaviours, delinquent or otherwise, which led psychiatry and the judiciary into the on-going debate concerning free will and legal responsibility. Further to this, the changes in civil law were influenced by conceptual developments in the notions of accidents, legal responsibility, insurance, and risk. Industrialisation, urbanisation, and transportation brought with it the risks of third party, in the pure form of accident, i.e., those that just happened to be there at the time. This was followed by the notion of error, in terms of mis-judgement, negligence, and inattention, which made someone liable for damages. Unfortunately, this burden could not be borne by many and thus changes in civil law allowed for the idea of no-fault responsibility. This set the model for penal law which quickly allowed the psychiatric exoneration of risk assessment in relation to the dangerous individual. 'With this untenable paradox of monomania and of the monstrous act, psychiatry and penal justice entered a phase of uncertainty from which we have yet to emerge. The play between penal responsibility and psychological determinism has become the cross of legal and medical thought' (p. 11) – then, as now.

Some recent and contemporary cases and social responses

In this section we wish to outline some notorious post-war British crimes that have impacted on the public to one degree or another and have influenced society's perception of the mentally disordered offender. The social mechanism of the media, by which these crimes are reported either in newspaper articles or books, is the tool adopted in this analysis. This, both, identifies and reinforces the social values that underscore the public response to these crimes.

Graham Young

In 1962, Graham Young, at the age of fourteen was convicted of poisoning his stepmother and attempting to poison his father, sister, and a school friend. He was committed to Broadmoor where he spent the next nine years. In 1971 he was pronounced 'cured' and released with a medical certificate that included the words 'he has made an extremely full recovery and is now entirely fit for discharge' (Chancellor Press, 1994, p. 26). By the end of that year he had murdered two work colleagues having gained employment as a storeman in a laboratory that manufactured photographic equipment. This environment was awash with poisonous chemicals. He was arrested and tried the following year in 1972 and given a life sentence.

The media coverage was extremely hostile, mainly because he had committed the same crime previously, been admitted to Broadmoor and pronounced 'cured'. Young brought into focus several issues that haunted society and the psychiatric profession itself. He was classified as suffering from a personality disorder but little was, or is, understood about this diagnostic label (Blackburn, 1993). The media were very sceptical about both the 'treatment' and the 'cure' and asked highly relevant questions regarding what exactly was the nature of the treatment he had supposedly received in the nine years in Broadmoor and what was the nature of the 'cure'? Graham Young remained in prison, dying of a heart attack in Parkhurst eighteen years later.

Ian Brady and Myra Hindley

In the post-war era it is, perhaps, the notorious combination of Ian Brady and Myra Hindley that evoke the greatest social disquiet. Brady and Hindley conjure up the personification of evil more so than any other murderers in recent times. Brady was illegitimate, born in Glasgow in 1938 and was brought up by a warm and loving couple who also had other children. Despite the relatively normal family life it is reported that he grew to be a loner, not belonging, and feeling that 'he needed to define his role in society' (Harrison, 1994, p. 25). He turned to cruelty and was fascinated by literature of a sadistic nature. He became emotionally isolated. Hindley also grew up outside of her natural home at her Grandmother's house in Gorton. Her upbringing was unremarkable and not uncommon. However, 'some of her teachers believed it had led her to form an attitude which set her apart from the other children . . . she was a loner . . . the Plain Jane' (Wilson, 1986, p. 14). Thus, independently, Brady and Hindley were loners, outsiders to society, and bore a grudge. It was the coming together to combine a chemistry of callousness that compounded itself into what is often described as 'evil'.

The corrupt combination sexually abused, tortured, and murdered several young children in the early 1960s, with other missing bodies still unaccounted for. The nature of their crimes were exacerbated with the tape-recording of one young victim begging for mercy and pleading for her 'mum' to help her. This tape played out in court produced a profound abhorrence towards these perpetrators.

Notwithstanding the extent of their depravity, and heinousness of their crime, Brady and Hindley produce a negative social reaction which appears to be greater than their peer serial child killers. Why is this? One contributing factor is possibly the fact that the death penalty in Britain was abolished one month after Brady was arrested and, therefore, these killers were one of the first to 'cheat the hangman' and 'escape' with life imprisonment. Another factor may have been the perceived multi-transgressional betrayal on the part of the female Hindley. She broke the law of the land by killing, she broke the law of nature by sex-offending (relatively uncommon in females), and she broke the law of maternity as a protective female 'mother'. In any event 'she is the most reviled woman in the British penal system and she has to contend with a sustained media campaign against her . . .' (Harrison, 1994, p. 194). Another factor may well be the continuing secrets that remain. Hidden bodies unrevealed. Details of their crimes remain unreported as Brady and Hindley refuse to tell exactly what they did, and we are left with the imaginative interpretation formed from the tape-recordings. Brady himself cast into the category of mentally disordered offender now spends his declining years in a special hospital. His continued secretive silence manifests itself in the vacillating psychiatric diagnoses of psychopathy and psychosis.

The extent of media interest in the Brady and Hindley case is interesting if only because of its endurance. From the trial itself – 'the judge [noted] that the case had attracted immense Press publicity . . .' – up to a recent interview with Brady – 'he was acutely sensitive to the hostile public attitude towards them' (Harrison, 1994, p. 147) – the media and the mass symbiotically perpetuate the myth of the moors murderers. Brady, somehow remains beyond the concept of a mentally disordered offender, residing in high security psychiatric facilities whilst Hindley continues her sentence in prison.

Peter Sutcliffe

Peter Sutcliffe was one of six children, shy and reticent, he played truancy from school on a regular basis hiding alone in the dark loft all day long, over a period of months. He did not like attention being drawn to him and always preferred to be at the back of any group of people. He had a need to hide away, to watch others without being watched himself: 'this odd need to hide, to make himself invisible, never left Sutcliffe' (Beattie, 1981, p. 116). His upbringing was relatively unremarkable with perhaps the exception of a strong emphasis on the Catholic faith and a teaching that suggested 'decent girls', like his mother, were placed on pedestals. However, his chaste and righteous mother had fallen from grace two years before Sutcliffe started his killing, by having an affair which rocked the foundations of the family. By then, Peter had a pathological hatred of prostitutes.

His employment record shows a series of unremarkable jobs interspersed by court appearances for petty theft and driving offenses. However, one job highlights a serious flaw in the character. Working as a grave digger several of his fellow work mates reported that Sutcliffe had a morbid fascination for the corpses he was burying or unearthing from earlier burials. He would often dismember the fingers containing jewelry and take pliers to gold teeth. He is reported as being engrossed by the bones he dug up and would laugh uproariously at the disgust shown by others at his behaviour (Beattie, 1981).

Between 1975 and 1980 Peter Sutcliffe brutally murdered thirteen women, attacking at least a further six, in the North of England. He used a ball-pein hammer to smash the skulls of his victims and then once dead he would grotesquely mutilate the bodies, sometimes slashing wildly, sometimes stabbing viciously. On one occasion evisceration took place with the intestines draped around the victim's neck, whilst on another occasion the girl was stabbed through the eyes. There does not appear to be any overt sexual assault with evidence of only one victim having endured intercourse whilst she died, although a suggestion has been made that Sutcliffe may well have ejaculated during the killing of the women. To begin with the victims were prostitutes but this changed to indiscriminately choosing any women out late at night.

However, apart from the personal tragedy of thirteen dead, seven seriously assaulted and psychologically damaged, twenty three orphans and countless family and friends in pain, it was two other aspects to this serial killing for which it will be long remembered. Firstly, the economics of the six year reign of terror. Sutcliffe was in police hands on at least nine occasions during the time that they were hunting the 'Ripper' but was allowed to go free each time. This enabled him to continue his slaughter and the financial costs of the investigation were said to be causing a great deal of alarm. At the two year stage of the inquiry there were 300 police officers using 343,000 man hours, having interviewed 175,000 people, taken statements from 12,500, and checked 101,000 vehicles (Beattie, 1981). The following year the cost was £2,000,000 and by the end of the case a total cost of £4,000,000 was estimated. However, others did make money from the case as the telephone line set up for callers to listen to the notorious Ripper tape recording (hoax) netted the General Post Office £40,000. Secondly, the media coverage and public concern was staggering. At first it was the 'seething outrage of Leeds citizens' (Beattie, 1981, p. 42) and then the 'near hysteria in the North of England' (p. 54). By 1979 the 'story was international news' (p. 73) and it was concluded that 'Rippermania had come to town' (p. 105). The public outcry was verging on frenzy as 'mob-fury erupted'. When he was finally caught the crowd 'bayed for blood "Hang the Bastard!" "Killer" they screamed ... several people held up home-made nooses' (Beattie, 1981, p. 106). The Yorkshire Ripper now occupies a place in Broadmoor.

Fred and Rose West

25 Cromwell Street, was the scene of police excavations in the spring of 1994. This house, of Fred and Rose West, became known as the 'House of Horrors' as the remains of nine girls were unearthed to reveal a macabre and deeply disturbing history of sado-masochistic sexual torture, rape, and murder of young women. Night after night the charnel house of Cromwell Street grew in notoriety through media coverage beamed around the world. The victims included waifs and strays from broken homes and tormented backgrounds, including two of Fred's own children, whose disappearance would, by and large, go relatively unnoticed and unreported.

Fred and Rose were quickly psychopathologised. Fred had suffered two head injuries in his youth with one coma lasting a full week. His parental upbringing was poor with a father whose sexual appetite was said to be a 'talking point' (Sounes, 1995) and much influenced Fred's care-free disregard of the girls he claimed to have enjoyed. It would later be claimed that Fred's sexual abuse of his own children was rooted in his fathers sexual abuse of Fred as a child. Whatever the facts of the matter, by the time he was twenty years old Fred was in trouble with the law, standing trial for the sexual abuse of a thirteen year old girl. Although he walked free the family were horrified, particularly the mother who then rejected him. In the small village community a social bond had been broken, seriously broken. It has been reported that 'at the age of twenty Fred was a convicted thief and widely believed to be a child molester. His moods were volatile and he may well have suffered brain damage. Shunned even by his own family, he had already become an outcast of society' (Sounes, 1995, p. 33). The relationship between mental abnormality (brain damage) offender (thief and child molester) and social outrage were clearly established at an early age.

Both of Rose's parents were mentally ill. Her father was a violent schizophrenic and her mother a depressive. Whilst in the womb Rose was to receive ECT via her mother. Rose's upbringing was harsh, cruel, and austere. From a very early age 'dozy Rosie', as she was to be known, was different. Sexually precocious in puberty it was later believed by the West's family that Rose had been sexually abused by her stern, prim and proper father.

These two figures, Fred and Rose, were to meet, fall in love and create a bond that would enable them to engage together in lustful sexual depravity with countless men and women over a period of twenty five years. They were to entomb their terrified victims in bondage, masking their entire heads with only a small tube inserted in the nose for breathing, strung up on butchers hooks in the cellar of 25 Cromwell Street. For days on end, to be abused and tortured at will, until murder relieved them of their suffering. Finally, Fred was to dismember the bodies, decapitate them, remove certain digits and bones, before unceremoniously dumping the remains into holes beneath the cellar.

What is it about this case that makes society shudder? There are differing levels of analysis in understanding this. Firstly, they do not fit the typical profile of serial killers who are usually male, of lower middle-class, and of normal or above-average intelligence.

Fred and Rose were, to all intents and purposes, a respectable married couple bringing up a family in a mortgaged house in Gloucester. They were hard working and neighbourly if a little eccentric and obviously of below average intelligence. In the case of Rose, female serial sexual killers are rare. Secondly, they both were apparently sexually abused as children and both suggest evidence of some early psychopathology and developmental disorder. Thirdly, the very chance meeting and the finding of each other must be lethal. For two people to be so well matched and attuned to each other's sexual appetites coupled to their extreme form of sado-masochism must have been both fortunate for them, and disastrous for their victims. Finally, perhaps it is that these sexual urges lie deep within the norms of society only kept in check by social and psychological mechanisms and that Fred and Rose clearly 'went too far' merely serves to give us a glimpse into our own soul thus racking our moral and social sensitivities.

Again, the medium by which this technology of sexuality is stirred is the intense visual coverage by television. Hundreds of onlookers flocked to Cromwell Street, and Sounes (1995) claims 'the case attracted extraordinary media attention as the house surrendered its secrets' (pp. 270–271). Even the judge at the trial warned the jury 'not to be influenced by anything they might have read about the case which he conceded had its "sensational aspects"' (p. 292). As will be outlined later the media operate at that interface between society and its values, and it is no surprise that it was announced on 4 October 1996 that 25 Cromwell Street (and the house next door) was to be demolished with the bricks ground to dust and the wood burned, to deter souvenir seekers (ITV, 4 October 1996). The house sign had already been removed and on the same day Rose's solicitor announced an application for leave to appeal for an unfair trial had been lodged, due to the extent of media coverage.

Many of those family, friends and victims surrounding the case made, or attempted to make, through chequebook journalism, small fortunes out of the sordid affair. Even Detective Savage, and Fred's solicitor, attempted to sell their stories. Fred hung himself on New Years Day 1995 and Rose remains in prison.

Christopher Clunis

On the 17 December 1992, Christopher Clunis, a thirty-one year old London born Afro-Caribbean stabbed to death Jonathan Zito.

In the following inquiry it transpired that Clunis had been shunted between authorities and services in the absence of adequate follow-up procedures. A known paranoid schizophrenic patient, Clunis had avoided taking his medication and had become increasingly disturbed manifesting violent behaviour. For many reasons, including the avoidance of stigmatising a person from an ethnic minority and the lack of resources, the system failed to support either Clunis himself or his family. His condition deteriorated and he murdered a complete stranger, Jonathan Zito, on Finsbury Park tube station, without warning.

Society was outraged and the media horrified as the community care programme was supposed to effectively manage psychiatric patients in the community. This politically driven impetus was heavily criticised on the grounds of being under resourced and the repercussions of this failed political initiative could have been extremely serious. This sad, and tragic, case focused attention on the care and supervision of mentally ill persons in our society more than any other single case. In the ensuing report the central themes to emerge were concerned with Section 117 of the Mental Health Act referring to aftercare of hospitalised mentally ill; Health Circular (90) 23/LASS Letter 90/11 requiring Health Services and Social Services to establish the Care Programme Approach (CPA); Supervised Discharge Orders announced by the Secretary of State for Health in August 1993; and the introduction of Supervision Registers (NHS Management Executive, 1994). This 'flurry' of political will, some of which was rather hurried, can be seen as a direct response to public outcry over what was being perceived, in response to media reportage, as a failed government initiative.

Beverly Allitt

Beverly Allitt appears to have had an unremarkable upbringing with the only quirk noted by her teachers was for her to be a little accident prone. She was often seen wearing bandages or slings in school and it was felt that she enjoyed the attention that they brought. When she left school she began a pre-nursing course in Grantham. Her tutors on this course observed that she was frequently injured and seemed to gain considerable sympathy from others. They also contributed to a large amount of time off sick throughout her nurse training. In retrospect this amounts to an early diagnosis of what later would be called Munchausen Syndrome by Proxy (Clothier, 1994). Allitt passed her nurse training and became an enrolled nurse on Ward Four, a children's ward, at Grantham and Kesteven General Hospital (GKGH).

Between February and April, 1991, Beverly Allitt murdered four children and attacked nine others, some more than once. Whilst the murders and attacks were not discovered as such at first, suspicions were soon aroused at the sudden increase of infant deaths and collapses over a few weeks. Later investigations revealed that Allitt had injected some children will noxious substances, asphyxiated others, and injected insulin and air into still others. She now resides in Rampton special hospital.

Robert Thompson and Jon Venables

On 12 February 1993, on Merseyside, a little two-year-old boy walked off with two ten-year-old youths whilst they were playing truant from school. By the end of that afternoon the little boy, James Bulger, had been taken two and a half miles away, beaten, tortured, abused, battered to death, and his body left across a railway line to be severed in half by a train. The nation was shocked. The placid abduction was caught on a surveillance camera in the busy Liverpool shopping precinct from which James Bulger was taken. The blurred picture of little James trustingly holding one of his killers, to be, hand haunts the social mind. John Major, the then Prime Minister, suggested that it was time to 'understand a little less and condemn a little more'. The killing was particularly brutal and shook the very soul of our society.

In an attempt to counter the words of John Major there was a huge impetus to draw some sense around this despicable act of violence against the most innocent of victims. There were suggestions that its causal roots lay in video violence as the crime reputedly had similarities with the film *Child's Play 3* (Morrison, 1994) with both killers claiming to have seen the film, and many more of its ilk. There were others who claimed that this crime was connected to the breakdown in family values (Lilley, 1993) as both killers came from broken homes. There were the usual claims of 'evil' with 'the populist climate of "hang the bastards" linked with the familiar rehearsal of New Right law and order themes' (Jackson, 1995, p. 6). Finally, there were the hackneyed political outcries claiming poor housing, unemployment, parental neglect, and so on, as causative factors. In all this, David Jackson (1995) offered us an incisive account of the role of masculinity and power in understanding this gruesome murder. Revealing to us the struggling rites of passage of two pubescent youths, bullied and abused themselves, turning their macho power violently on a two year old, Jackson pleaded for social action: 'if you feel anything about . . . the distressing death of James Bulger, then it's high time to start breaking ranks and causing a fuss' (Jackson, 1995, p. 43).

Although Robert Thompson and Jon Venables were not, and at the time of writing are not, considered mentally disordered offenders it is the relationship between their crime and their characters that lays claim to their being considered 'sick' in the deviant sense. There were suggestions that they were 'evil' and 'monsters' (*Daily Star*, 1993) and should never be released. However, it is more than this that creates the social tension regarding this case. It is the desperate desire to stop those boys taking James away on that video, the need to intervene, the nightmares of those forty people who witnessed James' long walk to death along the streets of Liverpool seeing James bleeding and bruised and wishing they had done something. Amidst a busy bustling city James died alone.

Analysing the cases

In Foucault's (1978) paper he sets the scene by relating a brief exchange which took place at a trial in a Paris criminal court in that year. The dialogue was concerned with the silence of the accused who refused to speak in defence of himself. In despair a juror cries 'for heaven's sake, defend yourself!' to the silent alleged offender, and for Foucault, it is not the discourse of the crime, the events, or the way in which they occurred that is sought, but answers to the fundamental question 'who are you?' that is needed (Foucault, 1978). It may well be that these central questions concerning the events of the criminal action can be distinct from the constructs of the person engaging in them. However, it would seem to us that in the cases that we have presented the criminal action or event, its genesis, process and content has become inextricably interwoven into the question regarding 'who the offender is'. The fusion of mental abnormality and offending behaviour (or human action) is now so strong in our society that there is a belief that the scene of crime *reveals* the offender i.e., as in profiling or investigative psychology (Canter, 1989). Therefore, the major concern for our judiciary, forensic professionals, police, and public is to bear witness to the revelatory confession of the mentally disordered offender regarding the intricacies of his crime. By his discourse of divulgence the irrationality and illogicality can be penetrated by a psychiatric explanatory power. He must, at all costs, speak of his crimes, and reveal all. The noise of Fred West's intimate and detailed disclosure of his sadistic torture of young women is matched only by the dark silence of Brady's sexual murder of young children. As we say above, it may be that it is Brady's silence in regard to his crimes and the whereabouts of the missing bodies that maintain his social position as being regarded as the most evil man in Britain (Harrison, 1994). The closest glimpse into his crimes is the harrowing tape-recording of Lesley Ann Downey pleading for mercy while he, evidently, sexually abuses her. The judge, jury, victim's relatives, and the public must listen, not to the perpetrator who refuses to speak, but to the victim, in the desperate hope, and need, to hear something about the perpetrator.

The second theme to our examination is concerned with Foucault's incisive analysis of the relational structure between the perpetrators and their victims in the cases that he presented. This structure being, in short, domestic, occurring in the neighbourhood, and inter-generational. In moving towards an understanding of the relational structure in the cases that we present we can identify one looming construct, that of, the victims as representatives of a vulnerable group. Brady and Hindley preying on children, the West's hunting the young homeless and unwanted, Thompson and Venables abducting two year old James Bulger, Sutcliffe's soliciting of prostitutes, Clunis' attack on a stranger, and Allitt's murder of hospitalised babies, all depict vulnerable groups. These offenders' attack on the vulnerable in our society creates a social tension, in that, our own vulnerability comes into stark relief. All members of society are vulnerable at one stage or another in their lives. We are all strangers, we were all children, we may all become helpless. This vulnerability is also brought into focus by another aspect to the relational structure, and that is in some cases there is a double edge to the severing of trust. Allitt not only attacked young helpless babies in hospital but did so as a qualified nurse; Brady sexually attacked young children but Myra Hindley, his accomplice, betrayed her maternal instincts when Lesley Downey referred to her as 'Mummy' in her panicked pleadings; Fred West raped his daughter and many young girls who were held down and tied up by Rose West, again, forsaking her feminine role; Thompson and Venables not only tortured and murdered a two-year-old child but also betrayed the trust so evident in the harrowing video of James Bulger holding the hand of his killer whilst being led away. So, the extent of vulnerability carries weight in terms of perceived depravity, which takes the offender further into the domains of incomprehensible 'sickness'.

The third analytical theme that we draw upon revolves around the Foucauldian notion of surveillance. In the *Birth of the Clinic* Foucault (1973) reveals how the medical 'gaze' (perception) at first could not penetrate the body but merely had to be content with following its contours and palpating its invisible structures. Then, early speculums and probes allowed inspection into the orifices of the body, albeit for only a short distance, until medicine influenced the law and sanctioned 'the opening up of a few corpses' (Foucault, 1973). This permitted the previously invisible spaces of our bodies to be revealed, but only in death. Since then medicine has achieved remarkable sophistication in penetrating the hidden secrets of the human body in life, through fibre-optics, key-hole surgery, radiographic techniques, and numerous scanning procedures. The brain, the last bastion of defence, is bombarded with the full thrust of medical technology as it attempts to navigate its structures and chronicle its processes. Psychiatric surveillance is merely a part of the overall 'gaze' that focuses on the human mind and the set of human behaviours that accompany it.

The process of psychiatrisation of life (Illich, 1976) continues with the circumscription of the criminal as the 'dangerous individual' now termed the mentally disordered offender. The surveillance of this group has entailed the development of an intense police network that controls urban space, a systematic process of prosecution of both macro-criminal events and micro-infractions of the law, and the operationalising of psychiatry as a form of public hygiene (Foucault, 1978). In claiming the crime and the criminal as psychiatric territory we need to go beyond simplistic explanation of imperialism and focus on the interests of professional bodies. As Foucault puts it: 'crime then became an important issue for psychiatrists, because what was involved was less a field of knowledge to be conquered than a modality of power to be secured and justified' (1978, p. 6). To locate this target of professional power and legitimise its operational practice over its action it requires an ever-increasingly complex technology of surveillance. This technology includes the mapping of demographic variables in relation to urban structures and industrial problems, the expansion of explanatory frameworks to encompass the pathology of social disorder in terms of cause and effect, and the penetration into the private sphere of the criminal in action by development of the record. If the medicalisation of the body required the 'opening up of a few corpses' then the psychiatrisation of the mentally disordered offender requires the 'opening up of a few crimes'.

Surveillance is a central issue for the cases that we present on two counts. Firstly, in each case there is a 'twist' in the psychiatric surveillance in that they all appeared to have slipped through the psychiatric net. It is as if they either avoided being brought under the 'gaze' of psychiatry or that psychiatry itself failed to focus upon them. And, where it did so, it failed to respond. In these cases the psychiatric surveillance readjusts itself to retrospectively construct psychiatric symptomatology. Brady was at first a psychopath, Sutcliffe was paranoid, Fred West was brain damaged, Rose West was mentally ill, Thompson and Venables were disordered, and Clunis was schizophrenic. This psychiatric surveillance makes sense only *after* the event.

Secondly, surveillance as a record of the crime features large in some of our cases. Brady and Hindley left us an audio tape recording of the offence against Lesley Ann Downey, Thompson and Venables are recorded on a precinct security camera abducting James Bulger, and Fred and Rose West left us 25 Cromwell Street full of hidden horrors to be revealed on the television news. The ever-increasing surveillance of public places will inevitably, one day, record the very private criminal action of a person psychiatrised as mentally disordered. What surveillance actually does is to operate as a form of two-way mirror. One view is the surveillance of our social spaces, to scan and search for aberrant behaviours in the form of crime. Yet, another focus is turned upon the viewer, in a type of 'hall of mirrors', in which you see yourself watching you but from a different angle. When surveillance techniques are developed they are done so in the knowledge that we are devising technology to be used on ourselves.

The fourth theme to emerge from an analysis of our cases was the idea of an interventive strategy, either social of psychiatric. Foucault (1978) argues that *homicidal monomania* was abandoned shortly before 1870 for two reasons. Firstly, as was said above, the idea that a partial insanity unleashing a criminal act was replaced by the idea that a mental illness could affect the emotions and leave thought processes intact. Secondly, there was a development in the idea that mental illness could transcend the boundaries of cultures, communities, and generations. However, Foucault qualifies this abandonment with the phrase 'in the strict sense of the term' (1978, p. 11) which indicates to us that some element of *homicidal monomania* remains. Although the explanatory power of this psychiatric term has shifted considerably with the monstrous crime now being explained by an array of psychiatric terminology, its form remains in that inexplicable act which constitutes the social sickness and the social danger. Thus, forensic psychiatry must engage in social control.

Forensic psychiatry must intervene, in explaining the actions of the mentally disordered offender, in creating an understanding of the social/biological processes by which their actions came about, in inserting its power into prisons and communities, in the relationship between a crime and its punishment, and in controlling dangerous individuals. This urge to intervene is deeply rooted in our society. It almost goes without saying that those forty or so people who witnessed James Bulger's walk to his death must surely have wished that they had intervened, and there can be few, if any, of those who saw the hazy video of the two boys taking James away who would not wish to reach out and break the holding of hands of the killer and his victim. And, who amongst us would not want to rewind that harrowing tape-recording of Lesley Ann Downey and reach out to intervene in that scene.

Social construction of the mentally disordered offender

The focus of concern in this chapter has been the mechanism by which the mentally disordered offender is socially constructed in our cultural ideology. It can be said that 'ideology refers to a set of ideas which interpret the world according to the point of view (the interests, values and assumptions) of a particular social group' (Winter, 1989, p. 186). We thus all share a number of ideologies. In fact, we can now see that it is hardly possible not to belong to one ideology or another. A distinction can be drawn between formal ideological systems (intellectual) and lived ideology of ordinary life (common sense). Within this distinction there is an accepted transformation of concepts, a passage both from formal ideology to lived ideology, and the converse (Moscovici, 1984). The distinction between lived ideology and formal (intellectual) ideology can be briefly explained. Lived ideology refers to 'the ideology of an age or of a concrete historico–social group, e.g. of a class, when we are concerned with the characteristics and composition of the total structure of the mind of this epoch or of this group' (Mannheim, 1960, pp. 49–50). This brings the concept of culture and lived ideology in very close proximity with each other. These concepts are similar because both are geared towards describing the social patterns of everyday thinking in relation to the social beliefs and the operation of power. Formal, or intellectual, ideology, is more akin to a formal philosophy. Aron (1977, p. 309) wrote 'an ideology presupposes an apparently systematic formalisation of facts, interpretations, desires and predictions'. It is the theoretical and practical possibility of the passage of concepts between these intellectual and lived ideologies which is crucial to the idea of a social construction of the mentally disordered offender.

Social constructionism is concerned with the way in which these formal 'scientific' concepts are embedded in the everyday ordinary life and become a part of the reality of that culture. In relation to the mentally disordered offender we note the popularist notion that mental illness is commonly associated with the concept of dangerousness. This traditional lived ideology has been fanned and fuelled by the 'literature of our collectivity . . . in painting, photography, film, popular fiction, theatre and song' (Curt, 1994, p. 151). Others have added cartoons to this collectivity (Parker *et al.*, 1995, p. 64), and we are all aware of the influence of the media in this area from national news to tabloid journalism.

Conclusions

The medium by which the mentally disordered offender is socially constructed involves all aspects of this collectivity from the inverted psychiatrist, Hannibal Lecter, gone mad, in the *Silence of the Lambs* to the *Sun Newspaper* screaming 'Hang Her – Murdering nurse Allitt should die says families' (18 May 1993), and from the soap opera to the comic strips (Philo, 1994) the relationship between mental disorder and dangerousness is constantly reinforced. This reinforcement is a reciprocity between the media and the society that it relates to. To paraphrase Baudrillard, you do not only watch the television, it also watches you; and you do not only read the newspapers, they are also reading you (Baudrillard, 1983). What Baudrillard is referring to here is that the media are constantly sensitive to the dominant values of the society in which it operates.

It must remain responsive in order to feed back to the society the messages it predominantly wishes to hear in its 'news'. Thus, the media becomes a mirror for the social values of that culture. It must do this in order to survive as a medium. The social construction of the mentally disordered offender is therefore completed by a two-way relationship between the public and the media in all its collectivity, as Campbell and Bonner (1994, p. 47) observe:

> we have already noted that the media have a crucial role to
> play in forming, and then reinforcing, crowd behaviour . . .
> this is particularly dangerous when, as now, too many news
> and documentary producers have lost any sense of obligation to
> present an objective picture. Instead, they use the tricks of their
> trade to push a subjective and often prejudiced line. And this
> tendency to dress up opinion with all the trappings of objectivity
> is highly dangerous.

Once we have socially created the mentally disordered offender through the pathologification of, both, the monster crime and the minor infraction, we are compelled to provide psychiatric services for them. This is the focus of the following two chapters.

Chapter 5

Systems of services and structures of power

Introduction

We have attempted to identify some of the social forces that have contributed to the emergence of the mentally disordered offender. It is further contended that this field of expertise, or body of knowledge, is only attainable with the sanction and legitimation of the society in which it is set. At one level society appears to adopt a simplistic view of mentally disordered offenders, particularly in relation to heinous crimes, with the popular press calling for capital punishment, embracing outrage, and insisting that we 'throw away the keys'. However, it is through a series of complex interactive processes that society bestows the right of the profession to enact its occupation. Through the verbalised statements of 'mad' and 'bad' in response to abhorrent crimes being labelled 'sick' or 'evil', again as evidenced both in media coverage and through lay conversations, through the rebuttal of outrageous offenses society verifies the relationship between criminal activity as a function of mental aberration in terms of madness, badness, or both. Thus society sanctions psychiatry's hold on its subject. Furthermore, this social enactment can be seen in the tragedy of the lynch mob awaiting the prison transport that escorts the accused to court; a common scene in serious cases, where the crime is deemed to be beyond the pale. Police apparently stand by, offering only a token gesture of control, whilst a baying crowd direct abuse and assault toward the prison van. Such scenes are short lived, but socially important in reinforcing those values that construct the criminal and govern attendant responses. This interplay between the crowd, the offender in the prison van, the police at the scene, and the observers through the media, is a multi-faceted exchange of normative prescriptions in which each affords the other some degree of expression.

The crowd, having escaped the status of potential victim, now turn their fear into anger and victimise the offender. The circumscription of the dangerous individual is complete at the point of arrival in court; from this moment, the individual and the evoked responses, become public property. Within the vehicle, accompanied by prison officers, escorted by police, society surrounds the scene; the accused is about to enter the system that will decide the future and dispose the person.

This chapter, and the next, are concerned with the relationship between society, the professions, and the development of services for the mentally disordered offender. All services are rooted within society, and owe a debt of gratitude for their existence. Despite the fact that some organisations are located in remote, rural, areas there is an intrinsic relationship between the existence of the mentally disordered offender and the services that develop in the wake of their creation. This relationship is often tense, with public protest in response to the proposed siting of secure accomodation, yet there is a reluctant tolerance to the expansion of such services. However, we will note that the development of services for the mentally disordered offender also embraces a complex interplay of power relations between dominant groups in society who can manipulate public opinion on issues relating to this, generally, unpopular group of patients.

Systems of capturing

Society insists that the dangerousness of such offenders requires circumscribing. The populace in each cultural setting will devise strategies to identify those members who are considered aberrant and thus a danger to the perpetuation of that society. In Laos, in Indochina, a culture that does not have a Westernised system of psychiatry adopts a specific two tier mechanism for controlling and managing their equivalent of our mentally disordered offenders. They have available to them a series of restraints, from bamboo cords and forms of staked bonds to a form of stocks which are logs with grooves hewn out of them to accommodate the legs and are placed over the prone offender. It also includes pits that are excavated in the ground in which the *baa* (violently insane) person is placed (Westermeyer and Kroll, 1978). Their social legitimation for this system is derived from two sources: the law and morality. If police stations are in the vicinity then police officers will visit the restricted person and assess the appropriateness of the types of restraints that are used. In rural areas which do not have police then monks from the local monastery will undertake the same function (Westermeyer and Kroll, 1978).

In our society a similar system is in force, albeit in a more sophisticated manner. The legislative framework that allows for the compulsory detention of mentally disordered offenders is the Mental Health Act (HMSO, 1983). This provides the legal basis for the treatment of mental and psychopathic disorders as well as varying degrees of mental impairment. It also ensures that mentally disordered persons who engage the criminal justice system may be transferred to the mental health services, even against their will, and possibly forced to have treatment, again with or without their consent. Although there are superficial safeguards against abuse, and ostensibly mechanisms to uphold their civil rights, *de facto* their position is one of a 'medical hostage' (Mason and Jennings, 1997).

One level of analysis may suggest that the mental health act is a benevolent legislation to support and protect persons who require some form of psychiatric intervention. And certainly, we would not argue that the majority of mental health professionals are not motivated to relieve suffering where and when they perceive it to occur. However, at another level we can appreciate the Mental Health Act legislation to be merely a public legitimation to effect a means of social control. It becomes within the law to remove someone from the social sphere and hospitalise that person. The Mental Health Act is thus one system of capture.

Another social mode of appropriation of the mentally disordered offender is the police. It would be quite rare for a mentally disordered offender not to have had some police contact at one stage or another in their history. In fact Section 136 of the Mental Health Act is concerned with the power of the police to apprehend and detain in a place of safety a person considered to be suffering from a mental disorder. Regarding mentally disordered offenders specifically in the case of criminal acts it will usually, although not exclusively, be the police who have initial contact. There is growing concern within the police regarding their role in dealing with mentally disordered persons, and PACE has influenced developments in this area. Some forces now teach custody Sergeants some basic psychopathology to enable them to decide whether a vulnerable person requires a doctor's attendance. Also, with the move to community care and the increased number of mentally disordered persons on the streets the police force are encountering greater numbers of incidents with the mentally ill. What form these encounters take and the means of their resolution remains to be seen, however, we can see both formally, through PACE, and informally in the community, psychiatry is penetrating the police and effecting their engagement with mentally disordered offenders.

Morality, too, is a system of capture. The social mapping of morality in relation to the mentally ill is well documented (Foucault, 1967). Foucault argues that the rationalised discourse regarding the Unreason has allowed us to claim the high moral ground in relation to the 'mad'. This legitimates the exercise of power over those afflicted. We can, in symbolic imagery, keep the Unreason 'forever in transit' (Foucault, 1973). Thus, we now transport the mentally disordered offender from society to the hospital, then on a rehabilitative journey which for some is a 'Ship of Fools' (Mason and Mercer, 1998), and on back to the community under moral surveillance. What allows for this treatment of those deemed to be mentally disordered offenders is our acquisition of the moral ground on two counts: firstly, our state of reason over their unreason and, secondly, our upholding of the law over their criminal behaviour. This system of capture is total. From this framework of law, police, and morality the forensic mental health worker extracts their role. The functionary is a public hygiene and we are its agents.

Service availability and the circumscription of dangerousness

In analysing the development of services for the mentally disordered offender we depart, momentarily, from the usual chronology of legislative Acts emanating out of great reformist movements; ostensibly, libertarian improvements for the unfortunate sick. Rather, we seek to locate the creation, establishment, and expansion of services in relation to the social forces that provide motivation, legitimation, and sanction, despite the tensions mentioned above.

Organisations, institutions, hospitals, clinics, units, and departments, appear to exist independently of the people that occupy their space. Certainly, in terms of the architectural structures of walls, ceilings, and floors they are 'real' at the level of lay understanding, and most readers of this volume will probably belong to, or identify with, one or more sections of the foregoing establishments. However, we are fully aware that they need the operational agency of human beings to provide the vibrant quality that gives them their identity, ideology, and *raison d'être*. It is the subjectivity of the human agents within it that execute its function through interpretation of its intellectual philosophy, its practical policies, and its aims and objectives. From this, the application of its procedures are enacted at a micro level, as part of the daily activity of the establishment, by a workforce. We will return to the power relations referring to how the grand ideology is originally idealised later; here we turn our attention to the four basic paradigms in which the purpose of such establishments can be located.

Sociological paradigms

The first refers to the functionalist paradigm of organisational social theory. Functionalist sociology attempts to understand human affairs as a set of 'social facts', in a similar vein to the natural science explanations of the physical world. Functionalism is a mechanistic approach which views the structures of the social world, such as institutions for the mentally disordered offender, as part of a larger 'machine', or system. For the overall system to function, all the constituent parts must work correctly. Therefore, functionalism is grounded in the practical problems of society and is concerned with a regulation of order and maintenance of control. Analogies of the functionalist perspective have often been drawn to the mechanical engineering of a motor car, and the biological functioning of the body.

The second perspective refers to the interpretive paradigm, in which the major concern is to understand the social world from the subjective interpretation of the actors operating within it, rather than attempting to overlay some ideal notion of objectivity. In the interpretive paradigm the social world is created by the members of that society. Therefore, organisations, in themselves, as social processes do not exist. It is the individuals within them, and their concerns with social order, consensus, social integration, and cohesion, that are the extant organisation.

Thirdly, the radical humanist paradigm, which emerged from the interpretive perspective, is based on radical change theory from a subjective point of view. It is grounded in the conviction that individuals are governed by the ideological superstructures within which they operate, and is concerned with how these can be overthrown, or changed. Within organisational perspectives the radical humanist paradigm stands as a nascent anti-organisation theory.

Finally, the radical structuralist paradigm also offers a radical change theory but in this perspective there is an emphasis upon objectivity. These theorists share many of the former concerns, such as emancipation, modes of domination, conflicts, contradictions, and tensions. However, one main difference relates to the radical humanists' emphasis upon consciousness as the focus of change whilst radical structuralists identify social structures, *per se*, as the mechanism.

These paradigms, then, offer a sociological framework for an analysis of the role and purpose of organisations; in our case those dealing with the mentally disordered offender, as they are developed and perpetuated within society (Burrel and Morgan, 1979).

Dominant discourse, demographics, and design

The histories of the psychiatric asylum, the prison, and deviancy are as inextricably linked as are the circumscription of dangerousness, social control, and surveillance. Whilst accounts of the rise of the insane asylum vacillate between the benevolent force of public policy (Grob, 1966) and the malevolent 'means of managing the mad' (Scull, 1985, pp. 19–20), the rise of the prisons were said to be based on a 'mill to grind rogues honest, and idle men industrious' (Bentham, 1843, p. 226) or a place of detterrence where the 'filth of the prison, the *squalor carceris* as a proper and necessary instrument of terror' (Ignatieff, 1978). These many and varied interpretations of the developments of psychiatric and penal provision have one commonality; that is, they are all based on the dominant discourse of their time and the exercise of power. Such discursives are grounded in the continuing battle between law and medicine which, as we have seen in chapters 1 and 3, have laid a claim for the mad and the bad when conjoined in the mentally disordered offender. These powerful professions have been granted permission to stake such a claim because the regulation of dangerousness is the responsibility of the state.

Protection of the community is a founding principle within Plato's *Republic*, and little has changed since he penned that treatise. Thus, in various stages of our history Governments have listened to the dominant discourse and formulated policy on their persuasion. This has sanctioned the exercise of power by those professions resulting in the psychiatrisation of the criminal, the criminalisation of the insane, the penetration of psychiatry into the prisons, and the prisonisation of services for the mentally disordered offender. From this interplay of historical power struggles the dominant discourse has ensured that demarcation between the law and medicine, or the mad and the bad, has remained blurred whilst producing a dynamic representation of changing services.

Like prisons, most insane asylums, were built in remote areas on the outskirts of communities. This location suggests a certain social stigma to their occupants and an excluding, shunning, rejection of them. Geographically, and symbolically, this distances inmates from the society which they have, at one level or another, offended. With urbanisation, however, communities have grown around these institutions and the cities have sprawled out to incorporate them within their boundaries. It is interesting to note that, the contemporary move of the mentally ill to the community was, in fact, preceded by the move of the community to the asylum. Once the psychiatric inmates were again ensconced within the bosom of the society they were decanted out of the asylums and dissipated throughout the communities. It would be simplistic to believe that the collapse of modern day community psychiatric services is merely a question of lack of resources whereas the truth is probably more complex than that. Community care has failed because, in reality, the community does not care. This is clearly evidenced by the recent coverage of the NIMBY debate which refers to the laudable discourse of setting up services for psychiatric patients but on the proviso that they are 'Not In My Back Yard'.

In terms of the historical service developments for the mentally disordered offender, as distinct architecture, we note the purpose built Dundrum (1858) in Dublin, and Broadmoor (1863) in rural Berkshire. Both were based on the prison romanesque architecture of red brick, tall buildings, and narrow passageways. A century later we have the 'community' modelling of the custom built special hospital and the single storey, wide space and angular design. From the modern rationalisation of the carceral asylum, there is a move to the postmodern sense of invisibility of the images of incarceration. At the time of its opening, Park Lane (now Ashworth North) represented a 'state of the art' centrepiece in forensic design, attracting the attention of visitors from around the world. Adjoining, and symmetrical, wards made for an internal and external exactness, a mirror image of the other. Identified only by the names of literary figures, in alphabetic ordering (Arnold, Blake, Carlyle, Dickens, etc.), the movement of patients within the circuit resembled an illusory passage, a 'looking glass' journey; not so strange, perhaps, that the wit of Lewis Carroll (lover of small girls and twisted logic) should escape this poetic nomenclature. Within the confines of perimeter security, these bungalow dwellings were geometrically grouped around the focal point of bowling green and tennis court, with a precision that obscured any view of the encircling concrete walls. Towering above, infra-red cameras and high-mast lighting cast a prescient and nocturnal eye over all inhabitants with grid reference accuracy. In the planners' dream to recreate a 'village' (of the damned), the zoo of Bedlam became a theme park of horrors.

Currently, lavish investment has witnessed the construction of self-contained flatlets, in the guise of a mediterranean villa, as the embodiment of rehabilitation for personality disordered offenders; and, technological sophistry has permitted a panopticism worthy of the millenium. With a minimum of physical intrusion, the micro-level lives of 'residents' can be monitored, recorded, and dissected, in a delicate surgery of the soul. In a surreal approximation of 'life outside', the deception of 'life inside' is intensified. The average estate agent understands, better than most clinicians, that the desirability of a residence is measured in terms of environmental context; furniture and fittings, in a room without a view, may offer a comfortable cell, but that is all. The proscenium architecture of a psycho-social drama, its tragi-comic players are the direct descendants of De Sades' theatrical madmen (Del Quiaro, 1994). This trend towards the invisibility of security has become a defining feature of the smaller regional units; the functional intent of the buildings as an inverse to the cost of construction. The absence of any traditional apparatus of control (locks, keys, barred windows, high walls, and distinctive codes of dress), has produced a uniform style to compete with the ubiquitous blandness of motorway station fast-food outlets. Indeed, there are strong parallels: an over-priced product, consumed, disposed of, and forgotten – temporal markers of unending travel. Other sections in this volume explore the extent to which the discipline (knowledge) of forensic expertise has (or rather, not) kept pace with the discipline (technology) of confinement. Here, it is to be noted how the relationship between each, the discursive-practice, retains and extends an historically grounded constancy. Structural reforms which echo the mantra of em*power*ment, now entwine the disordered offender in an anonymous web of surveillance; so that 'this architectural apparatus should be a machine for creating and sustaining a power relation independent of the person who exercises it; in short, that the inmates should be caught up in a power situation of which they are themselves the bearers' (Foucault, 1977, p. 201). The in vogue 'hotel-isation' produces gardens and gadgets invoking images of Eden with surreal statues, rolling rockeries, and fashionable fountains. The glossy brochures, the potted plant foyers, and the tinted glass windows, dispense the veneer of slick businesses, whilst beneath the surface the subterranean lives are lived-out as they have always been. Today it is merely the fashion to create fashionable forensic fads.

What the foregoing reveals is the connection between the political will, the professional discursive, and the social commitment to services, or not as the case may be.

Creation of the asylum

The word asylum, in its original meaning, connotes a state of affairs in which a person takes shelter, seeks refuge, or claims sanctuary from some form of political, religious, economic, or psychological persecution. A preferable place of inviolable relief standing apart from another place of perpetual torment. However, latterly this noun has taken on the harsher semantic of a total institution from an anachronistic ideology, a place for society's unwanted (Goffman, 1962). A 'bin' for refuse rather than a place of refuge. This changing semantic emanates from, and is rooted in, the historical discourse pertaining to the mad and bad throughout the ages. According to Foucault (1961) the discourse on Western madness has known four distinct phases. In Medieval times it was regarded as a divination, a holy possession, a spiritual madness or badness, whereas in the Renaissance it was closely identified with a form of high wisdom, ironical reason, a sublime folly. Then, madness was no longer feared as a condition, but merely mocked the world to reveal it for what it was – another form of non-sense. Madness pointed to a meaning beyond reason, which created a new terror for society. This terror producing the expulsion of the insane from its bosom, symbolically on the 'Ship of Fools' the 'loonies' were sent away. Quite suddenly, in the mid seventeenth century madness ceased to be allowed its freedom and became a fixed entity for 'scientific' scrutiny and professional development. The symbolic ship had anchored and turned into the abysmal hospital (Foucault, 1961).

Foucault claims that

> at the end of the Middle Ages, leprosy disappeared from the Western world. In the margins of the community, at the gates of cities, there stretched wastelands which sickness had ceased to haunt but had left sterile and long uninhabitable. For centuries, these reaches would belong to the non-human. From the fourteenth to the seventeenth century, they would wait, soliciting with strange incantations a new incarnation of disease, another grimace of terror, renewed rites of purification and exclusion . . . Leprosy withdrew, leaving derelict these low places and these rites which were intended, not to suppress it, but to keep it at a sacred distance, to fix it in an inverse exaltation. What doubtless remained longer than leprosy, and would persist when the lazar houses had been empty for years, were the values and images attached to the figure of the leper as well as the meaning of his exclusion, the social importance of that insistent and fearful figure which was not driven off without first being inscribed within a sacred circle.
>
> (Foucault, 1961)

What is important in this rather long quotation is not so much the factual accuracy of the insertion of the insane into the supposed vacant lazar colonies but the relationship that is established between the images of sickness, discourses of knowledge, and the architecture of housing. It is not surprising that Foucault calls this period the Great Confinement, as it sequestered the mad, the dangerous, and the subject to a place, a location, and an epistemology.

The building of the early criminal lunatic asylums took shape from this relationship and can be seen in the early prison-type establishments, such as Broadmoor, with its large-scale buildings and its stark images of confinement. Although prisonesque they also incorporated psychiatric concepts of the time such as day rooms, terraces, and pleasurable views in the therapeutic armamentarium. Broadmoor was built by the prison architect, Joshua Jebb, who must have been versed, or briefed, in the ethos of Connoly's treatise (1856) on the liberal treatment of the insane without mechanical restraint. Similarly, contemporary establishments being built for the mentally disordered offender embrace a small-scale structuring, state of the art technology of surveillance, and invisibilities of control, cradled within a therapeutic discourse.

Penetration of psychiatry into the prisons

Note has already been made of the strong historical links, in Britain specifically, between maximum secure psychiatric services and the prison system; each sharing, for many years, a centralised management structure and common physical plant. At the level of operational practice, the ideological proximity of therapeutic custody and penal custody is mirrored in procedures which focus upon public protection and preventive detention; routine and regular searches, the censorship of mail, and the escorted movement of patients (monitored by UHF radio) within and without perimeter security (Burrow, 1998). Until very recently, staff in the special hospitals wore a prison style uniform and cap, were almost exclusively represented by the POA, and enjoyed civil service rather than NHS status. Terms such as 'parole' and 'canteen' (hospital shop), derive their origins from prison policy and practice; while the occupational and institutional argot of staff and patients reflects a richly expressive, collective, culture. Despite differential claims of a treatment philosophy and rehabilitative ideal, secure hospitals are defined by the carceral aim of enforced and protracted segregation: 'An inmate, in whatever institutional custody, is confined against his/her will in conditions which they have not themselves chosen and this constitutes an unequivocal captivity' (Burrow, 1991, p. 27). Attempts to integrate high security hospitals into the wider health-care system have struggled to reverse this legacy; yet on-going concerns, crises, and inquiries indicate illusory, rather than illuminating, advances (Mercer and Mason, 1998). Here, however, an interesting paradox emerges, the significance of which is diminished by the uni-directional discourse of the reforming zeal. If the impact of the penitentiary upon the asylum has, to some extent, been challenged, the expansion of psychiatry within the prison has steadily progressed. Thus, any sociological exploration into the (diagnostic) construction of the mentally disordered offender, must embrace the (disciplinary) convergence of professional power.

Discussing the impact of deinstitutionalisation in the USA, and its British parallels, Palermo *et al.* (1991) lend support to the thesis of 'progressive transinstitutionalism; where the penal institutions have become a repository for the mentally ill, as a group of misdemeanants and 'pseudo-offenders'. Retrospective analysis of national census data, reveals a statistical significance between psychiatric and legal variables: 'These correlations strongly suggest that there may be a two-way flow of people from prison to the mental health system and back again, which indicates that many of the jail/prison inmates may be inappropriately sentenced or held because they have incapacitating mental illness' (Palermo *et al.*, 1991, p. 103). The measure of this increasing pressure on the criminal justice system has a more human dimension, in terms of overcrowding, unrest, riot, and predatory sexual violence; all of which hide depths of suffering and need. It is in this sense that one can argue for high standards of health care generally, and psychiatric intervention particularly, in the prison setting. However, in attempting to define an ethic of professional responsibility for prison psychiatry, any initial optimism is clouded by contextual tensions and divided loyalties; typically, *prison medicine* versus *medicalised prisons*.

Thus, Smith (1987) urges that reform and advancement be disentangled from a narrow 'forensic' application; carefully negotiating the complexities of double stigma, coercive pressure, and institutional collusion with custodial regimes. By targeting those 'obvious mental illnesses' which legitimately warrant treatment in the wider community, and excluding character or personality disorders, a laudable, even spiritual, goal is set: 'The highest levels of clinical skills and accountability are required to ensure that care is not suborned to the punitive purposes of prisons. It is time for physicians to make the pilgrimage to the prisons as an act of faith, hope, and commitment to our ultimate professional purposes' (Smith, 1987, p. 722). Yet, any meaningful distinction between the prisoner-patient and the mentally disordered offender calls for a move beyond discussions of medical practice to a sociological critique of medical power.

The origins of the Prison Medical Service, in Britain, are usually attributed to the eighteenth-century reformer John Howard. His report 'The State of the Prisons', published in 1777, catalogued appalling conditions, abuses, and neglect, as a national scandal and prompted legislative action. An act of 1779, required that a physician be appointed to each institution with legal responsibilities for the welfare of prisoners (Bluglass, 1990). Yet, if the initial emphasis was directed at the maintenance of minimum health standards, the dominant discourse was concerned with the maintenance of social order. Successive developments have been described as a march of progress, embracing and conjoining the physical health of prisoners with the mental health of offenders: 'In fact, in consequence of this, prison medical officers became eventually, before the last war, to be regarded as the original forensic psychiatrists' (Topp, 1977, p. 261). Only recently, have critical histories emerged to challenge this model of benevolence, and explore the political role of prison medical workers in a wider disciplinary project centred upon danger and deviance: 'Categorisation through observation not only has contributed to the doctors' claims to be treated as professionals but also ideologically has sustained the individualized views of criminality and its restricted class-based location that have come to dominate popular and academic analyses of the problem' (Sim, 1990, p. 10).

The role of prison medicine, then, has a longstanding tradition of 'discipline and punish' (Foucault, 1977) in relation to the lives of the confined. The multiple functions of individual doctors crystallise around the 'health' of inmates, and the 'safety' of society. This contradiction has fuelled widespread criticism of the abusive exercise of psychiatric power, notably around the misuse of diagnostic labels and prescribed medications (Coggan and Walker, 1982; Owen and Sim, 1984). Beyond the issue of illicit control, though, is the more significant trend that it signifies: 'What concerns us more is the medicalization of control in prisons: the definition of "troublesome" behaviour as a medical problem in need of a medical solution, for this represents a new and potentially sinister development in the logic of containment' (Fitzgerald and Sim, 1982, p. 121). At precisely this interface, of individual threat and societal fear, the mentally disordered offender is most likely to become ensnared in the webs of surveillance.

In relation to prison medicine, Sim (1990), advances the Foucauldian idea that any structure of power, no matter how oppressive, contains sites for productive resistance. One such example, pertaining to the mentally disordered offender, might well be the case of Alan Reeve, a tragic biography from the prisons and special hospitals. In the style of Jackson's (1971) manifesto of prison struggle, he reconstructs 'psychopathy' as a brutal tool of political oppression. His derisory words on the mechanisms of indeterminate psychiatric 'treatment' pose a question that remains unanswered: 'the result of this is that prisoners detained on allegedly psychiatric grounds may continue to be detained in a place legally defined a psychiatric prison, without recourse to any legal protection, for reasons determined by political considerations' (Reeve, 1983).

The rise of the medium secure unit

The enforced exodus of patients from asylum care to care in the community began to take shape theoretically throughout the sixties, and in practice in the seventies, and coincided with the end of deviance as an epistemological subject. Most asylums of the period had the facility of a locked ward which housed those patients considered to be dangerous, and with a deinstitutionalisation ethos came the practical concerns regarding their release. The 'silent' special hospitals had conducted their business of containing the deranged for over a hundred years with little, if any, public or professional awareness of their inner workings. Between the locked wards of general psychiatric hospitals and the closed system of the criminal lunatic asylums lay an expansive area for the development of a stratified system of secure provision. This area is not dissimilar to the Foucauldian 'margins of the community, gates of the cities, and the reaches of wastelands where this sickness had ceased to haunt'. The trigger for this development was the closure programme of the large asylums.

Locked wards in general psychiatric institutions were considered anathema in a climate of post-war liberalism, and the 1960s saw the conceptualisation of both the closure of these asylums and their locked facilities. However, they were transposed in the form of the Interim Secure Units (Snowden, 1990). This era saw not only a growing concern in mental health policy and service provision but also an increased awareness of the plight of the mentally ill in prison. Through a series of Government initiated reports into services for the mentally disordered offender in, both, mental health and criminal justice systems, the political will was galvanised into providing funding for each Regional Health Authority to create a facility specifically catering for this patient group. If the professions and the politicians saw the need for these facilities, the fund-holders were not yet convinced and misused the allocated monies for other purposes. They achieved this, presumably, by arguing that other services were more needy which acquired the societal sanction of the general public. If the special hospitals existed to cater for the dangerous and violent mentally disordered offender then that provision could suffice, despite their overcrowding. For the development of the Interim Secure Unit programme the special hospitals would need to be criticised, and be seen to have failed in the provision of their service. This began in the mid seventies with a savage documentary about Rampton, the 'secret hospital'.

Structurally, the special hospital system was seen to be corrupt and incorrigible with ever increasing calls for their reform or abolition (Pilgrim and Eisenberg, 1985; Richman and Mason, 1992). Throughout the eighties radical humanists and structuralists saw the special hospitals as sinister societies which functioned on the fringes of psychiatric provision. As the special hospitals shuddered under the penetrating gaze of public scrutiny, the Interim Secure Unit metamorphosed into the Regional Secure Unit and the building programme gathered momentum. The large-scale institutions were considered too big and unmanageable, against the appeal of these much smaller facilities. The special hospitals were institutions with a long-stay population, whilst the Regional Secure Units restricted themselves to relatively short-term clients; the special hospitals were portrayed as static, whilst the Regional Secure Units promised dynamism.

Throughout the eighties Thatcherite philosophy was rooting itself ever deeper in the social fabric. Few places did not feel the cold face (coalface) of this extreme form of capitalism in which the market dictated the survivors; evidenced in the National Health Service with the move to Trust status and a business ideology. However, commodification of the patient is one thing when that person can exercise choice in relation to hospitals, doctors, and treatment; it is quite another if they are compulsorily detained, and forced to receive interventions that they do not want. This period saw the economy of the mentally disordered offender emerge with the patient as product; yet, as is often the case with an inchoate profession, early models soon appear out-moded and of limited value. In terms of the mentally disordered offender, the main players in this equation are those professionals who manage the services, those who purchase them, and the public whose protection is paramount to their existence. The recipient of these services, the patient, remains without influence.

Throughout the nineties, Regional Secure Units have continued to be built and, at the time of writing, there are approximately thirty such establishments. Again, their development is closely allied to criticisms of the special hospitals, and the nature of the changes within them. During the first half of the 1990s the special hospitals were under the auspices of the Special Hospitals Service Authority (SHSA) which began the process of reform amidst a public inquiry at Ashworth (HMSO, 1992). This damning report ushered in restructuring, reorganisation, and rethinking by a combination of new and old management. Unfortunately, the pendulumatic swing to change for change's sake produced a rudderless uninspiring superficiality which culminated in another public inquiry regarding allegations of paedophile activity within the institution. Other allegations included the widespread use of pornography, involving both staff and patients.

In 1996 the SHSA was disbanded and replaced by a High Security Psychiatric Services Commissioning Board, with a purchaser–provider relationship established between themselves and the three special hospitals. As the *High Security* Psychiatric Services Commissioning Board developed, the Regional Secure Units began changing their name; the *Medium Secure* units and clinics had matured. Thus, the level of security was structured, and the service rooted in society. Currently, again at the time of writing, there are several small-scale units, or wards within hospitals that have locked doors, and are calling themselves *Low Security* units. This structuring has taken place, and continues to take place, alongside the expansion of services for the mentally disordered offender in other community settings which will be discussed in the next chapter.

Assessment of risk

If there is one central task for those involved in the care of the mentally disordered offender, whether they be in high, medium, or low security establishments or within any number of services throughout the community, it is to ascertain and evaluate the extent to which that person is a risk to others. The tripartite structural relationship between the perpetrator, the victim, and the professional lies at the heart of forensic mental health work; and there is probably as much concern regarding potential victims as there is for the rights of the offender. The hue and cry over those patients incarcerated for many years who, in effect, would not have re-offended pales into insignificance in relation to public and political outrage regarding a released patient who does re-offend. This difference locates the primary function of forensic services as the protection of the public rather than the welfare of the patient. This historically driven impetus has bedeviled forensic mental health services, as it is both its *raison d'être* and its Achilles heel. Inextricably entwined, forensic psychiatry claims an area of expertise, whilst realising its hopeless inadequacies. This single fact has served to govern the development of services for the mentally disordered offender, with every bar, lock, and fence as testimony. The explicit system of services, and the implicit technologies of security and surveillance, operate to conceal the reality of this ineptitude.

If the professional forensic mental health worker finds this protective function so difficult, we should ask why have they not abandoned it and merely focused upon the welfare of the patient? The answer is simply stated: their existence is sanctioned on the proviso that the public are safeguarded. Society could as easily slip back to the punishment of the body under penalty and penance in prison rather than allow the more subtle means of confinement through psychiatric treatment (Foucault, 1988). The reason why it endorses such a system as forensic psychiatry is that it pays homage to notions of sickness and its curability, to breakdown and its repair, and to sin and its forgiveness – but only as long as society is not at risk. This risk is central to the development of services for the mentally disordered offender, and has its roots in the emergence of the dangerous individual during a period of industrial development.

Risk is, inherently, an insurance term which dates back to the sixteenth century, but in those times it was, more-or-less, restricted to individual risks. It was not until the nineteenth century that with the development of industrial techniques, increased effectiveness of mechanisation and transport, and the growth in size of urban structures that the idea of third-party risk emerged (Foucault, 1988).

> The employer exposed his employees to work-related accidents; transport companies exposed not only their passengers to accidents but also people who just happened to be there. Then, the fact that these accidents could often be linked to a sort of error – but a minor error (inattention, lack of precaution, negligence)

committed moreover by someone who could not carry the civil
responsibility for it nor pay the ensuing damages.

(Foucault, 1988, p. 147)

From this emerged the concept of no-fault responsibility based
on a number of principles. First, a focus not on an error, but on
causes and effects with responsibility for an action based on the
side of cause rather than fault. Second, the causes are of two types:
one in which the chain of events create the happening; and one
in which risk has been created through behaviour, equipment, or
enterprise. Third, although risk should be reduced wherever possible it was understood that it could not be eradicated completely.
Finally, since the no-fault liability relates to a risk that cannot be
completely removed, insurance does not operate as a form of punishment but as a form of repair and compensation. Furthermore,
through lessons learnt with each new insurance claim there is
an element of tending towards a constant reduction of the risks
(Foucault, 1988). We can now see, alongside the emergence of
the dangerous individual, that the notion of no-fault liability and
the inherent risk that the offender poses may well make him responsible for the act but that, in one sense, he is not at fault. Therefore, 'the purpose of the sanction will . . . not be to punish a legal
subject who has voluntarily broken the law; its role will be to reduce as much as possible – either by elimination, or by exclusion
or by various restrictions, or by therapeutic measures – the risk of
criminality represented by the individual in question' (Foucault,
1988, p. 148).

Conclusions

We have argued that the systems of services for the mentally disordered offender have emerged from a complex interplay of social
forces that are evidenced in the organisational structures and their
processes of operationalisation. With the societal need to protect
communal members from the ravages of mentally disordered persons, the circumscription of dangerousness became a driving force.
Professions engaged in claiming this group of offenders as part of
their domain of expertise influenced the creation and expansion
of institutions that became part of the forensic psychiatric system.
Through discursive practices, and the construction of scientific discourse, the forensic system materialised; sanctioned and legitimated

by institutions of law and medicine. Allowed to function by the society it represents, the systems of services grew, slowly initially but with increasing speed during the last previous three decades.

The forensic psychiatric systems have now become subtle and sophisticated, with technologies of control, surveillance, and containment refined to such an extent that society is assured and the social conscience salved. This state of affairs is tranquil only as long as the mentally disordered offender is not released to threaten society again. The reticulate systems of services spreads its tentacles through society, penetrating the structures of our community, and claiming new territory in its colonial expansion. Having created its institutions, units and clinics it now leaves behind its home in search of new sites of power.

Chapter 6

Service development: capture, contagion and community

Introduction

We saw in the previous chapter the rather slow emergence of services for the mentally disordered offender with the rise of the large asylum in the age of the Great Confinement. Little changed for over a hundred years until the evolution of the medium secure unit concept. However, the medium secure units themselves were slow to develop as capital funding made available was spent elsewhere. Forensic services during the sixties and early seventies were, as yet, of low priority and relatively unpopular both within the professional domain as well as the public one. However, through the eighties and nineties there has been an 'explosion' of forensic services which has taken on an impetus and drive that is staggering. Not only are there services being built physically as in the construction of secure units and clinics but also in terms of a wave of medicalised initiatives that embraces ever-wider notions of disorder. Moreover there is an increasing drive for the services to penetrate further into the criminal justice system as it infiltrates the prisons, the courts, and the police stations, and an increasing number of professions and professional areas are claiming some expertise in the area of forensic. In fact, for those working in the related fields of mentally disordered offenders the word 'forensic' has become so popular that to prefix one's job title with the word is now considered normal practice, albeit often a little asinine. This growth in popularity needs further elucidation.

Most accounts of the development of psychiatry and its provisions identify a close relationship between the personal attributes and charisma of influential individuals who drive services forward, whether they be politicians or professionals. This is usually coupled to periodic reform in legislation to take account of changing public opinion and professional views. However, this traditional view of the history of psychiatric provision is usually a slowly evolving process with only minor sudden surges. This is in stark contrast to the fifteen year eruption of contemporary forensic service provision which is apparently driven forward by a number of social factors that have crystallised to provide this changing force. We have discussed some of these at length in earlier chapters and include the yawning gap created by the end of deviance during the seventies as a scientific discipline which was quickly filled by the inchoate specialty of forensic psychiatry. This opportunity to seize a professional 'scientific' territory was taken by early stakeholders in the profession who held positions of influence. Such a growth in experts had to equate with a corresponding growth in forensic knowledge and thus the product champions were born. This claim on 'expertise' being a call for the establishment of a specific body of knowledge pertaining to the mentally disordered and their offending behaviour. However, there are other social forces at play as society must legitimate this growth of services it follows that it must have some degree of trust, or belief, in the benevolent interventions of psychiatry as applied to offenders. Thus, there appears a combination of public acceptance, professional interests, and political will brought together to produce policy development. What we need to explore further in this chapter is (a) the nature of the service development to capture clients and (b) how this is achieved.

Personal problems, public hygiene and the social body

Medicine has always had a close relationship to the body, from early times when it mapped its contours and palpated its hidden internal arrangements, to the penetration of probes and speculums via its orifices, to the 'opening up of a few corpses' for structural investigation, and to the contemporary navigation of its genetic structures through fibre-optic exploration and magnetic resonance techniques, the body is the site of medical power. However, where there is power there is resistance (Foucault, 1967). At one level we can see that the encroachment of medicine is a laudable enterprise undertaken in the spirit of benevolence for those requiring, and desiring, such medical interventions. But, what of those who do not wish it? What is the nature of their right to decline such medicine? In terms of medical conditions one may say that a person who has cancer may well refuse treatment and that decision be considered a rational one. However, what of physical conditions that have some degree of psychological overlay such as anorexia nervosa? Would refusal of treatment in this case be considered a rational decision or would psychiatric power be wielded in support of forced medical intervention? Furthermore, the picture becomes more confused if the person with either cancer or anorexia nervosa seeks treatment but not from traditional Western medicine but from an 'alternative' health belief system. This now becomes apparently more rational in terms of seeking treatment but irrational in terms of the health belief system that is adopted. Thus, the personal problems are a question of relative evaluations in relation to the services available and those requested.

The main question here involves the risk to a second party. In the cancerous patient and the anorexic the risks are clearly relating to their own personal well-being. However, should their disorder begin to have an effect on another member of society, say in the case of someone having an infectious disease, the community considers it appropriate to protect itself by removing that person from social contact. Legislation exists to forcefully remove them and ensure that they receive treatment in a hospital for infectious diseases. This principle holds true for the mentally disordered offender in our midst who may be considered a risk to others and be forcefully removed to a secure unit via the legitimation of the Mental Health Act (HMSO, 1983). The crucial point is that the dangerousness caused by the offenders condition is similar to the dangerousness caused by the infectious person's contagion. Both the infected person and the mentally disordered offender being considered 'sick'. Without this 'sickness' the dangerous person cannot be removed from society before the act of danger had been committed. There are many released prisoners each day who may well be a danger to society but are not considered ill, disordered, or sick and therefore cannot be detained.

Therefore, the function of forensic services is a form of public hygiene. As in outbreaks of infectious diseases measures are undertaken to reduce the risk of contamination by various tactics. These may include removing infected persons from the community but also may involve restricting their movements, their behaviour, or their interactions. Moving away from individually infected persons there may be legislation passed to enforce processes of control and surveillance as well as government policy guidelines to ensure safe practices. So it is with the mentally disordered offender who as an individual may be removed but also trigger the setting up of legislation and government policy based on general principles pertaining to all mentally disordered offenders. Thus service development is driven by a public hygiene to safeguard the social body. This is, both, in terms of the action taken against individuals and the formulation of general principles.

This public hygiene requires its inspectors, its agents, and its police which must be enacted through surveillance; a constant vigil to ensure the early capture of dangerous individuals. The function of this operation being the maintenance of social order with the biggest threat being criminal activity. Thus, we see that the two forces of psychiatry and policing are brought together as one function in the systems of forensic services.

What is being cleansed in this public hygiene is the notion of danger, as it is this that links mental disorder with offending, and psychiatry with prison. Not a linkage based on *a priori* causation but on linguistics.

> And yet, all the same, when you look closely at the penal code, whether it is of an Anglo-Saxon or a Napoleonic type, *danger* has never constituted an offense. To be dangerous *is not an offense.* To be dangerous *is not an illness.* It is not a symptom. And yet we have come, as if it is self-evident, and for over a century now, to *use* the notion of danger, a perpetual movement backwards and forwards between the penal and the medical. The penal says: listen, I don't really know what to do with this man, I'd like your opinion about him – is he dangerous? And if the psychiatrist is told: come now, you must reply to *this* question, will reply: obviously, 'danger' is not a psychiatric notion – but it is the question *asked me by the judge.* And there you are! If one considers the whole thing, taken together, one sees that it all functions on the notion of danger.
>
> (Foucault, 1988, p. 191)

The early capture of the mentally disordered offender is, therefore, not surprisingly, located at the interface of policing and psychiatry. The Court of Law is one point of penetration. There are over one hundred court schemes (Backer-Holst, 1994) in which psychiatric services function as screening processes for those with some form of mental aberration. It matters little whether these schemes are court diversion schemes in which the mentally vulnerable are diverted from the criminal justice system to the mental health system or whether they are court liaison schemes in which they exist as a point of referral for psychiatric assessments. The important point is that, no matter what they are called they function as an area of psychiatric expertise in dangerousness and serve to move this condition from the criminal justice system which is limited in its ability to restrict dangerous people to the mental health system which is not. A dangerous paedophile given a ten year jail sentence walks free after serving that time, whereas the same person sent to the mental health system for treatment of his predilection can be detained for life.

In another service development, rather than mental health professionals penetrating the domain of the law we see the psychiatric expertise being instilled into non-mental health professionals. The police are being trained in basic psychopathology with custody sergeants receiving special training. Police are now encouraged to identify those with a mental disorder as early as possible in their policing activity. This is ostensibly to ensure that this 'vulnerable' group receive early attention from the mental health system. However, from differing perspectives we can see the operationalisation of the conjoint roles of police and psychiatry in a perfect sense with these officers actualising psychiatric power.

Prior to a court appearance the mentally disordered offender must reside in a police station, and prior to his residency there he must be arrested somewhere in society. The earlier that psychiatric authority can be applied the greater the chance that he will be embraced by that power. Psychiatry is, thus, seeking new ways of penetrating that space as early as is possible.

Later capture

In all of the developments discussed above, there is a shared ideal of contemporary social policy that offenders with mental health difficulties should be diverted *away* from custody. Such is premised on the assumption that health and social agencies will provide a more appropriate, and locally based, service; these can embrace serious sexual offenders, as well as petty lawbreakers. The bulk of sex-offender work in Britain is currently undertaken by social workers, and members of the probation service: 'The majority of convicted sex offenders are dealt with by non-custodial disposals, such as fines and conditional discharges' (Epps, 1996). Without undermining the intent of these initiatives, they can be seen to represent an extension of the therapeutic enterprise into the structures of the community. The paedophile who attends a group treatment programme, almost as an out-patient, is saved from the stigma of incarceration, but not without conditions. Understandably, supervision and surveillance are an important mechanism for reducing risk, but at another level signify new technologies of intervention linked to the treatment model.

As we move on to consider the issue of 'later capture', the typology of 'sexual offender' can be used to illustrate a number of issues. Firstly, in terms of disposal it appears that the decision regarding a penal or psychiatric placement is arbitrary; with special hospitals, perhaps, becoming a repository for the more disturbed, and disturbing, offenders. Ironically, though the prison system currently delivers a national, and systematic, treatment programme for the perpetrators of sexual crime; it is one which cannot be equalled by the secure psychiatric hospitals. Aimed at the practical goals of reduced recidivism, and public safety, this psychologically driven innovation coincided with the Criminal Justice Act (1991), with provision for community disposal and post-release supervision (HMSO, 1993).

For sexual offenders within the special hospital system, the operation of therapeutic groups to address sexually violent behaviours presents a number of ethical concerns. Despite the premise of being detained for treatment, individual patients retain the right to volunteer, or withdraw, their participation. Increasingly, though, secure units which offer the usual route out of high security settings insist on some measure of progress before considering any patient for transfer. In a tightly controlled, and sexually segregated, world there are few indicators of behavioural change, and even less regarding emotional or fantasy life. Given this, the notion of voluntarism assumes a sinister twist, and compliance with treatment (as far as the patient is concerned) is expected to offer longer-term rewards. And here resides the ultimate contradiction of forensic practice, where the promise of medicine conflicts with the politic of control. The therapist–patient discourse is exactly that which constructed the 'dangerous individual' in the first instance. We are, again, returned to Foucault's (1978) spectacle of the courtroom; the more a defendant tells, the more closely entwined they become.

The way that offenders become entrapped within secure services has been conceptually described as 'biographical shunting';

of lives spent in transit, on a journey decided by others, that is
without destination. At a micro-level it describes well the, semi-
official, management strategy for dealing with difficult and disruptive patients. Thus, frequent ward moves, initiated without
notice, mean that the individual remains a transient figure among
peers. At a larger level, these moves are between institutions; with
few belongings, and no permanent home, they become the 'bag-
people' of the secure services. For those prisoners who move into
the psychiatric system, the alleged luxury of 'nutting out' is not
without a high price. Within mental health legislation (HMSO,
1983), is the provision to detain transferred prisoners (now
patients) beyond the expiry of their release date; if their mentally
disordered status is 'notional', their 'capture' is very real.

Specialist roles

As we pointed out, briefly, earlier, the claim on a specific area of
expertise pertaining to the provision of services for the mentally
disordered offender either asserts that it is a unique body of knowledge that stands independently of the other epistemologies or
it professes to be based on general psychiatric principles merely
applied to a specific target population. Put another way, it is either
a new claim for a type of *homicidal monomania* or it is the exercise
of psychiatric authority on criminal conduct. However, this particular polarised view is one in which there is little chance of extricat-
ing oneself and the contemporary writers in this area are aware
of this aspect and tend to adopt a relational position, whilst not
totally dismissing either poles. Eastman (1993) eloquently displays
this in his definitional account of British forensic psychiatry: 'it
is, as most commonly perceived in Britain, a clinical discipline
practised in relation to mentally disordered offenders (or, more
correctly, those showing the coincidence of mental disorder and
antisocial behaviours, rather than offending per se). Additionally
it is the application of law to all mentally disordered patients'
(Eastman, 1993). Eastman (1993) then goes on to identify the focus
of developments in the British forensic system over the past two
decades and claims: 'running through the review is the conclusion that there has been a high degree of concentration in British
forensic psychiatry on development of services rather than on individual patient treatment methods, albeit that substantial *gaps* in

services explain why this should have occurred' (Eastman, 1993; emphasis in the original). It is perhaps this statement that truly reveals the thrust of contemporary trends; service development rather than treatment progress.

We have discussed at length throughout the book the strong relationship that exists between society and the dangerous individual and we have also noted the popularisation of the mentally disordered offender in *relation* to forensic psychiatry. Nowhere is this more popularly performed than in the film and book *Silence of the Lambs*, in which the brilliant psychiatrist Hannibal Lecter, who is a deranged cannibalistic madman, is pitted against the psychiatrist who is an arrogant, brusque buffoon, but who is entrusted with the task of treating him. In this alarming story, the application of psychiatric treatment is lost amidst an overpowering battery of security procedures designed to contain the danger that Hannibal Lecter poses. These ultimately fail, with Hannibal escaping to have his psychiatrist round for dinner! (i.e. cannibalism). The irony of the novel being that it applauds the power of psychoanalysis as an investigative tool whilst distorting its use to create the mentally disordered offender. Although highly dramatised it is this fascination with the wicked wonders and the wonderfully wicked of the world that contributes to the success of such films as this, and it is also some explanation as to why a Madame Tussauds house of horrors is one of the more favourite holiday outings. If Foucault was right in stating that forensic psychiatry first proclaimed itself a pathology of the monstrous (Foucault, 1978) then we can see that the contemporary popularity is grounded in the fascination of this monstrosity.

The popularisation has also been part of the professional domain with psychiatrists claiming forensic expertise, professorships in forensic psychiatry being developed, and departments, units, and institutes growing from this pathologisation. Nurses shadowing their psychiatrist counterparts adopted the title of forensic psychiatric nurse with an abundance of committees, courses, and conferences, as well as an associated body, an RCN form, and an expanding journal for forensic mental health workers. Lectureships and senior lectureships in forensic nursing are established and Professorships now abound. The British Psychological Association, after long and contentious debate, has recently succumbed to the guile of 'forensic' and now recognises it as a branch of psychology. Forensic Social Workers are now in vogue and have produced documentary evidence of their 'expertise' in this domain (Central

Council for Education and Training in Social Work, 1995). Some community psychiatric nurses are now Forensic Community Psychiatric Nurses.

Other professional expansion techniques involve the term 'mentally disordered offender' rather than 'forensic' with specialist probation officers claiming some authority. This particular service is keen to establish some academic, but practically orientated, rigor in their profession and most probation officers will have had some mentally disordered offenders on their caseload. Some Occupational Therapists working with mentally disordered offenders attach 'forensic' to their title and become Forensic Occupational Therapists and, again, it is a little uncertain as to whether they lay claim to specific occupational therapeutic knowledge for mentally disordered offenders or are merely adopting generally recognised occupational therapy skills and applying them to this specific patient population. Some individual lawyers as well as some law firms have specialised in the area of mentally disordered offenders and enjoy a growing body of proficiency with a captive client population and a lucrative source of fees.

Finally, forensic psychiatry and forensic psychiatric nursing may no longer raise any eyebrows as they have received professional recognition and, perhaps to a lesser degree, become accepted at a societal level. However, as other services begin to adopt the title in their quest for expansion the appellation at first sounds odd and clumsy. For example, there are currently claims for a specific area of expertise in Forensic First Aid (presumably on the basis that injuries sustained in this environment are somehow different). Another secure establishment is developing a Mother and Baby Unit, and referring to the specialist professional practice of forensic midwifery!

Community developments

It seems an odd paradox to discuss the service developments in the community for the mentally disordered offender as it is a place from which they have been excluded because of the danger that they represent to that community. The reconciliation of this, at one level, employs rationalistic discourse pertaining to the benefits of community existence, the appropriateness of inclusion strategies into the communal spirit, and rehabilitative impetus of social existence. At another level the discourse is concerned with the denigration of institutional housing, the demoralisation of asylum care, and the dysfunctional nature of the organisation. And, whilst at still another level, the discursive plays with symbolic images of movement, progress and advancement, portraying the mentally disordered offender as 'forever in transit', at another level it is concerned with fiscal considerations and the rationing of services. Finally we see the expansion of services for mentally disordered offenders into the very heart and soul of the society in which they are constructed as a question of exorcism. The exorcism of dangerousness from our midst. The rationalisation of the existence of forensic services. The 'proof' required to convince society that the dangerous individual can be neutralised, corrected, and cleansed.

The great asylums that were built over the previous 300 years to house the insane, and the dangerously mentally ill, were established to remove those afflicted from the community that they represented a danger to. Throughout the history relating to the confinement of the mad the one central theme that has remained constant is the stratagem of containment. The mechanisms by which they have restricted, confined, and regulated the insane may have changed with the mores of their time, often subtle tactical shifts have been sufficient but at other times dramatic inversions were necessary. For example, the contraptions that were developed to discipline the weaknesses of the insane were variations on a theme of terror under the medical guise of modern therapy, however, the switch from the chains and manacles fashioned from iron to the more fashionable iron rule of quaker morality was effected by the discourse of benevolence and libertarianism (Foucault, 1973). Thus, the mechanics of confinement changed but the end result of containment remained. The asylum was justified.

The deinstitutionalisation programme of the last three decades has witnessed the closure of many of these large-scale asylums with an influx of the mentally ill and mentally handicapped into community care provision. However, with the under funding of such resources in the community this has led to an increase in these patient populations becoming the homeless and destitute. They have been returned to the conditions that led to the Vagrancy Act (HMSO, 1744) and now occupy the 'cardboard city' in many towns of Britain. However, this is tolerated to a large extent as they 'disappear' with the light of the day and are kept on the move throughout the streets. But, what of the dangerous individual? When the asylum closure came, the dangerous insane could not be allowed to roam the streets as their non-dangerous counterparts were, they needed the development of methods of containment that would continue to safeguard the community to which they were supposedly destined. If the move from the iron chains of confinement to the moral imperative of containment required the overlay of a benevolent discourse then the deinstitutionalisation of the dangerously insane would require their reinstitutionalisation through dissimilar, more subtle, means of containment. This was achieved with the rise of the medium secure units replacing the locked wards of the asylum, but with a discourse of modernity and a denigration of previous practice which, presumably, was similar to the piety of Pinel and Tuke, the French and British libertarians, at that time.

The contemporary thrust of service development for the dangerous individual is undertaken amidst a legitimating discourse of modernity. The really dangerously insane are maintained in the institutions of the Special Hospitals as they have long done so, the nearly really dangerously insane are contained in the medium secure units, and the not so dangerously insane are confined to the growing number of low dependency psychiatric units. However, to fulfil the spirit involved in the move to community care requires further sophisticated mechanisms which provide an image of developing expertise but at another interpretive level and are merely astute means of containment. These are the community developments.

As was mentioned above, the dangerously mentally ill have traditionally been removed from society, and in fact still are. However, the community care programme has created a need to produce services for mentally disordered offenders in the community. Alongside the community care programme was the move of health authorities to become trusts which itself caused particular concern for those managing mentally disordered offenders. With patients being transferred to lesser security services comes the potential for harm to others and although, as we will see in chapter 8, the majority of discharged mentally disordered offenders do not go on to re-offend the few that do can cause sensational media coverage and extreme political repercussions. One such service development designed to maintain some degree of containment of the mentally disordered offender is the Care Programme Approach. This approach calls for a full review of the patient who may be considered for discharge prior to him leaving the specialist psychiatric service. It includes an assessment of health and social care, a key worker to co-ordinate the programme, a regular review, interprofessional collaboration, and consultation with users and carers (Sallah, 1994). This is clearly an approach designed not only to establish responsibility for those discharging patients but also a mechanism which extends the surveillance through into the community. This is further indicated in the After-care of Conditionally Discharged Restricted Patients (Home Office and DHSS, 1987) document which was a precursor to the circular H.C.(89)5 Discharge of Patients from Hospital (DOH, 1989), which 'emphasises the importance of ensuring that, before patients are discharged from hospital, proper arrangements are made for their return home and for any continuing care which may be necessary' (p. 1). This circular goes on to highlight a number of concerns regarding discharge arrangements and the necessity for adequate follow-up. The community surveillance was increased with the Introduction of Supervision Registers for Mentally Ill people (HS[94]5) (NHS, 1994) which is maintained for those at significant risk of suicide, violence to others, and severe self-neglect. Although laudable in themselves they provide the social legitimation for psychiatric surveillance within the community and represent the spreading net of containment.

The forensic market place

Throughout the eighties and nineties the dominant political ideology of, what became known as, Thatcherism dictated that health care provision was placed in the 'market' That is, the provision of health care was competed for by services that attempted to provide facilities more efficiently, or more effectively than others. This involved issues of quantity and quality with the main thrust of the system being the establishment of patient power to choose services as consumers of that provision. Set amidst the Conservative agenda, for example the Patient's Charter and the Health of the Nation (DOH, 1992), consumerism and marketisation produced health as a commodity to be bought and sold. The totally free market place, outside of purely private provision, was not achievable within the historicity of the National Health Service which was still being financed by the majority of the population. Thus, in 1989 the foundations were laid for the division of the NHS into those that would become quasi-autonomous trusts operating in a purchaser–provider relationship. This would eventually involve more and more services who would bid for contracts with health authorities and general practices purchasing on behalf of their patients.

This system may be flawed in many ways, however, in terms of mental health and forensic psychiatric services, it is unworkable in the strictest ideological sense. This has been noted by Eastman (1993) who argued that because the system is based on assessment of need it determines the quantity and definition of the services that are delivered. However, he goes on to point out that 'assessment of need is difficult to define and operate in medicine generally, psychiatry particularly, and in forensic psychiatry very particularly' (p. 12). The reasons for this are numerous. In social constructionist terms the specialised knowledge of the expert, i.e. the doctor, has been built up over thousands of years to form a universe of meaning which is legitimated both by members of that profession who operate its codes and by the lay public who fulfil their role as believers of this expertise. When one is purchasing a car or washing machine this expertise is shared to a greater degree between purchaser–provider than when one is purchasing some aspect of health provision which may be concerned with life or death. In buying a car the purchaser may 'know' that he or she wants a particular model, colour, size, insurance rating, etc., and the provider may have the expertise of a salesperson to sway their decision. However, in health care provision generally the purchaser tends not to know what they want other than to get better whilst the provider assumes the status of all-knowing expert in this matter.

In terms of mental health provision there is the added burden of rationality. Whereas a purchase of a general health care service may well be considered to be based on a rational choice, in the mental health arena rationality, or the supposed lack of it, lies at the heart of its operational philosophy. If a person is considered to be mentally ill, i.e. irrational, they will almost undoubtedly be considered to have an inability to function as a reasonable decision-maker as to what are the most appropriate psychiatric services they require. Therefore, the purchaser–provider relationship embroils a third party, the mental health worker, who decides what services are considered the most appropriate for the patient. Thus, the requirements of true consumerism are not fulfilled.

Now with the mentally disordered offender we have another complicating factor. Not only do we have the same conditions as those mentioned above but we also have the added dimension of the victim (actual or potential). In this, the decisions regarding which services are most suited to the patient's requirements are taken completely from the recipient and are placed in the hands of the law and mental health professionals. This then expands the calculus by the involvement of the Home Office and civil servants. The true consumer of secure psychiatric services now appears to be the general public as the potential to become victims. This distortion blurs further with the issue of the treatability of the 'mad' and 'bad' (Eastman, 1993). As we have seen earlier, offending behaviour is often seen as merely 'bad' or psychopathic and therefore the general public tend to consider disposal to prison as more appropriate than transfer to psychiatric services. This then begs the question as to whether we have gone full circle on the issue of consumerism in that the public, as consumer, knows best what its requirements are. The difficulty now is that the decision for service requirement is in the hands of a third party, the mental health professional, the law, the civil servant, and the potential victim.

As far as the main consumer, purchaser, and patron of services for the mentally disordered offender are concerned we need to know what are the constituent parts of the commodity that is being bought and sold. In terms of general health settings we may see the results of a blood test or the outcome of an operation, and in mental health services we may note the drugs being taken, an altered mental state, of length of stay in hospital. However, with mentally disordered offenders the outcome measures of the effectiveness of the commodity are more concerned with the patient no longer being a danger to others. This involves issues of treatability and continued dangerousness, and will form the basis of the next two chapters.

Conclusions

The idea of forensic psychiatry as a mode of public hygiene has been advanced through discussion of the escalating growth in service provision for mentally disordered offenders. As the management of the dangerous individual has shifted away from the institution, disparate criminal justice, health, and social agencies have consolidated into a network of surveillance. Through the treatment of the offender, medical power (sited in the body of the patient) has infiltrated the societal body of the community.

Following this, services have been outlined in terms of the 'capture' of lawbreakers, both the knowledge which constructs them, and the structures that contain them. Therapeutic language, as a discursive practice, not only initiates the career of the disordered offender, but perpetuates their journey with each re-telling of the story. Finally, in the market economy of contemporary health care, the forensic patient emerges as a reluctant consumer and a dubious product.

Chapter 7

Treatment and management from a social perspective

Introduction

In the previous chapter we discussed the developments of forensic services and saw how the major thrust was concerned with broadening and extending the surveillance mechanisms throughout society. Early forensic psychiatry may well have started with the pathology of the monstrous and their incarceration into criminal lunatic asylums, but the contemporary forensic concern now involves a plethora of minor infractions alongside the heinous crime. As the forensic 'net' has been cast wider to capture more disorder so the large-scale service has been fragmented to penetrate the social body. Now forensic services include forensic psychiatric outpatient departments, forensic community psychiatric nurses, and forensic social workers who are dealing with the political and professional issues of service development such as supervision registers, care programme approach and compulsory treatment in the community. At the time of writing we are witnessing a break up of the large forensic institutions with recommendations for more small-scale establishments (Reed, 1992) which is underpinned by this penetration of small services into society itself.

The debate on the treatment and management of the mentally disordered offender crystallises into several dimensions. The first dimension involves notions of the effectiveness of such therapeutics and regulation. Unlike other medicalised arenas in which treatment inefficiency may lead to serious consequences for the patient themselves, in the field of forensic psychiatry there tends to be a third party involvement, the victim. Thus, the efficacy of the treatment and management of the mentally disordered offender issue immediately become of professional, public, and political concern; in other words, very much located in the social sphere.

A second domain involves the question of which treatment and management model should be applied. By a historical benchmark it is psychiatry and the medical model that dominates the approach, not only in understanding the nature of mentally disordered offenders, but also in their treatment and management mode. This medical model has a number of variations but can be briefly explicated as comprising a process of identification, classification, diagnosis, treatment, and prognosis. It also involves notions of 'disease' equating with 'disorder' in some form of tentative relationship of pathology. However, this medical model of mental disorder has its critics (Szasz, 1960; Sarbin, 1967). Psychological approaches challenge the medical model by aiming beyond the mere relief of symptoms into the area of personal growth and the development of coping skills (Blackburn, 1993). However, the term 'psychological approaches' is a necessarily restricting one and in reality can encompass a wide array of interventions which may be as much political as they are economic (i.e. the short, sharp, shock approach). Although sociological theories to understanding offending have made a significant impact on the conceptual plane, in the practical enterprise of treatment and management they remain inchoate. Some sociological approaches may fit loosely into the 'therapeutic community' or 'milieu therapy' rubrics, however, the area of social therapy is grossly underdeveloped. Whatever model is applied it seems clear that the crux of the approach is the extent to which it is effective, and this inevitably involves the rate of recidivism.

A third domain to the treatment and management issue involves the setting in which it is undertaken. Treatment and management of mentally disordered offenders occurs in prisons, on hospital wings and is undertaken by psychiatrists and, in some cases, psychologists and nurses. There are also the special hospitals and medium secure units which function at varying hierarchies of security from maximum to low. These establishments, as was stated earlier, are usually populated by compulsorily detained patients who are forced to have treatment. This coercive approach in relation to the establishment of therapeutic relationships has yet to receive the degree of critical examination it justly deserves. A further area of forensic work is now undertaken in what can be loosely termed the 'community' (Vaughan and Badger, 1995). This may involve out-patient clinics, hostels, and homes with support services comprising social workers, probation officers, and community psychiatric nurses, as well as psychiatrists and psychologists in specialist treatment centres.

First and foremost forensic psychiatry exists to protect the public from dangerous individuals and to prove its efficacy it must return mentally disordered offenders to society without them causing harm to others. The increase in forensic structures within the community, such as those mentioned above, are mechanisms of surveillance in order that such mentally disordered offenders may be monitored for signs of dangerousness. Although, as we will see in chapter 8, the majority of mentally disordered offenders released into the community do not go on to re-offend, those that do become sensationalised by the media and cause serious questions to be asked of the forensic psychiatric profession itself. These cases tend to cause some considerable political embarrassment and may result in damage to personal careers. If forensic psychiatry is to succeed in convincing society of its effectiveness then it must continue to safeguard the public from harm and, should it fail to do this, society has the power to demand that the dangerous individual be incarcerated in the criminal justice system rather than the mental health system. Thus, society is ever watchful of forensic psychiatry.

This chapter is concerned with the treatment and management of the mentally disordered offender but from a social perspective rather than from a purely psychiatric or psychological approach. We will set out the main points in the debate between punishment and therapy in which the treatment of prisoners is contrasted with the punishment of the mentally ill. Social therapy will then be discussed in relation to whether it is the social that is considered the cause of sickness or the source of therapy. Finally we will highlight some main issues in the forensic social structures of supervision registers, compulsory treatment in the community, supervised after-care orders, assertive and passive outreach, and case management of mentally disordered offenders.

Punishment versus therapy

The care and management of mentally disordered offenders within institutional settings is bedevilled by an on-going debate about therapeutic custody (Burrow, 1991). Seemingly irreconcilable tensions between enforced detention and treatment goals have mutated the dual statuses of both staff and inmates, the carer/ custodian and the prisoner/patient. Whilst some of the literature has attempted to unmask a rhetorical confusion of professional practice as political control (Burrow, 1993), there remains considerable naïvety in terms of resolving these difficulties. It has been suggested that systems of confinement can be 'fine-tuned', and an equitable balance achieved. However, recent events at Ashworth Special Hospital on Merseyside (the investigation into alleged paedophile activity and the extreme use of hard pornography), being illustrative of larger trends to democratise maximum secure psychiatric provision, is testimony to poor management, with limited vision, presiding over the greatest forensic debacle in the global history of the service with appalling consequences. Allegations of neglect and abuse, precipitating a major public inquiry, generated managerial reorganisation underpinned by a 'culture change' programme; the setting up of an Independent Advocacy Service and Patient's Council, directly enacted recommendations of the Blom–Cooper report (HMSO, 1992). More significantly, though, these changes imparted a new language of 'user' involvement, collaboration, and empowerment. Conjecture at the time permitted cautious, if optimistic, predictions for the future (Bingley, 1993). Yet, within five years the answer was furnished as Ashworth faced a second major inquiry and judicial review. A re-emphasis on security, backlash towards reform, and allocation of structural slant towards the Prison Service symbolised more than a localised service crisis; such struck at the very function and future of forensic psychiatry. Critical sociological analysis offers some insight into this entanglement of 'language games', connecting those discursive practices which construct the disordered offender to a wider scenario of politics and power; not delineating therapy from punishment, but identifying their ideological symmetry.

Longstanding concerns about the sharing of populations between penal and mental health systems (Penrose, 1939), in questioning the scientificity of disposal decisions, paved the way for a critique of the 'therapeutic state' (Kittrie, 1971). More recently, it has been suggested that the 'revolving door' of the asylum is a far from forgotten chapter of mental health history. In contemporary terminology it is, perhaps, better described as a transcarceral network of services and agencies spanning institutional and community provision; representing an endless forensic journey for those ensnared within its gravitational field (Menzies, 1987). Passionate debates about the disposal of law-breakers, from legal bar to public bar, as *subjects* for treatment or *objects* of punishment are manifestations of ideologically discrete approaches to crime; and, of greatest importance in the context of this volume, the relationship between *criminal responsibility* and *mental disorder*. There is a need to focus on the criminological enterprise not as a body of objective knowledge, but as a powerful force in shaping theory, research, policy, and practice. In shifting attention away from the language of *causation* to that of *context*, or of *cure* to *control*, is to begin unravelling the interwoven ideologies which underpin mental health and criminal justice; and in so doing move us towards a 'history of the present' (Foucault, 1977).

As Blackburn (1993) notes, 'the relationship between mental disorder and crime reflects changing interactions between criminal justice and mental health systems as much as *scientific* concern' (emphasis added). Yet, the quest to identify an aetiological link between two distinct human experiences (mental illness and criminality), has overshadowed the larger issue of social construction mediated by professional power (Ingleby, 1985). However, a number of seminal works, rekindling and revitalising the libertarian critique of the 1960s have laid the foundations for a critical analysis of the medical appropriation of insanity and crime. Iconoclastic histories of the asylum and the penitentiary (Foucault, 1973; 1977; Ignatieff, 1978) counter the received wisdom of compassion, reform, and neutrality, whilst illuminating the operation of state institutions in contemporary society. Though the theoretical perspectives of the authors differ, these writers 'each emphasised a historical position that eschewed benevolent progression for more structural dimensions of political economy, social class, ideology and power' (Sim, 1990). Here, the genesis of psychiatry and medicine in the prisons and mad-houses of the eighteenth century was inextricably linked to the maintenance of order amidst a new set of capitalist social relations.

Explanations of disease and illness have varied over time, and between cultures. Until the late eighteenth century, European medicine comprised a combination of both 'personalistic' and 'naturalistic' systems, respectively seeing sickness as the result of external forces or an imbalance of body elements (Morgan *et al.*, 1985). However, from the early nineteenth century, a changing conceptualisation of disease, as aetiologically specific and universal, accompanied the consolidation of professional medicine based upon the scientific paradigm. The bio-medical model assumed a dominance which has continued to the present, and 'resulted in health and illness being seen in individualistic terms, with the causes of illness and responsibility for health largely residing with the individual' (Morgan *et al.*, 1985). Though generally portrayed as the triumph of rational knowledge, critics have pointed to the social factors, and forces, that shaped the ascendancy of medical power. That disease categories, rather than existing independent of the physician, are socially interpreted and constructed (Freidson, 1970; Illich, 1975).

In terms of mental illness orthodox texts, similarly, suggest that the 'nineteenth century takeover of the field by medicine, and its consolidation in recent years, demonstrate the progressive spread in our society of principles of reason and humanity' (Ingleby, 1985). In stark contrast, critical histories have vigorously attacked the application of medical metaphor and methods to so-called 'diseases of the mind' (Laing, 1960; Cooper, 1972). Indeed, for Conrad and Schneider (1980) the historical development of mental illness is 'literally the original case of *medicalised deviance*' (emphasis added). The emergence of a unitary concept of mental illness, and an expanded psychiatric nosology, was derived from the philosophical tenets of positivism; the idea that the social world, like the natural world, was accessible to empirical investigation, measurement, prediction, and control.

Concepts of diagnostic classification were accepted and advanced despite the lack of either a demonstrable somatic pathology, or any effective treatment; ironically, medical prestige was enhanced by an investment of faith in its methods, rather than a measure of its validity. Graphic examples such as 'drapetomania', an 'illness' causing slaves to run away from plantations, illustrate the Eurocentric and imperialist infrastructure of the nascent discipline (Fernando, 1992). Disease labels could be attached to any behaviour at variance with a normative view of the world, including crime (Conrad and Schneider, 1980).

This debate clearly assumes a key prominence as we move towards a consideration of the role of medicine in relation to legal or moral transgression. An ever-expanding list of behaviours has now been transferred into a psychiatric arena; along with the victims of domestic violence and child abuse we can include the perpetrators of those acts, other forms of sexual offending, drug addiction, alcoholism, prostitution, violence, and political dissent (Miller, 1980). Indeed, from shoplifting to serial killing the expertise of the forensic psychiatrist can be invoked, and the concept of punishment replaced with that of treatment. To begin asking why this should be so is to explore the nature of both crime and criminality, an ideological relationship which like mental disorder is rooted in history.

Like madness, definitions of deviance (the transgression of societal values) and crime (the transgression of criminal law) are historically and culturally specific, as are the types of sanction and punishment evoked in response to socially proscribed behaviour; be they religious, legal, or medical (Miller, 1980). These conflicting, and at time entangled, systems of social control impact powerfully on the management of offenders, and embrace wider debates about retribution, reform, and rehabilitation. Criminology has broadly been defined as 'the study of crime, of attempts to control it, and of attitudes to it' (Walker, 1983a). If this description adequately outlines the administrative mainstream of the discipline, its focus is upon the twofold search for individual causation and organisational effectiveness in criminal justice. For critical theorists, correctional criminology represents 'the face of the enemy' (Hester and Eglin, 1992), and has been met by attempts to 'demonstrate theoretically the connections between law and the state, legal and political relations, the economic basis and functions of crime' (Hall and Scraton, 1981).

An understanding of shifts in the organisation of penology has to be located in the wider social relations of a society undergoing radical change (Garland, 1990). Classicist explanations of the eighteenth century interpreted crime as a rational activity, deliberately chosen based upon a calculus of odds. Correspondingly, justice embodied in the notion of a 'social contract', sought deterrence through a scale of penalties proportional to the degree of harm produced. Thus, the individual was seen as responsible for his/her actions and punished accordingly (Young, 1981).

Writing from a Marxist perspective, Melossi and Pavarini (1981) offered a pioneering contribution to exploring the connections between prisons and the social structure; an historical analysis written against the backdrop of increasing ferment and protest within a penal system in 'crisis' throughout the western world. Punishment as public spectacle (whipping, branding, and execution) or the privation of personal assets (money, property, or life) struggled to survive the breakdown of a feudal economy (Giddens, 1989). In the context of a capitalist economy a new form of retributive punishment was required, commensurate with exchange value and waged labour; the penitentiary represented a clear relationship between the *means of production* and the *means of punishment*. Thus, it is argued that 'in every industrial society, the institution has become the dominant punitive instrument to such an extent that prison and punishment are commonly regarded as synonymous' (Melossi and Pavarini, 1981).

As criminality merged with the disease epidemics that followed industrialisation, confinement became part of a changing discourse about public hygiene based upon a surveillance of points of contact between the individual and the social body (Foucault, 1973). The disciplinary regime of the penitentiary paralleled the moral regime of the asylum, sharing alike a concern to maintain social order through a resocialisation of *reason* in inmates and felons (Ignatieff, 1978a; 1981b). The reforms of Pinel and Tuke, typically interpreted as the symbolic turning point in enlightened care, represent here a triumph of medicine over crime and insanity. It was an expansion, and legitimation, of discipline to embrace the mind as well as the body; and one 'intended to transform the mad, sad and bad into the disciplined and docile workforce required for the purposes of industrial capitalism' (Dobash and Dobash, 1992).

It was in these carceral institutions that criminologists such as Caesare Lombroso commenced their search for the criminal man, as doctors and jurors wrestled for the soul of the 'dangerous individual' (Foucault, 1978). Crime was redefined as a disease, innate and inherited, commited by those abnormal in body or mind; punishment no longer deemed appropriate was replaced with indeterminate detention for treatment. At the same time the focus of analysis shifts attention away from the contextual structure in which human action takes place and any human meaning attached to it. Though now obsolete relics of the past the early ideas of 'stigmata' and 'atavism' are echoed in a lineage of scientific testing of incarcerated populations (Sapsford, 1981). Depending upon fashion and technology, prisoners have 'had their heads measured for irregularities, their bodies somatotyped, their unconsciouses probed and analysed, their intelligence rated, their personalities typed, their brains scanned, and their gene structure investigated' (Box, 1981).

Suggestions that the development of psychotherapeutic approaches represent an emancipatory break from the past warrant closer scrutiny. Thus, it has been suggested that the contribution of Freud merely moved the dialogue from 'biogenic determinism' to 'psychogenic determinism' (Conrad and Schneider, 1980), extending the medical model of madness to a wider range of emotional problems. The historical and cultural construction of 'hysteria', which remains contested as a disease category, connects clinical practice, sexual division, and patriarchy to the structural dimension of gender (Showalter, 1987). If women who dare to affront the norms and role expectations of a male dominated society are less obviously oppressed by contemporary society, medical knowledge reflects and reinforces popular prejudice. It is another irony that the profession which for so long actively silenced the voices of female survivors of sexual abuse (Masson, 1985a, 1990b; Salter, 1990), should transform into their therapeutic salvation. The discourse which emphasises personal pathology in abused and battered women, according them the status of patient or client, has been accompanied by a massive escalation in the numbers of professionals allied to the mental health movement. Sexual-political and economic problems are masked by clinical language, and change equates with the process of individual therapy: 'The objective now appears to be perfection of self through counselling and psychotherapy' (Dobash and Dobash, 1992).

Grendon Underwood, Britains first psychiatric prison, may be seen as an experimental venture, outlasting an era of therapeutic optimism, and peripheral to the overall penal system. Rapists are no longer viewed as 'sick' (Karpman, 1954; Watts and Courtois, 1981), but the ideology of 'treatment' has remained professionally potent, and politically prudent; evidenced in the implementation of a national strategy, in 1991, for imprisoned sex offenders. If chemical castration (tablets) has been replaced with group therapy (talk), the 'beast' ('tamed' not 'maimed') remains as a species of medico-legal discourse. And today, the judicial machinery of punishment, as much as the technology of forensic science, requires this dialogue: 'When a man comes before his judges with nothing but his crimes, when he has nothing else to say but "this is what I have done," when he has nothing to say about himself, when he does not do the tribunal the favor of confiding to them something like the secret of his own being, then the judicial machine ceases to function' (Foucault, 1978, p. 18).

Social therapy

As we pointed out in chapter 2 certain theoretical perspectives view society as 'sick' in terms of its social structures, inequalities and divisions as causative factors in the production of psychopatho-logical disorder. Thus, attempts to treat individually disordered persons without changing the society in which the disorder arose is an incomplete therapeutic task and is highly likely to fail. Such contemporary social perspectives are rooted in the close associa-tions between psychoanalysis and anthropological interpretations. As early as 1931, Louis Wirth writing from the University of Chi-cago, made an argument for Clinical Sociology in which he distin-guished between the social psychiatrist, the social worker, and the clinical sociologist. In short, he believed that the cultural approach of clinical sociology could be beneficial when behaviour was per-ceived as a problem when it represented a deviation from the defining qualities that prevailed in a particular cultural milieu. Only then could such behaviour be understood, controlled, and modi-fied in relation to this cultural background. Wirth believed that manipulation of the social world and the modifications of attitudes, beliefs, and prejudices were the major therapeutic concern of the clinical sociologist. This interactive, and adaptive, model suggests that social forces act upon individuals, who then adapt their be-haviour in response, and develop attitudes which are then con-stitutive of aberrancy. Thus, altering the social forces will, arguably, produce changes in the person's attitude.

In a similar vein, Thomas and Thomas (1929) had argued the case for 'beneficence framing' as a method of social therapy for children, in which deliberate manipulation of the child's environ-ment was undertaken. This could be the manipulation of the fam-ily, the school, or community in order to make it more responsive to the child's wishes through the achievement of social objectives. They attempted to substitute socially disapproved values for more socially appropriate ones which involved modifying the attitudes and behaviours of members of significant others in the child's social world which presented two major therapeutic techniques. Firstly, a modification in the child's attitude towards both his social world and the significant others in it, and, secondly, an adjustment in his conception of himself. The fact that these are clearly inter-related was not overlooked and began an unresolved dilemma in terms of the 'chicken and the egg' scenario of which comes first, the social forces producing the aberrant attitudes or the personal-ity traits that respond to the social forces in such a way as to pro-duce aberrant attitudes. The dilemma is further complicated by attempting to identify the target of such 'social therapy', i.e. directed at social factors, at the aberrant individual, at significant others in their social world, or a combination of all three.

Construction of the group

The post-war years saw an expansion of interest in social psychology, particularly with the work of Michael Argyle, in which there was a conjoining of psychological understanding with a growing knowledge of the influence of social situations and group formation. This involved more specific work on the person–situation debate, particularly in relation to cross-situational behavioural consistencies (Bem and Allen, 1974), the prediction of individual and group behavioural patterns (Epstein, 1979), and the way people change situations whilst acting in them (Argyle, 1976). Taking up the early work of the symbolic interactionists and ethnomethodologists Berger and Luckman (1966) analysed situations in relation to their interactive and communicative strategies between group members whilst Garfinkel (1967) studied the rational properties of groups by disrupting their natural order. From an objection to the foregoing the ethogenics of Harre and Secord (1972) suggested that social action was more than rule-following behaviour and also included a dramaturgical self-monitoring component. Kelley's (1972) typology of information processing within the theory of attribution was outlined as (a) consensus, the extent to which people act the same in similar situations as the person under study; (b) consistency, the extent to which the person under study acts the same in different situations; and (c) distinctiveness, the extent to which the person under study acts differently for a specific situation. Finally, there is an abundance of functional theories of social situations emanating from the work of Merton (1949) and Parsons (1953) in which, despite the critics, there is an analysis of individual and group action relating to the social situation and includes the following:

1 Dimensional Approach – which calls for methods of measurement of a person's perception or reaction to social situations along bipolar scales

2 Componential Approach – which involves an analysis of the components and elements in each situation and an understanding of the relationship between these elements. The elements include rules, roles, concepts, triggers, props, etc.

3 Environmental Approach – which includes an analysis of the physical features of situations such as space, audience, heat, noise, light, etc., as well as the symbolic and social significance of these features

4 Ecological Approach – which is closely related to micro-sociology and anthropology which uses detailed analysis and description of physical, temporal, and social aspects of naturally occurring social situations

5 Ethogenic Approach – in which there is a detailed analysis of the rules and roles of social episodes usually taken from the testimonies of the social actors in these situations.

There are, of course, other methods of studying social behaviour in the social setting but the above categorises the major approaches as outlined by Argyle, Furnham, and Graham (1981).

Activities of living

Another interpretation of the constituent parts of the construct social therapy pertains more closely to what are known as 'activities of living'. These activities include the appropriate organisation, planning, and management of aspects of daily life such as eating, washing, cleaning, recreation, and sexual gratification. It is premised that a malfunctioning in these areas leads to frustration, isolation, and social withdrawal of both self and others. Therefore, the social therapy would involve education and training in shopping, budgeting, preparing meals, and the cleaning of clothes as well as attention to personal hygiene. Through this it is anticipated that the person becomes a more sociable animal and through the complex self-reinforcing interactive components in social situations they begin to function within societal rules.

Interpersonal relationships

Another perspective on social therapy is to view the interpersonal relationships with others as a central component of effective social action. Thus, aberrant behaviour is seen as a corollary of poor social relations. The logical connections to this state of affairs, simply stated, is that poor social relationships with others leads to frustration, rejection, isolation, anger, etc., with the resultant turning against others and the corollary of violence, aggression, and other forms of deviant behaviour. It is an obvious statement to make that personal relationships with others are an important aspect of human existence. Groups, clans, gangs, and clubs, of all manner of descriptions, exist as testimony to the importance of relating to others. This relationship is context bound, and complex in nature, as the common maxims of 'opposites attract', 'birds of a feather flock together' and 'honour among thieves' clearly show. However, most successful relationships are formed through a generalised process which involves (a) the meeting of strangers and the selection activity employed, (b) the development of a relationship including self-disclosure and general courtship, (c) maintaining relationships and their reinforcement, (d) understanding the processes involved when relationships break down, and (e) how to put them right, or not as the case may be (Duck, 1988). People unable to operate these social processes of relationship formation, sustainment, and repair may well become social misfits.

The relationship between the social misfit and mental disorder is well documented (e.g. Hersen, 1979) and the socially inept not only stand out very quickly but appear to be in a spiralling social deterioration. That is, the more they socially interact the more they socially fail, and the more they fail the more socially inept they become. According to Trower (1985) the social misfit fails in a number of social dimensions. First, in the scripted and unscripted social situation which involves strict adherence to rules and roles of a given situation especially in the former scripted, but less so in the latter unscripted. An example of a scripted social situation would be the restaurant script in which there are rules, roles, and props that occur in a sequence with clearly delineated outcomes. A second social situational dimension is in the tension between explicit and implicit scripts and their rule accessibility. Explicit rules are more readily available and are often rehearsed, i.e. as in a marriage ceremony, whereas implicit rules of informal social situations are more difficult to detect and decode. Third, situations have hierarchies of rule significance with fundamental ones considered important to adhere to, with the consequences of transgressing them being more serious. A fourth dimension involves the high versus low skill repertoire required for dealing with social situations. Unscripted and unfamiliar social situations may call for a wide variety of skills, however, the complexity is considerable as even in highly scripted situations there may well be an intricate variety of rules. Fifth, there is a tension between the public and the private objectives in the social situation which can lead to a conflict of interests. A sixth dimension concerns the specifity–generality of social situations in which, in the former they may be unique whilst in the latter they are more common. A seventh dimension involves the selectivity of the social situation. That is, the extent to which we are selected or unselected for a social situation, i.e. selected for an exclusive club but unselected to join a bus queue. Finally, there is the extent to which social situations provoke self-awareness. Those situations that involve self-presentation, scrutiny by others, and the potential for loss of face create the possibility for self-awareness.

However, the social situation not only involves the foregoing dimensions but also includes the characteristics of the actors within them. A social misfit is considered to have inconsistencies in components of persona related to operating in social situations. These include a tendency towards a restricted rather than an elaborate social skill repertoire, inappropriate situation schemas in which the wrong script is chosen, inappropriate perceptions of self or others, subjective internal monitoring or self-evaluation, high and low self-consciousness distortions, tension between demanding and non-demanding goals and standards, and finally discrepancies between high and low outcome expectancies (Trower, 1985). Thus, we can see that the dimensions of the social situation and the dimensions of the personality govern the extent to which the person 'fits' into social life, or conversely highlights them as a social mis-fit.

The therapeutic community

The idea of a therapeutic community arose in the 1940s and the 1950s in the UK and the USA respectively and now embraces a wide range of therapeutic group endeavours including the all-embracing, but inadequately defined, milieu therapy. That living in a particular communal environment tends to infuse the person with the ideology of that group, albeit often only temporarily, is not new. This adoption of the spirit, ethos, and philosophy of a community is exemplified in religious groups, cults, and Kibbutzim as well as street gangs and the criminal fraternity. The similarity between these groups is the adoption of, and internalisation of, a given ideological framework which then sets the parameters for the members' behaviour. It is not surprising, then, that the historically well-versed social structural formation of group cohesiveness would become medicalised as the therapeutic community. Although, as we say, there is now a wide range of approaches subsumed within the therapeutic community enterprise the common threads are grouped into the democratic–analytic and the concept-based therapeutic communities (Blackburn, 1993). In the former there is an emphasis upon the resolution of conflicts, tensions, and contradictory behaviours through a democratic process of community living, rule formation, power sharing, social tolerance, reality confrontation, and group application of sanction. These types are more common in the UK in such establishments as the Henderson Hospital, Grendon Underwood Prison, and the Barlinnie Unit in Scotland. In the latter, concept-based therapeutic communities, which are more common in the USA, there are hierarchically structured social groups based on self-help philosophies. They have been established in prisons and juvenile correctional facilities and share the following basic features '(1) an informal atmosphere; (2) regular community meetings; (3) sharing the work of running the community; (4) recognition of residents as auxillary therapists' (Blackburn, 1993, pp. 386–387). All therapeutic communities pivot on the notion of creating self-control with the main approach being to create individual responsibility within the social group. This is most effective when the person has a long history of non-responsibility, uncaring attitudes towards others, and has received little positive regard from societal members. A good example of this is with the Barlinnie experiment in Scotland. Prisoners within the penal systems who are disruptive and non-compliant, and who engage in destructive violence consistently, tend to suffer from an increasingly degrading strategy of control which may include management on hospital wings, segregation units, and punishment blocks. This may send the prisoner on a spiralling, downwards, trend of disruption and further sanction until there is an organisational impasse in which prisoner and prison officers are becoming injured. Barlinnie's therapeutic community approach was to take the most disturbed, and disturbing, prisoners in the Scotish penal system and to re-establish respect, and responsibility, for the inmate. Trust was established and the prisoners were involved in organising the rules of the unit as well as formulating what sanctions needed to be applied to fellow prisoners should they transgress the community rules. The regimes were relaxed and comfortable and disruptive prisoners soon came to respect the role that they had to play within the therapeutic community.

What is interesting in these therapeutic community approaches, in terms of mentally disordered offenders, is the patient groups for which they cater, i.e. the psychopathic, sociopathic, personality disordered, juvenile delinquent, drug and alcohol abusers, and neurotic. They very rarely, if at all, admit those that are deemed psychotic. The therapeutic communities are for those who are cognitively intact and can respond to peer group pressure, accept responsibility, adjust behaviour according to group rules, and respond to social denigration for rule-breaking behaviour. In short, despite their aberrancy, they are socially aware and not socially incapacitated. Their pathological conditions are seen as malfunctioning in social structures and thus treatment is reliant upon correcting their group social action through their belonging to a therapeutic community. Seen from an anthropological point of view sociopathy (psychopathy in Britain) can be seen as a social adaptation equating with cheating in human interactions (Harpending and Sobus, 1987). Encounters in daily life usually have joint payoffs for all participants, and over time, reciprocity of payoffs was the normal state of social affairs. However, sociopaths tend not to play the reciprocal payoff game in social interactions and thus are known as 'human cheaters' in that they receive their positive payoff but leave their social interlocutor without a reciprocal positive feeling. A further development in the social understanding of psychopathy (sociopathy in the American literature) concerns the nursing management known as the 'Alpha Dog' as outlined by Moran and Mason (1996). In this approach the social dynamic of a ward community of psychopaths and their management approach is said to contain certain nursing principles including (a) usufruction, in which the ward dynamic should be enjoyed rather than feared; (b) never be surprised at the sudden change in the social action of a psychopathic patient; (c) employ humour where appropriate; (d) adopt honesty at the expense of comfort; (e) destabilise the static hierarchical ward structuring; (f) adopt rule-flexibility within legitimate boundaries; and (g) understand that all are vulnerable in the interactive encounter with psychopaths. What this recent work shows is the social nature of this group structuring and the authors note this by their use of the ethological social dynamic of the Eskimo Huskie Alpha Dog as an analogy (Moran and Mason, 1996).

However, this only deals with a certain segment of the patient population and is concerned with therapeutic communities within established systems of control, be they prison or hospital, what we need to focus upon now is the wider social community and their understanding of what constitutes treatment and management of mentally disordered offenders.

Social meaning of a mentally disordered offender

There is an ever-growing list of theoretical outlines of the causation of mental disorder – too numerous to reproduce here. The long debate concerning whether mental illness derives from genetic abnormalities, chemical imbalances, environmental influences, or a combination of all three is not overly relevant to our current project as we wish to focus on its occurrence and the impact it has on the person concerned, their family, and their community. We are well aware that whether or not the mental disorder arises from within the social interaction between the afflicted person and their society, its manifestation, in whatever form, will have an impact on their social relations. This is not dissimilar to the contracting of cancer which may well be genetically determined but once known, has a profound impact on the person's social processes.

The mentally disordered person will quickly be identified, in his family interactions and his social setting, as his behaviour becomes differentiated from his previously known patterning. Once the psychiatric profession is involved his behaviour will be subject to scrutiny for the absence of, and presence of, certain signs and symptoms of what is considered normal and abnormal functioning. He may well not be doing something that he ought to be doing and he may well be doing something that he ought not to be doing. In any event, it will be the absence or presence of some behaviour *in relation* to his social configuration. This may well issue forth any number, and manner, of assessment procedures for social skills deficits, social skills training, and psycho-social interventions. The point being that, in this approach, the emphasis is upon the normalising of the social functioning of the disordered person in order that others in the setting do not see, or do not know of, a difference.

Unfortunately, it is the known, or known about, that carries the stigma of mental disorder. The communication of the presence of a psychiatric illness in a family member is one of the first, and most difficult, decisions to be made. An early study, still highly relevant today, on this issue reveals the complexity: 'Communication is determined on the basis of a clear demarcation of "ins" and "outs". There are certain people whom you tell, and not others. The "ins" are variously defined, (a) there are those who will know because they are part of the problem or have been involved in the hospitalization of the patient, or (b) they have a "right" to know, or (c) they are people who will "understand"' (Yarrow, Clausen, and Robbins, 1955, p. 37). In some cases the communication is deferred until there is no other option or situations are manipulated so that communication is avoided. Within families there may be a conspiracy to maintain secrecy of a member's illness whilst in others circumvention is achieved through restricting discussions. What is apparent in all strategies adopted is the extent of stress this applies to members due, mainly, to the perceived shame of the stigma involved.

Differences in communicational strategies occur in differing social contexts. The meaning of the communication is different if friends, neighbours, or professional personnel are informed. Furthermore, the stage of the illness/hospitalisation also influences the meaning of the communication which differs if the person is being admitted, is an inpatient, or is about to be discharged. These are referred to as 'open' communicational systems by virtue of the fact that they transcend family boundaries. Communication of mental illness within family boundaries are usually relatively 'closed' systems depending upon how far the 'family' is extended. The social meaning alters according to the extent to which concealment is achieved or responsibility is levelled. For example, children are often told that their afflicted parent is in hospital with a 'bad leg' or a 'tummy ache' whilst the Grandparents may be held responsible for making their son or daughter the way that they are.

Informing external family members can lead to many problems as most people are highly selective who they inform and what they tell them. This leads to elaborate strategies of camouflage and avoidance which tends to isolate family members. The longer that the situation continues the worse it becomes with increased tension, isolation, uncertainty, and apprehension.

Once the word is out, the reactions of others are crucial but, sadly, all too familiar. Initially, there are waves of reassurance, expressions of sympathy, and verifications of the rightness of the decision to seek help. There may be strategies of communicative support for the relative which range from stories of others who have recovered to offers of lifts to the hospital or repairs to the house, etc. Differences in responses between those afflicted with a physical illness and those with a psychiatric illness are reported as:

> Normal expressions of concern for the welfare of one who is ill such as visits, written messages or gifts are avenues little used for the mental patient. According to the wives' reports, 50 per cent of

> the patients in this study had no visitors outside the family during all the months of hospitalization, 41 per cent had only a single or a very occasional visitor, 9 per cent had frequent visitors. Friends telephone the wife to inquire about her husband, with vague promises of 'wanting to go to see him', which never materialize.
>
> (Yarrow *et al.*, 1955, p. 44)

Mental illness is, thus, rarely a private matter and once the information becomes public the stigma dictates the social reaction to the mentally disordered.

Are mentally ill people dangerous?

The popular perception, as we have seen, is that the notion of madness equates with dangerousness. However, in research studies this is somewhat inconclusive. Gunn (1978) found that 31 per cent of randomly selected prisoners in the south east of England could be viewed as mentally disordered given that the main conditions found were personality disordered prisoners and those with alcoholism. In a later study (Gunn *et al.*, 1991) the overall rate of psychiatric disorder in a prison population was 41.8 per cent with a breakdown of substance abuse (23 per cent), personality disorder (10 per cent), neurosis (6 per cent), psychosis (2 per cent), and organic disorders (0.8 per cent). Turning the approach around, the research which looks at criminal activity in psychiatric populations have shown conflicting results. Early studies indicated that low numbers (6.9 per cent and 9.4 per cent) of psychiatric patients were arrested after a nineteenth month follow up period (Steadman *et al.*, 1978), however, more recent studies have suggested that the situation is more complex than merely recording arrest rates. Toch and Adams (1989) found that previous offences of mentally disordered prisoners tended to have occurred during periods when they were psychiatrically disturbed. However, empirical studies only tell one side of the story. In lay terms, fuelled and fanned by the popular press, there is a common understanding that mental illness and irrational violence are inextricably related. However, the nature of this relationship is often biased against the mentally ill group by the use of denigratory media coverage. Certainly, it would seem to be the case that there is a paucity of work in the area of media reporting and mental disorder, however, the Glasgow University Media Group have offered some important and stimulating commentary regarding how public perception, manipulated by media attention, can influence and reinforce the notion that mentally ill people are dangerous. This is achieved not only by direct language referring to mental illness and dangerousness, such as the 'mad axeman' or 'crazed sex offender' but also in a much more subtle fashion by establishing perceptual linkages between bizarre or eccentric behaviour and forms of strange or odd behaviour. It is the

> sheer frequency and penetration of such terms into everyday language that gives it the power to become *popularly known* and *common sense*. For example, we are all familiar with the headlines 'the barmy right', 'the loony left', Motorway 'madness', and more recently 'road rage' which all indicate a relationship, however tenuous, between a mental state and some form of perilous behaviour.
>
> (Glasgow University Media Group, 1993)

These are said to generate anxiety within societies through creating 'strong emotional responses in their viewers and readers' (Glasgow University Media Group, 1993)

Turning our attention away from both the sensational headline referring to the one-off heinous crime and the minor discursive practice of relating odd behaviour with mental instability, we can focus upon the scientific research in this area. The two main thrusts of this type of research are, firstly, to focus on rates of violence in mentally ill populations and, secondly, to study the prevalence of mental illness in criminal groups. However, as we pointed out in chapter 3 it is not clearly established that a group of mentally ill persons are any more dangerous than their non-mentally ill counterparts. For a relationship to be established it requires a stratification into sub-populations of specific psychiatric symtomatologies (Hodgins, 1993).

Yet, the scientific evidence does not weigh heavily on the social mind. Reporting on a patient from a high security psychiatric hospital who absconded whilst on a rehabilitation trip in Blackpool the *Daily Star* alerted the public with the headlines 'PSYCHO II AT FUN PARK . . . most worrying of all it's now plain that dangerous patients of every description are being allowed to mingle with the rest of us on a regular basis' (*Daily Star*, 1996a). Following in the same vein two weeks later the *Daily Star* kept the alarm ringing with 'how many more dangerous mental patients will be allowed to go walkabout before the message gets through *its the public who matter not the perverts and paedophiles'* (*Daily Star*, 1996b; emphasis in the original). It is through this type of reporting that the public are kept in a high state of anxiety and, although in the above case no harm came to anyone, should they have gone on to hurt a member of the public the media response would have been even more ferocious. This media attention brings the public into a high state of apprehension which in turn causes politicians to become concerned.

Social construction of the community

We can see that the mentally disordered offender bears two major social stigmata. The first is concerned with the social meaning of the mental disorder itself which brings the shame and embarrassment whilst the second involves the transgression of a social rule in the form of the committing of an offence. However, the dynamic interplay between the mental disorder and the offence is further complicated by the 'type' of offence committed. Sexual crimes and crimes against children produce a greater negative social reaction than does, say, armed robbery. Furthermore, the extent to which a society was terrorised by an offender, for example, in the case of a serial killer, and the degree of perceived irrationality to the crime are additional structures to the dynamic of the social reaction. A community may well consider a mentally disordered offender as irrational and not culpable for his actions or he may be perceived as 'evil' and merely attempting to trick society by claiming a supposed mental illness. Therefore, the community itself is important in not only understanding the nature of the offence and the social reaction to it but also in terms of understanding the mentally disordered offender's return to that community in the future.

We are all aware of certain 'areas' in our community that are considered 'good' areas or 'bad' areas or 'rough' areas and unless we delineate them according to, say, 'posh' areas or 'slum' we have few ideological differences between them. For example, all sub-areas have territorial imperatives in which human behavioural forms exist to disperse intruders and to reinforce group membership. These social territories are said to exist to help designate a whole range of associations in which individuals can feel comfortable and reassured (Suttles, 1972). To maintain them they may need some degree of aggression to ensure distancing, and may also require the formation of vigilante peer groups. The street-corner gang is but one example.

In the thrust of community care, the replacement of mentally disordered offenders back into society does not often take cogniz-ance of the social structures to which they are destined. Certainly, from the paucity of published material in this area, it is surprising that the contemporary focus on social therapy makes little attempt to understand human behaviour in relation to the meaning of social action within their specific community setting.

Case management

Through the move to deinstitutionalise long-term psychiatric patients forensic patients too have been caught up in the welter of enthusiasm for the ethos of community care provision. It was some considerable time before it was recognised and accepted that the level of services for long-term psychiatric patients was insufficient to adequately maintain them in the community. Hostels and hous-ing were inadequate, follow-up and support services were disjointed, and there was little cohesive planning or strategic thinking to the overall provision of services. The result of this was an increase in mentally ill and mentally impaired homeless people marginalised on the fringes of society. Yet, the majority merely blend into the shadows rather than stand out as 'troublesome'. However, with the forensic patient whose 'troublesomeness' may well be a serious danger to other members of society there is an added impetus to ensure that someone is overseeing them.

Case management quickly became a recognised term which emerged to counteract the failures of the community care approach. The major theme that runs through the notion of case management is that it attempts to overcome what is seen as a frag-mented service (Brunton and Hawthorne, 1989). The constituent parts of case management include case identification, assessment, need analysis, service design, implementation, monitoring/observ-ing, evaluation, and re-assessment. There are a number of models of case management which include the service brokeridge model in which the case manager acts as a patient advocate linking ser-vices to needs but is not usually a budget holder; the social entre-preneurship model where the case managers are budget holders within an agency, usually social services, and can purchase services for the patient; and the extended co-ordinator model which is based on a multidisciplinary team approach with a key worker attempting to co-ordinate services (Beardshaw and Towell, 1990). Whichever model is used there is usually an emphasis on the operationalisation of the theoretical underpinnings. That is, putting theory into practice. Case management is concerned with ensuring that the patient receives the appropriate services to maximise their potential for social living. It is often the case that a case management model will comprise of a number of strands from other mainstream models. For example, Berzon and Lowenstein (1984) designed a flexible model in response to a specific target group of young adult clients who characteristically act out, who are geographically mobile, who resist treatment, and who tend to abuse alcohol and drugs. The model was designed around three teams of staff who established good relations with all services in their catchment area and devised individual programmes for their clients. Shared staffing and shared information was the key to operationalising this case management model which adopted an interventive strategy in actively pursuing the young persons into the community setting.

Case management of mentally disordered offenders in the community has developed out of the Care Programme Approach (DOH, 1990) and, again, adopts varying approaches which are, as yet, disparate and somewhat disorganised as far as a national strategy is concerned. The general thematic approach is to maintain contact between the mentally disordered offender and the psychiatric service, and to ensure that the forensic patient is provided with support services. These services include housing, employment, finances, and recreation, and is based on the principle that if the stresses and strains of poor housing, poverty, and unemployment can be avoided there is a greater chance of preventing relapse. A number of professions are involved in contributing information to case managers and include court diversion schemes, police initiatives, specialist solicitors, community mental health workers, voluntary agencies, and many more. This shows the expanding web of services for the mentally disordered offender as growing public, political, and professional awareness is raised with every patient who slips the net and goes on to re-offend. Social tolerance is extremely low in the face of media outrage.

Passive and assertive outreach

Modern living is a highly complex endeavour and causes increased levels of stress through competition for housing, jobs, and status. Social administration, bureaucratic structures, public welfare, and social security entitlements are increasingly more difficult to understand, apply for, and acquire. Therefore, those with incapacitating mental illnesses or learning difficulties may soon withdraw from such competitive pressures with the corollary of social isolation and marginalisation from the community that is supposed to hold the key to providing care. In the case of the mentally disordered offender this can be a dangerous state of affairs for other potential victims. In managing enduring mental illnesses in a community setting, outreach approaches have been developed as techniques for ensuring that the patient receives the correct level of services. Outreach has been delineated into passive and assertive. Passive outreach is a gently supportive model which relies on encouraging the patient to take up the services on offer and although it relies heavily on the motivation of the patient to attend for clinics and appointments it is based on the principle of the maximum liberty of the patient and freedom of choice. Assertive outreach, on the other hand, is a more resolute approach which may involve searching for patients who fail to attend for outpatient appointments and ensuring that follow-up contacts are maintained. It also involves aggressively acquiring services for patients such as accommodation or financial assistance from social security. There is an added sense of urgency in this second approach.

Forensic outreach, or outreach services for the mentally disordered offender have not developed independently but have tended to overlap with other forensic mental health work approaches. A growing body of specialist knowledge with outreach for mentally disordered offenders indicates that this group of patients has always been in existence but only recently deemed important enough to receive specific resource allocation (Pederson, 1988). Expanding the general community psychiatric nursing role, Moon (1993) includes such aspects as risk assessment in relation to violence and criminal intent, anti-social behaviour, and liaison with forensic services. Cooke *et al.* (1994) argued that mentally disordered offenders who do not have many of life's little luxuries are more likely to deteriorate and re-offend. They claimed that in managing this group in the community 'it seems vital to target services at developing *something to lose* for clients who commit offenses' (Cooke *et al.*, 1994, p. 62). This suggests that mentally disordered offenders, like most of us, prefer to live in the community to which they belong and to feel a part of that society they need some form of investment. Certainly, with 'nothing left to lose' society creates a most dangerous individual.

Supervision registers

It is a sad fact of life that some patients, for many different reasons, do not manage to acquire, or maintain, the appropriate level of services or the required level of behaviour in the community despite the programmes of care that are applied (Anthony and Blanch, 1989). In many instances this failure, although sad and tragic, directly involves that specific patient who may attempt suicide or may drift into serious self-neglect. However, when, in some cases of failure, the injured person is an innocent third party the media attention, political outrage, and professional condemnation tend to fuse together causing a backlash of scapegoating and policy change.

A series of events, including a schizophrenic patient, Ben Silcock, jumping into the lions' enclosure at London Zoo and the killing of Jonathan Zito by a perfect stranger, Christopher Clunis, at a London tube station, highlighted, in different ways, the failure of the community care programme (see chapter 3). Had it not been for the chance private videoing of the lion mauling the mentally ill Silcock who believed himself to be immune from attack, and the images acquired by the media who beamed them around the world in news broadcasts, then the story may not have had the public and political impact that it had. These video images displayed to the world the failure of the British community care programme. The murder of Jonathan Zito was also witnessed by a number of shocked bystanders and the resultant inquiry revealed a catalogue of missed opportunities, by a number of services that may have prevented this tragedy. The upshot was the introduction of the Supervision Registers on 1 April 1994.

The Supervision Registers required that all provider units 'set up registers which identify and provide information on patients who are, or are liable to be, at risk of committing serious violence or suicide, or of serious self-neglect, whether existing patients or newly accepted by the secondary psychiatric services' (NHS ME, 1994, p. 1). However, this legislation was merely an attempt to slide out of the ethical and legal dilemmas inherent in the civil liberty rights of patients in the community, the deinstitutionalisation programme, the right-wing fiscal preoccupation, the lack of community resources, and the need to identify an accountable professional scapegoat in the event of something going wrong. The Supervision Registers would allow the Government to slip the hook of responsibility.

Supervised after-care orders

After-care of mentally disordered offenders discharged or transferred from hospital falls within the legislative framework of the
1983 Mental Health Act under section 117. The legislation calls
for District Health Authorities and local Social Services Authorities to provide, in co-operation with relevant voluntary agencies,
after-care services for any person to whom this section applies. This
provision pre-dates the Supervision Registers and is clearly the fore-
runner of the latter service development. In the advice for the
'Guidance of Social Supervisors' we note the relationship between
public concern, political responsibility and professional involvement. The purpose of the formal supervision resulting from conditional discharge

> is to protect the public from further serious harm in two ways:
> first, by assisting the patient's successful reintegration into the
> community after what may have been a long period of detention in
> hospital under conditions of security; second, by close monitoring
> of the patient's progress so that, in the event of subsequent
> deterioration in the patient's mental health or of a perceived
> increase in the risk of danger to the public, steps can be taken
> to assist the patient and protect the public.
>
> (Home Office, 1987, pp. 5–6)

The same document highlights the role of the Home Office in
relation to: (a) patients transferred from prison, (b) those transferred or discharged who are restricted, (c) the preparation of
documentation for Tribunals who are hearing restricted patient
cases, (d) following the conditionally discharged patient by authority of either the Home Secretary or a Tribunal through monitoring
the patient's progress and giving consideration to the variation
of conditions, and (e) recalling to hospital or absolutely discharging patients as circumstances require. This, in effect, shows the
involvement of a Government Department, i.e. the Home Office,
in the progress or otherwise of mentally disordered offenders, who
understandably represent the general public and are responsible
for their safety. It is all the more illuminating when we note that
the Division of the Department charged with this responsibility is
staffed by people who 'are not specifically trained in law or medicine but the Division has wide experience of restricted patient cases
and detailed knowledge of the relevant legislation' (Home Office,
1987, p. 5). Thus, the link between the general public concern

and the political responsibility for the safety of members of the community is firmly established.

Compulsory community care

As we have seen, the history of the psychiatric colonisation of the criminal began with the pathologisation of offending behaviour. Once fully brought within the domain of medicine, offenders were compulsorily detained in asylum care and forced to have some form of treatment irrespective of their wishes. In contemporary times this is achieved through effective mental health legislation and ineffective rights of refusal via an extremely poor second opinion system. With the advent of deinstitutionalisation and the care in the community impetus it is not surprising that *compulsory* treatment in the community quickly followed. Forensic psychiatry needs the captive patient population to exercise its power as few mentally disordered offenders would voluntarily seek their service. Thus, attempting to manage mentally disordered offenders in the community needs, not only a reticulate of psychiatric surveillance techniques, and legal powers to return the offender to institutional care, but also a mechanism whereby it can exercise its control at the very point where it will ultimately be judged – the community. As Blackburn (1990) noted: 'while it is mental disorder rather than offending behaviour *per se* which justifies diversion to the mental health system, we cannot avoid the fact that alleviation of the disorder is expected to reduce the risk of further anti-social deviance, and our performance is ultimately judged by reduced recidivism, not by the greater happiness of our patients'.

Conclusion

There are many conceptual, practical, and moral problems with compulsory care in the community which we do not wish to engage with here. Rather, we would like to conclude this chapter with a few comments relating to the social response to compulsory community care which is noticeable on two distinct levels. The first is concerned with the well versed dialogue relating to the 'not in my back yard' scenario. We have already raised questions regarding the community placement of mentally disordered offenders, and in particular sex offenders, whereby it may well be a common agreement that some should be cared for in community settings but, unfortunately, there are few members of the public willing to have them in their vicinity. Recent media attention has focused upon whether police should inform members of a community when a sex offender moves into that area. This, again, shows the close interface between the public, the profession of forensic psychiatry, and the political sensitivity of managing mentally disordered offenders. The second main area of concern refers to the social response when things go wrong, as they inevitably will from time to time. Society, via the media, is a harsh task master, in that, there is little praise when successes, however they be judged, are known, and ferociously punitive when failures occur. We have already commented upon the ex-Prime Minister's (John Major) words when the killing of James Bulger was first reported, i.e. 'society must understand a little less and condemn a little more'. However, they are worth focusing upon once again as they epitomise the groundswell of social response to heinous acts within the realms of the 'mad' and 'bad' debate. Outside of asylum care there is no hiding place for the mentally disordered offender. The community is their stage, their spotlight, and their microscope. They perform on it, in it, and under it – as does forensic psychiatry.

Chapter 8

Re-offence and recidivism

Introduction

In the previous chapter we dealt with the idea that if it is the social space of the community in which the mentally disordered offender is created, and from which he is excluded, then it is also to this domain that he must return once the cure is effected. If the medicalisation of the criminal is to be a completed project then treatment must be seen as effective and accurate prognosis achievable. We also discussed how the inner dynamics of community living, in terms of the social, has become a treatment modality in itself. Social therapy, in all its diverse forms, is now a major treatment perspective for mentally disordered offenders as it is within this social space that they must successfully function. The deconstruction of this social space has involved the analysis of group dynamics, from the formation of groups and the interpersonal relationships with others to the community itself as a therapeutic enterprise. Simply stated, mere incarceration of the mentally disordered offender does not require the force of medicine; it is the return of 'cured' to the social space by which the profession will ultimately be judged.

To achieve a recognised professional status forensic psychiatry must fulfil the requirements of the medical undertaking. That is, it must be seen to have the skill and knowledge to complete the process in which successful treatments are applied with the corollary of reduced recidivism. Irrespective of academic interest in a causal nexus between mental disorder and criminal behaviour it is the lay belief in such a relationship which will have the greatest influence on the judgement of forensic efficacy. If mentally disordered offenders are not an acceptable option in the criminal justice system, and for them to remain languishing in hospital servitude is not deemed appropriate, it falls to forensic psychiatry to do justice to its claim to be able to progress the patient along his mental health career. If this is focused on care and management of psychopathology alone, and not related to the dangerousness of the patient, then long-term secure psychiatric facilities are going to be a necessary requisite. Furthermore, if this were the only scenario, then one would need to be extremely accurate in this prediction of dangerousness. However, clearly the system would soon 'silt up' with a shortage of beds if some patients did not progress, through transfer and discharge, back to the community.

In this final chapter we focus on the response of society to those mentally disordered offenders who are returned to the community and are deemed 'successes' or 'failures'. The space given to the 'successes' is relatively short as these patients, by dint of being a success, do not come to the attention of the public. However, conversely those that do go on to re-offend cause alarm in the public, consternation to the profession, and apprehension in the politician; therefore, this group receives greater debate. Moreover, we will focus more generally on the societal response to recidivism by mentally disordered offenders as this tends to have the greater impact on professional development and service delivery than any other single factor.

Back to the community

In the post-war years there has been a growing number of research studies on the attitudes of the public towards mental illness (Bhugra, 1989). In fact, the volume is such that it lies beyond the scope of this chapter to review it completely, therefore, we intend to limit ourselves to the narrower field of mentally disordered offenders. In doing so it is worth noting at the outset that much of the published material in this area is American, yet its relevance to the UK perspective is by no means diminished by this.

In an early paper Nunnally (1961) argued that the popular perception of the mentally disordered is closely associated with the normal offender. This association being linked, stereotypically, by propensities of both groups towards violent and dangerous behaviour. It is the prejudicial nature of this attitude which not only forms the lay relationship between crime and mental disorder but also creates the belief that where the mentally disordered and the offender are located in the community the crime rate will increase (Swarte, 1969). In this latter study the author found that certain forms of crime were more closely associated with the mentally disordered than other types of offending. For example, sexual crimes and offences against children were associated more with the mentally disordered than with normal offenders, and crimes against property associated more with the latter group than were offences of a violent nature.

The intolerance of members of society to both offenders and the mentally disordered is observed in a study by Tringo (1970) in which disabled and deviant groups were hierarchically structured. The physically disabled were more tolerated than any other, with the least tolerance shown to the four deviant groups: ex-offenders, mentally impaired, alcoholics, and the mentally ill, in descending order. We can see from this that the general public tend to view mental disorder as somewhat distanced from notions of a physical illness and more akin to a form of deviancy. However, it becomes more alarming in later studies to discover that contemporary society now views the mentally ill 'to be dangerous and believes that they are likely to act violently and commit horrific crimes' (Appleby and Wessley, 1988), particularly offences of a sexual nature (Levely and Howells, 1995) (cited in Colombo, 1997, p. 24).

Although it is fair to say that other studies may well have found a more positive association between mental illness and attitudes of the public towards criminal offending (Skinner *et al.*, 1995) the recurring theme of the mentally ill as a stigmatised group remains consistent.

Community alarm

An interlinking social concept within the public domain regarding the mentally disordered as being more likely to commit crime is the dual perception that offenders, *per se*, are dangerous. Regarding the dangerousness of offenders generally we note that community fear is raised for many reasons and not least of all because of the ubiquitous view that violence is on the increase (Last and Jackson, 1989). Furthermore, other authors have claimed that there is an increasing tendency for the public to call for tougher action on criminals from the criminal justice system (Hindelang,

1974) with more severe custodial sentences demanded (Walker and Hough, 1988). Although this is limited research it is supported by evidence on media reporting of crime in which it is usually claimed that there is an overall increase in the crime rate and that society is generally becoming a more dangerous place in which to live (Levi, 1995).

A major concern in relation to the attitudes towards the dangerousness of offenders refers not to those actively engaged in offending, as this understandably causes public anger, but to those ex-offenders who have served their time, paid their penance, and are reformed. In these cases the few studies available would suggest that the social stigma against offenders is maintained to the degree of active prejudice against them long after they have served their time. It would appear that when an offender commits a crime against society it equates with an immorality that ensures the perpetrator forfeits their community status and certain civil rights. 'Thus, the only way to restore their former status would be to convert the public away from the view that ex-offenders are eternally damned' (Colombo, 1997, p. 26).

Reed (1979) studied the attitude of a number of social groups towards reinstating certain rights for offenders, such as privacy, the right to unlimited mail for prisoners, the right to fulfil jury service, and applying for specific jobs for ex-prisoners. The author reported an overall reluctance to reinstate those rights for those serving time or for those who had completed their sentences. In another study of this area Schwartz and Skolnick (1962) showed a clear relationship between the offer of employment and the presence or absence of the candidate having a history of criminal activity. More specifically, on mentally disordered offenders Steadman and Cocozza (1978) highlighted the public alarm at the release of such patients into the community: 'public conceptions of the criminally insane are dominated by fear of the extreme danger they are seen as possessing, and this danger is substantially greater than that posed by former mental patients who have been shown in previous studies to be highly rejected and feared individuals themselves' (Steadman and Cocozza, 1978, p. 527).

However, it should be pointed out that this attitudinal formation and the exercise of such prejudice is not static but actually changes, however subtly, over time. We are aware, even if only at an intuitive level, that societies have differing attitudes towards certain topics from generation to generation, and differing attitudes from society to society.

Recidivism rates

The prospect of having mentally disordered offenders at large in the community is a daunting one indeed, both to the general public who constitute the potential victims and the mental health professionals who are responsible for their freedom. Should there be a relapse and the offender commits a further crime the response from the media, the public, and the politicians is usually one of outrage and anger. This results in a farrago of emotional reactions for those responsible for the patients' release and may include guilt at the creation of a victim; anger at the perpetrator for the breaking of trust; resentment towards those who criticise; and sadness for the impact it has on the professional career. However, as we stated above, mental health professionals are, and must be, involved in the release of mentally disordered offenders back into the community if the psychiatrisation process is to be completed. Yet, assessing the recidivism of this group of patients cannot be judged only on the media response to the one-off sensational 'case' that sadly occurs from time to time, we require more appropriate mechanisms of assessing the outcomes.

One such method involves the follow-up studies of mentally disordered offenders with the most famous being what are known as the Baxstrom studies. Johnnie K. Baxstrom, a patient in a high security State Hospital in America, claimed that he was being detained illegally following his transfer from prison to the State Hospital. The basis of this claim was that he continued to be hospitalised after his sentence had expired. The United States Supreme Court adjudged that 'Baxstrom had been denied equal protection under the law by being detained beyond his maximum sentence in an institution for the criminally insane without a new hearing' (Halfon, David and Steadman, 1971, p. 518). This ruling, in February 1966, meant that not only was Baxstrom being detained illegally but also that almost one thousand patients fell under the same legal principle in this American State. Therefore, all 967 patients had to be released from the high security psychiatric establishments into a number of residential settings including ordinary hospitals, community homes, and to family and friends (Hunt and Wiley, 1968). This transfer occurred over several months between March and August of 1966.

The repercussions were many and varied. The public were alarmed and predicted a massive increase in the crime rate. The media launched a campaign of terror which fuelled the public fear and anxiety. Staff at the receiving establishments demanded special units be built, claimed to require specialist training, and requested more pay in the form of 'danger money'. The court ruling did not allow for this 'special' treatment insisting that the, now termed, 'Baxstrom patients' be treated as the rest of the population. Further repercussions were that the sudden reduction of almost a thousand patients in the two State Hospitals led to some redundancies for the staff and, moreover, questions would now be raised as to the involvement of the mental health professionals and their role in the illegal detention (Steadman and Halfon, 1971).

Hunt and Wiley (1968) reported on the Baxstrom patients at the one-year follow-up stage stating that 'at the end of the first year the most striking news is that there is no news' (p. 136). Of those that were transferred to civil hospitals approximately half remained there voluntarily whilst the other half were held on court orders but without any trouble reported. There had been one hundred and seventy-six discharges, sixty-two placements in convalescent care, twenty-four deaths, a few on family leave, and a very small number of absconders (Hunt and Wiley, 1968). It transpired that at the one-year follow-up only seven patients were deemed too difficult to manage and were returned on a judicial determination back to the high security State Hospitals, with only twenty-six being returned at the four-year stage (Steadman, 1973). At the one-year follow-up of those released there was only one arrest for petit larceny. The conclusion reached was that the original psychiatric assessment of the patients' dangerousness was grossly inaccurate.

The Baxstrom studies, and there have been numerous of them now, have been criticised on the grounds that they were not a representative sample of mentally disordered offenders as they were (a) predominantly schizophrenic, (b) a long-stay population, (c) institutionalised, and (d) elderly. However true this may be, the Baxstrom situation is a good example of the release of a large number of mentally disordered offenders and the community response to them. Furthermore, it has prompted many other studies of such offenders, in many different countries. For example, Dell (1982) and Bailey and MacCulloch (1994) in England; Lidberg and Belfrage (1991) in Sweden; Sheppard and Hardiman (1986) in Ireland; Yesavage et al. (1986) in France, to mention but a few. The overall result of these studies suggest that around a third of all released mentally disordered offenders go on to re-offend, which means, of course, that two thirds do not (or that they do not get caught). The problem with this is that whilst in secure psychiatric provision the prediction of which two thirds are safe to be released and which one third continues to be dangerous is notoriously inaccurate (Monahan, 1984).

Margaret Norris (1984) produced a book entitled *Integration of special hospital patients into the community* in which she reported that a patient's lifestyle should receive close attention in rehabilitative endeavours. The main thrust of the argument being that the lifestyle post discharge was a central issue in success or failure of the mentally disordered offender. However, this 'lifestyle' was a hugely complex interplay of personal attributes, social interactions, and support mechanisms. Although the main objective of high security psychiatric services was said to be the reintegration of patients back into the community in which they were indistinguishable from other members of society there was little as to the public's view of re-offence and recidivism. In an earlier work Dell (1980) outlined the long waiting list for patients to be released from special hospitals. They were considered by the special hospital staff to be ready for transfer to NHS facilities of lesser security but the staff in those facilities were negatively inclined to take them. Dell (1980) reported that the reputation of the special hospital was likely to impede transfer as much as the clincial picture of the patient. An illustrative example is offered 'a man described in his transfer report as "co-operative and courteous to the point of diffidence"' is considered suitable for transfer by the consultant psychiatrist but then the consultant claims 'that his staff would not accept him because another patient currently in the hospital had recently attacked a nurse. Two years later he was still waiting transfer.' Thus, we can see the power of the stigma of special hospitals, even for mental health professionals. John Bailey and Malcolm MacCulloch produced a series of research reports on released mentally disordered offenders in the 1990s from the custom built special hospital Park Lane. Having transferred many patients from Broadmoor some were assessed as no longer requiring high security establishments and were released. These authors reported that of 112 released 54.9 per cent that were considered personality disordered reoffended whilst only 21 per cent who were considered mentally ill went on to reoffend. Overall, this produced a re-offence rate of 36.6 per cent which shows that the majority did not reoffend, and considering that one special hospital considered them dangerous the Park Lane psychiatrists did not, shows the somewhat arbitrariness of incarceration.

False positives and false negatives

In terms of mentally disordered offenders and psychiatry's ability to treat them it is the extent to which the idea of 'cure' fits within the social context. Society barely tolerates serious offenders being catered for within the mental health system as they see this disposal as a 'soft' option or as 'easy time'. However, as they are released back into the community, or transferred to conditions of lesser security, society becomes anxious. We have seen this tension with the NIMBY campaigns (Not In My Back Yard) and the popular headline's 'sex killer' referring to all mentally disordered offenders from a special hospital whether they are in fact sex offenders or killers, or neither. However, it is when the released mentally disordered offender goes on to commit a further crime that society's reaction is the severest. This brings us to two important issues in psychiatry's ability to predict such dangerousness. They are, the issues of false negatives and false positives.

In this prediction of dangerousness psychiatry makes statements concerning the treatment of mentally disordered offenders, undertakes assessments whatever they may be, and formulates a prediction regarding the likelihood of them re-offending. We know from follow-up studies of released mentally disordered offenders (i.e. those considered safe to be released), that some actually do re-offend and this group are known as false positives. In simple terms they are 'failures'. The major problem, of course, is that their failure or, if preferred, psychiatry's failure usually leads to the creation of victims with their concomitant and related suffering, which results in media coverage and political concern. It is the fact that society considers that if they have been 'treated' by a psychiatrist and deemed, in lay terms, to have been 'cured' then the re-offence stands as stark testimony to psychiatry's inefficacy. This does not occur to the same degree with released dangerous offenders from prison who go on to commit further crime as the failure is depersonalised as an attack on the penal system itself.

On the other side of the prediction coin, however, are those mentally disordered offenders who are considered to be dangerous and therefore are not released into the community but detained in hospital *ad infinitum*. Unfortunately, we also know from such scenarios as the Baxstrom situation that some of those detained are, in reality, not dangerous and would not re-offend. The only trouble being that we do not know accurately which ones are which. These are known as false negatives. It is predicted that they are dangerous but in fact are not. The major concern in this scenario is that patients are unduly incarcerated.

Although both false negatives and false positives are undesirable they do not have the same social consequences. Those considered 'safe' and released but re-offend have the weight of societal outrage against them whilst those who are considered dangerous and incarcerated but are, in reality, 'safe' must rely on the civil liberties lobbying. Thus, if the prediction of dangerousness is not adequate enough, we must understand how it is being arrived at.

Risk assessment

The contemporary state of the science of risk assessment in terms of dangerous behaviour is notoriously poor with a success rate approximating to a third of predictions being accurate (Monahan, 1988). This is bad enough, but made worse by the knowledge that there is such a wide disparity of methods used in arriving at such predictions. For the sake of brevity and space these methods can be subsumed under two broad approaches. First, statistical, or actuarial, methods and, second, clinical approaches.

The use of statistical methods incorporates probabilistic theory pertaining to whether the presence of certain variables will give an indication that a person will be a danger to others (Menzies *et al.*, 1994). These variables are known as predictor variables and may be factors related to the persons history, the manifestation of previous dangerous behaviour, and the person's mental state. For example, a description of predictor variables from a persons history may include time with parents, school achievements, occupation, recreation, relationships, use of illicit drugs, etc. Factors relating to previous dangerous behaviour may include a seriousness score, type of behaviour, use of alcohol or drugs, victim details, premeditation, etc. (Quinsey and Maguire, 1986). These variables receive a weighting, or score, which are then used to produce a statistical probability of future dangerous behaviour. The statistical procedures adopted in these quantitative approaches are as numerous as the approaches themselves. Although, as we say, they are by no means accurate, there is a growing belief that by adopting a combination of statistical, or actuarial, approaches this may enhance the overall accuracy (Blackburn, 1993).

The clinical prediction of dangerousness involves the mental health professional considering factors related to the person, the situation, and their interaction, and is used to arrive at a decision based on previous experience, clinical traditions, and knowledge of the relevant literature (Blackburn, 1993). Different workers adopt differing approaches with some believing that current offence, cues during the interview, childhood factors, and family circumstances were important in such predictions (Menzies, Webster, and Butler, 1981). However, when these approaches have been tested they have been found to be less reliable than pure statistical measures. Thus, the general conclusion in the scientific world is that rather than continue in the quest for empirical predictors of dangerous behaviour we should focus on the decision-making process. This leads us to ponder Mulvey and Lidz's (1984) early suggestions that the best that we can hope for is an informed judgement (Blackburn, 1993).

The foregoing, of course, is the mental health professionals' point of view in relation to the assessment of risk but in relation to the release of mentally disordered offenders back into the community it is the society at large that bears the brunt of the failure of accurate predictions. The media are quick to respond to the situation in which a released mentally disordered offender commits a further crime and such procedures as risk assessment, risk management, and informed decision-making receive short shrift in the press. Such 'risk' is unacceptable in society's eyes when a further victim has been created (see below) and there is usually a call from the tabloids to incarcerate the offender permanently. What are rarely discussed, as they lack the sensation of the failures, are the successes that do not re-offend. Unfortunately, we know as little about this group as we do about the other.

Desistance

The statistical fact being that approximately two thirds of mentally disordered offenders released from psychiatric detention do not go on to re-offend tells us little about what factors contribute to their desistance from criminal behaviour (bearing in mind that there may well be some mentally disordered offenders who are released and do re-offend but are simply not caught). Desistance refers to those factors that contribute to an offender ceasing offending behaviour. Although this has received some attention in penology and criminology there is a paucity of research undertaken in this area with mentally disordered offenders. In delinquency studies Knight and West (1975) identified several factors that they considered important in distinguishing between those delinquents who offended temporarily and those who continued to do so. These factors included seriousness of the juvenile record, motives for juvenile offenses, offending in company, involvement with adolescent peer groups and psychological variables. The thrust of their work focused on the reasons why temporary delinquents desist and continuing delinquents do not. They reported that: 'among the reasons for giving up delinquency volunteered by the temporary delinquents themselves the most prominent were the consequences of being caught' (Knight *et al.*, 1975, p. 47). Continuing delinquents, however, were more casual about their conviction experiences and found penal experience neither beneficial nor a deterrence.

In a later study Osborne (1980) suggested that home environment was a major determinant of delinquent behaviour. This was a complex factor which was difficult to unravel but, for this author, it was a central issue in future offending behaviour. The study focused on background factors relevant to future offending and the rate of moving home. Taking a different perspective Shover (1983) focused on changes within the delinquents over time as major determinants of desistance. This study identified four areas of interest. Firstly, the temporal contingencies included an identity shift in middle age, incommodious time (time as a diminishing entity), and aspirations and goals that develop later in life. Second, the interpersonal contingencies such as ties to another person and ties to employment. Thirdly, interdependence contingencies in which the former two sets did not occur in a fixed sequence, and, finally, negative cases in which offenders felt it was 'too late' for them to change. A more recent author, Tarling (1993) found that careers of offenders changed with the age of the offender, when they no longer associated with delinquent friends, with marriage, when they developed a critical and detached perspective of criminal youth, and when they had a change in aspirations.

The major difficulty in these foregoing studies is that they are not generalisable to the mentally disordered offender population. Without research in this area we can only speculate that the factors that contribute towards mentally disordered offenders desisting from further offending may well include aspects of their clinical condition and their compliance in taking medication as well as more mundane, but equally important, aspects of life such as housing, occupation, and regular finance. What is important to note from a sociological point of view is that when released offenders re-offend there is some public concern and a call for incarceration but this does not appear as sensational as when a released mentally disordered offender commits a further offence. Society is less tolerant of this latter group of criminals as the creation of victims is considered, in part, the responsibility of the mental health profession and their inability to cure the patient, rather than some inherent criminal wickedness existing in the general offender.

Victimology

Victimology has long been concerned with the relationship between offender and victim, not in terms of laying blame on the victim, although this has often occurred, but more in relation to the role of the victim in the criminal event. The close proximity of the perpetrator and victim is a major concern of the legal profession and of public interest. Von Hentig (1948), an early scholar in this field knew the importance of this:

> here are two human beings. As soon as they draw near to one another, male or female, young or old, rich or poor, ugly or attractive – a wide range of interactions, repulsions as well as attractions, is set in motion. What the law does is to watch the one who acts and the one who is acted upon. By this external criterion, subject and object, a perpetrator and a victim are distinguished. In sociological and psychological quality the situation may be completely different.
>
> (p. 383)

Although Von Hentig's focus is upon the role that a victim plays in contributing to the perpetration of a criminal event this was in relation to how the eventual victim may have initiated or exacerbated the offence. He was not necessarily suggesting that some persons were born victims but that some people tended to be prone to becoming victims.

This led Wolfgang (1958) to outline his concept of victim precipitation which 'applied to those criminal homicides in which the victim is a direct positive precipitator in the crime' (quoted in

Fattah, 1979, p. 202). Later this idea was developed by Amir (1971) who used this concept in the offence of rape: 'the victim actually – or so it was interpreted by the offender – agreed to sexual relations but retracted' (p. 262). However, by this time the notion of blame was, at least implicitly, being firmly laid at the victim's door, and although attempts were made to dispel such views the idea that victims could be partly responsible for contributing to the crime persisted. Terms such as victim-facilitated, victim-initiated, victim-induced, and victim-invited served to apportion blame (Fattah, 1979). Similarly, some contemporary victims have been seen as partially responsible, for example in date-rape in which cues have been purportedly mis-perceived. Unfortunately, it is this blame laden aspect of victim creation that has burdened the science of victimology.

However, it is not this blame laying aspect that we wish to focus upon in our project but the intricacy of the relationship between the victim and the mentally disordered offender within the criminal event, and the extent to which blame on either side is dissipated and relocated on third party involvement. The victim is generally viewed as merely unfortunate enough to be in the wrong place at the wrong time, and in the wrong company, whilst the perpetrator is viewed as not responsible for their actions – at least on one level. The blame is attributed to the mental health worker who failed to treat the mentally disordered offender more effectively, or failed to intervene early enough, or merely lacked the skills to do either. When mentally disordered offenders are released, or not effectively treated by the system, society views victims as having been created by the mental health professional.

Victims and blame

In one sense the general public view the mental health profession as an area of scientific expertise which involves the effective treatment and management of mentally disordered offenders. The natural corollary of this leads to the expectation that once discharged to the community such offenders will be successfully managed and live without causing harm to others. Yet, as we have seen, in terms of the false positives, i.e. those considered 'safe' but go on to re-offend, and the false negatives, i.e. those considered dangerous but in reality are 'safe', such professional expertise is unconvincing. Taken together the research shows that, at the time of writing, we are less than 50 per cent accurate in both predictive directions, i.e. false positives and negatives (Monahan, 1988). Morally, both states of false predictions are equally unsatisfactory. However, it is the false positives which we would wish to deal with here.

Civil liberties as well as professional accountability urge the release of 'safe' mentally disordered offenders into the community. To effect the full extent of the medical model, in terms of prognoses the profession must be seen to have some success which means the safe maintenance of returned offenders back into society. Again, as we have noted, many mentally disordered offenders do indeed function safely in the community. However, some do not do so well and go on to re-offend, and although re-offences vary in degrees of severity the few that lead to serious offences involving death or sexual attacks result in public outcry. What we should not forget in this state of affairs is that most re-offences produce victims (Young, 1988) who are difficult to scale in severity due to the variance in emotional and psychological trauma that results. For some victims, a relatively minor offence can produce major damage whilst for others serious crimes may be well-managed psychologically. The important point being that some suffering usually occurs.

For mental health professionals who are held responsible when things go wrong and re-offence occurs come under serious scrutiny, and are often criticised, for their role in the decision-making process. The catalogue of public, and internal, inquiries into the disastrous cases in which mentally disordered offenders have gone on to murder is growing steadily and the public concern centres on those who are seen to be responsible for releasing them into the community. Bypassing the offender themselves, society's outrage is directed at those who can be identified as the decision-makers and, thus, they are in a skewed sense considered more harmful than the actual offender. Blame could well be levelled at the offender in which cases calls for crackdowns are the usual response (Elias, 1986). Or blame could be laid at the victims' door for their role in precipitating their victimisation (Walklate, 1989). Or, again, the community itself may well be targeted as failing the mentally disordered offender (Hope and Shaw, 1988). Finally, Government policy may be responsible for the lack of appropriate resources and are, thus, responsible, at least in part, for the failure. However, these 'targets' are usually avoided, at least in the initial wave of outcry, and society, through the media focuses upon the mental health professional and their supposed expertise as the locus of failure.

'Throwing Away the Key'

Mentally disordered offenders who have received treatment from psychiatric services, considered safe and released, but who then go on to re-offend are a difficult group to manage. The reasons for this difficulty are manifold and include political, professional, and moral considerations. For example, as we have seen above society is less tolerant of a mentally disordered offender who has re-offended than they are regarding a recidivistic ex-prisoner. The creation of a victim is considered avoidable given that psychiatry's claim for 'treatment' would suggest some form of 'cure' for those released into the community. From a lay point of view when this goes tragically wrong there is public outrage and a strong sense of injustice with calls for, at the least, incarceration. For those mentally disordered offenders who are legally classified as psychopathically disordered there may well be calls for jail sentences as their re-offending appears as evidence for their untreatability; whilst those who are considered to have enduring mental illness long-term institutional care is the usual media request. However, the policy planners and service developers have a much more onerous, and less clear cut, task facing them.

The main thrust of the Reed Report (HMSO, 1992) was concerned with a retraction of high security psychiatric services accompanied by an expansion of smaller-scale medium secure units. Although laudable in themselves these recommendations have some practical and conceptual difficulties. Firstly, they would require some considerable capital expenditure in an arena of health care which is not considered a popular area. Furthermore, the establishment of medium secure units, in terms of planning permissions and public inquiries, would meet with considerable resistance. Secondly, reducing high security psychiatric hospitals in size would ensure that the condensed patient population would likely be those extremely difficult and intransigent cases who are non-resistant to treatment approaches. This would lead to a 'dead-end' mentality and, in effect, the creation of the psychiatric 'supermax' (Mason, 1999 in press).

On the other side of the coin there are suggestions that mental health care facilities should be developed within the prison system itself. However, there are those who consider an expansion or further encroachment of psychiatry into prisons as anathema. Moreover, mental health legislation is not readily transferable into the criminal justice system and changes in the law would certainly be required.

In another vein, it may well be considered appropriate to attempt to develop more effective treatment strategies, which in terms of long-term psychiatric provision for mentally disordered offenders involves several issues. Firstly, this raises questions as to the effectiveness of contemporary forensic practice; secondly, there are issues regarding those patients with enduring mental illnesses whose psychopathology is such that they are non-responsive; and thirdly, there are those patients who actively choose to resist treatment. This latter group often consider themselves to be 'political prisoners' compulsorily detained against their will and coerced towards engaging a therapeutic enterprise that they consider to be malevolent. Often they refuse to engage and adopt silence as a strategy of resistance.

Conclusions

Psychiatry's project is to take a mentally disordered offender, apply some form of intervention and return them to the community from whence they came. For this to be successfully achieved the person should be free from mental disorder and, by association, should not re-offend. However, when they do re-offend the public reaction is one of outrage which carries greater insult than in the case of a released prisoner who may re-offend. The reason for this indignity is that psychiatry claims to be an effective medical enterprise in which the public expect the production of a cure. On the other hand there are those patients who are considered dangerous but who in reality would not be so should they be released which is, again, an aspect of psychiatry's failure but which is often overlooked. The relationship between forensic psychiatry and the public is a tenuous one in which the creation of victims by mentally disordered offenders is not tolerated, and once the public become jittery regarding the role of psychiatry in this patient population so too do the politicians who rely on their votes. Thus, we see huge vacillations between public sympathy and political support for this inchoate profession.

Chapter 9

Conclusions: contemporary picture and future problems

Introduction

We have argued that the mentally disordered offender, as an area of study, emerged following the convergence of a number of factors. These factors included the death of deviance caused by a loss of faith in difference and rationality, the move to deinstitutionalisation and the expansion of the community care programme, and the growth in interim and medium secure units. This academic focus on the criminal allowed the medical 'gaze' to focus on this new territory of psychiatric colonisation. At this inchoate stage of development the contemporary pioneers staked a claim for the efficacy of psychiatric principles to control and govern the aberrancy of criminal conduct. A claim made to satisfy the will to professional power through the acquisition of the criminal. Laid bare this psychiatric authority must produce the successes of its application and hide its failures, and must convince its scrutineers of its scientificity. However, the project has sailed into 'choppy waters' with the growing concerns of poor risk assessments and management strategies, and the extent of false positives and negatives. Those mentally disordered offenders considered safe and released but who go on to re-offend cause alarm and even panic among the public, fuelled and fanned by media sensationalism, and those considered dangerous and detained in hospital but who are in fact safe is a morally outrageous abuse of psychiatric detention.

By emphasising the sociology of the mentally disordered offender we have attempted to show how society itself is influential in governing how forensic psychiatry develops. Society will ultimately adjudicate on the profession and should it consider it a failure then the project will fold. Therefore, forensic psychiatry must attempt to convince the public of its efficacy and undertakes this via narratives of dangerousness, with an affirmation on the expertise to control it. Through dangerousness and its circumscription forensic psychiatry functions as a form of public hygiene on the social body. Policing its aberrant and governing its difference, it is granted the power to compulsorily detain people against their will and force them to have treatment that they do not wish. Few question the nature of these 'treatments', or the expertise of those applying them, or their availability. Few would dare.

In concluding this book we would like to review the current condition of forensic psychiatry in relation to the services for the mentally disordered offender and to highlight some potential problems for the future. By doing this we would wish to re-emphasise the role that society at large plays in shaping this and the function it serves in creating the mentally disordered offender.

Contemporary scene

The span of time that the academic encirclement of the mentally disordered offender is concerned with, i.e. 15–20 years, is of such a relatively short period, in real terms, that it can only be regarded as a sapling branch. However, the huge advances over this short period in related fields have ensured that the impact has been, and continues to be, influential on the development of forensic mental health. Often the impact has been such that the forensic services have been unable to respond positively which has resulted in huge difficulties for them. At other times they barely keep abreast and appear to be unsure and unsteady in their response to changing times. Certainly, in postmodern terms, the shrinking time and space of contemporary living with its concomitant shifts in world economies, political parties, technological advances, and human global relations have converged to influence thinking in philosophy, science, and politics. There can be few areas of life left untouched by the expansions of global markets and the widening gap between the rich and poor, and the powerful and powerless. These social structures have a large impact on individuals and communities around the world with success and achievement equating with high status, and failure being the stigmata of the worthless.

Mentally disordered offenders occupy that social space between the two poles of these binary oppositions: first, as the mad forced insane by crushing external pressures and unable to resist due to presumed inner psychic weakness; second, as the bad, the criminal, the offender, and the monster.

At the time of writing we are fast approaching the turn of the millennium, that period which in *Anno Domini* we have only witnessed once before, i.e. at the turn of the year 999 to 1000. We can only guess at the issues (outside of hunger, disease, and death) facing those ancestors and their hopes for their new millennium. As we move into the year 1999 and towards the year 2000 there appears to be a world taking stock of events and their roles within it. This is as much the case in the field of mentally disordered offenders as it is in many other walks of professional life. Let us review the decade to set the scene for a signpost to the future for forensic psychiatry and the services for the mentally disordered offender.

The 1990s were ushered in with the newly formed Special Hospitals Service Authority (SHSA), an authority set up to move the intransigent special hospitals towards the wider NHS and the expanding market economy of UK health care delivery. Although focusing on the special hospitals the SHSA was also influential in developing a number of related initiatives pertaining to the mentally disordered offender. Their official remit ranged from protecting the public through to promoting research and development, whilst their unofficial agenda appears to have been to wrest the control of the special hospitals from lay discourses of dangerousness to professional rhetoric of treatment. It was always about power. Prizing the special hospitals open to public scrutiny and forcing through change was rooted in the politics of Thatcherite economics in which the commodification of everything was to be at the vagaries of the market. The mentally disordered offender was to become a commodity on which a product (a poor one at that) was to be forcefully applied. The only 'market' force being the third-party purchaser who was to decide on the provision.

The contrived Blom–Cooper Inquiry (1992) provided an added thrust to change and the report was used strategically to create disruption and disenchantment with the maximum security hospital. Questions, long heard previously, were raised once again about the need for such archaic organisations. However, politicians and public were becoming increasingly concerned over the move towards Trust status for the special hospitals. The concern was with the anticipated release of mentally disordered offenders on to the streets of Britain, uncontrolled by the traditional gatekeepers, the Home Office. If local authorities refused to pay the extravagant fees for residency in a special hospital it may well be that they would be released. This gave the medium secure unit system an added growth spurt as regional areas realised that they may require such facilities after all.

The medium secure units throughout the nineties have acquired the high professional ground over the high security hospitals on two counts. Firstly, they are portrayed as manageable, short term, and successful placements for mentally disordered offenders, whereas the special hospitals are viewed as the contrary. This popular and professional perspective remains despite the inquiries at a number of medium secure units and the relatively successful period enjoyed by Rampton special hospital. Second, the medium secure units are perceived as professionally advanced whilst the special hospitals are seen as archaic in professional terms and unable to attract quality higher echelon professionals. Up to the time of writing, at the close of 1998, we await the publication of the Fallon Report on the second major inquiry at Ashworth Hospital in 1997/98. This inquiry was doubly damning. Firstly, because it was concerned with a range of issues relating to the alleged setting up and systematic operation of a paedophile ring within the maximum security hospital by established, and known, paedophiles ostensibly under treatment by professional mental health practitioners. Second, because the management that presided over what is considered to be the greatest forensic debacle in the global history of the services were recruited as 'experts' following the first Blom–Cooper Inquiry in 1992.

Whether the 'specials' survive remains to be seen but one can predict with some degree of certainty that they face another wave of change, probably including a good degree of shrinkage in size. Total abolition is always going to be difficult because, like them or loathe them, they continue to represent the 'bastions of society's nightmares' (Richman and Mason, 1992).

Another area of contemporary scrutiny is concerned with professional content. That is, the popular pursuit of prefixing the word 'forensic' in front of job titles and claiming an area of expertise. In the wake of the false positives and the false negatives it is not surprising that society is beginning to question such self-acclaimed 'expertise' and raise serious misgivings regarding the many and varied on the bandwagon. As forensic psychiatry is increasingly restricted to the prescription of drugs the forensic bio-chemists may surface to claim this territory; as the forensic psychologist takes over the psychopathology the forensic sociologist may assume responsibility for correcting social relations; and as the forensic nurse becomes ever more unclear as to what their role actually is, the advocacy groups and security guards may emerge as the agents in psychiatric authority. The early signs of a professional convergence can be seen with the professional splitting of disciplines and the jockeying for areas of 'expertise'. Social therapy and the personality disordered are two of the contemporary forensic fads.

With the Ashworth Inquiry (Fallon) focusing on those with the legal and clinical labels of psychopathy and personality disordered, society forces the profession to explain the nature of these conditions and the role of mental health professionals in their treatment and management. The hive of activity surrounding these issues, at this point in time, reveals an element of panic. If psychiatry has failed with this group of patients, and psychology is considered dormant, then the natural shift is to claim something social. Thus, social therapy was created as the panacea for these ills. Reminiscent of the fictitious *homicidal monomania*, with its inexplicable constructs, social therapy is invested with, and adorned by, 'experts'. Yet, this brings us to a particular thorny issue, as yet unaddressed by those involved. It is proposed to undertake this social therapy either in a maximum security psychiatric hospital or in a prison, both being far removed from the society in which social rehabilitation is purported to be required. Furthermore, it is stark testimony to the distance, real and symbolic, that people with these conditions actually are from any notion of community care.

The final social structure worthy of mention in the contemporary scene of the mentally disordered offender is the legal framework that surrounds them, and the extent to which this may change in the near future. Currently the mentally disordered offender is legally detained by the Mental Health Act (1983) with, up until recently, a clear distinction between the Mental Health System and the Criminal Justice System. Under the former legislative framework compulsory psychiatric treatment is permissable but under the latter it is not. Therefore, those in the Criminal Justice System who developed a mental health problem were, ideally, transferred to hospital under the Mental Health Act for treatment – and back again once cured, again in ideal circumstances. However, with changes in the focus of treatment and management for those with personality disorders if this is to be undertaken in prison then changes in the mental health law will be required. Whilst the current hybrid order allows for movement between hospital and prison it does not allow compulsory treatment in the prison setting. This would be an onerous step to take but one which is being considered.

Anticipated problems

The growing need to define the function of forensic psychiatry is likely to become a burgeoning problem into the millennium. As psychiatry, the pivotal power-base profession involved in the care and treatment of mentally disordered offenders, moves, or is pushed, down the road of the corporate drug companies, psychiatrists may well lose sight of the fundamental problems of their trade. The bio-chemical quest necessarily emphasises the mental disorder side of the forensic equation which deals with psychiatric disturbance, amine imbalances, neurochemical transmitters, and the like, all said to be causative factors in the psychopathological processes. However, only a few diehards actually believe in the single causation model of mental illness. Yet, even with an acceptance of the social aspects of mental disorder such as expressed emotions, disrupted familial relationships and double-bind theories, or the political contributions of homelessness, poverty, under achievement opportunities, and low status there remains an imbalance in the equation. This being the relationship between a mental state, condition, or disorder and offending or criminal behaviour. Whilst some, the idealists, may argue that it is the mental disorder alone that is the focus of forensic psychiatry others, the realists, will state it is the re-offending by which they will be ultimately judged. In social, political, and moral terms forensic psychiatry will not be able to avoid addressing this relationship in the forthcoming years.

This theme links into the second major problem facing those whose focus of mental health work is related to mentally disordered offenders, and is concerned with the shifting sands of risk assessment and management. Although it is difficult, at this juncture, to foresee a time when the plethora of actuarial risk assessment tools, instruments, and measures will be abandoned, this day must surely come. Similarly, it is even more difficult to envisage a time when psychiatrists will desert the claim to the seat of knowledge in respect to the clinical interview and the 'science' of intuition. This too, will not be tolerated forever. The problem facing those working with mentally disordered offenders is that there is a growing crisis in the notion of scientific measurement of human nature, particularly in relation to predicting behavioural outcomes from such a huge reservoir of human emotions and possibilities. it may be regarded, at some future time to be yet another fictitious Holy Grail in which the spirit of the crusade was enough, temporarily, to convince some to keep searching. Once the idea that forensic mental health workers cannot fulfil the risk assessment prediction then management, that is management of failure, is all that is left for society.

This is the third problem to be faced. Society is well versed in the risk assessment and management ethos of policing their own insurance requirements. They assess the risk by their method of worth, and they manage that risk through a series of precautions and payment of premiums. Yet, they know that with the best protection in the world, houses fall down, earthquakes and floods happen, and burglars bypass the most sophisticated alarms. When this happens the major focus is upon *liability*. The identification of those deemed responsible either in causation or through non-protection is of central importance. Accountability is considered the route to compensation. There is usually an added impetus, beyond the payment of basic insurance cost, to seek redress from those considered responsible. This will be the increasing scenario facing forensic mental health workers whose risk assessment and management of mentally disordered offenders is deemed to be incorrect and thus they will be considered liable. Their problem to be faced is establishing mechanisms of no-fault liability.

Of course, the problem now to be addressed is what to do with those persons who have re-offended following release or are considered to be too dangerous to be released in the first instance. What psychiatric application can be attempted in these cases when release is now no longer an option? What now the price of forensic success? It may be the case that the societal conscience is somehow salved with the notion that the mentally disordered offender is *hospitalised* rather than *imprisoned* but how much longer will it take for society to realise that incarceration in psychiatric servitude is possibly the greater immorality. When 'terminal' forensic cases are held for decades, and in some cases for life, are continually coerced to conform to therapeutic regimes, and all this without any real possibility of release, then we are left with a less than convincing argument surrounding quality of life issues. If the argument is concerned with the relief of distressing symptoms then that is certainly a case for general psychiatry, however, without the 'forensic' relief of dangerousness it is the latter profession's sad indictment. Furthermore, what of the psychopaths and personality disordered languishing untouched within a forensic psychiatric system void of any real offerings? Will this abuse of psychiatric authority be allowed to continue? Unlikely, in our view. Therefore, the problem will be to do with the development of long-term *high* security psychiatric services or the development of long-term *medium* security provision. Once the level of security has been established we will, in effect, have returned to the locked door scenarios within the old asylum system.

The final problem that we wish to deal with is concerned with the expansion of psychiatry into the prison system. Although this debate is not new, and adequately covered in a number of texts, we ought, in our view, to focus the last few words of this book on reiterating the position but from a future perspective. What appears to be different in this forecast is that whereas the historical analysis refers to the penetration of psychiatry into the prisons as a form of professional will to power, in the future scenario it is likely to be based on the collapse of forensic psychiatric credence in the mental health services, particularly the high security hospitals that deal with psychopathy and the personality disordered. Should this penal psychiatric expansion occur, probably via these lego/clinical conditions, then the law will need amending to legitimate and sanction this psychiatric expansion. One is left hoping that the prisoners in the criminal justice system do not suffer the same fate as their forensic counterparts in the mental health services: that of being silenced by psychiatry, abandoned by law, and symbolised by society.

References

Adshead, G. and Morris, F. (1995) Another Time, Another Place. *Health Service Journal.* 9 February, 24–26.

Agnew, R. (1991) The Interactive Effects of Peer Variables on Delinquency. *Criminology.* 29: 47–72.

Akers, R. (1990) Rational Choice, Deterrence, and Social Learning Theories in Criminology: The Path not Taken. *Journal of Criminal Law and Criminology.* 81: 653–676.

Allen, H. (1987) *Justice Unbalanced: Gender, Psychiatry and Judicial Decisions.* Milton Keynes: Open University Press.

Allen, J.E. (1952) *Inside Broadmoor.* London: W.H. Allen.

Alperovitz, G. (1996) *The Decision to Use the Atomic Bomb.* London: Fontana Press.

American Psychiatric Association (1994) *Diagnostic and Statistical Manual of Mental Disorder.* Washington: London.

Amir, Z. (1971) *Patterns of Forcible Rape.* Chicago: University of Chicago Press.

Anthony, W.A. and Blanch, A. (1989) Research on Community Support Services – What have we Learnt? *Psychosocial Rehabilitation Journal.* 12 (3): 55–81.

Appleby, L. and Wessely, S. (1988) Public Attitudes to Mental Illness: The Influence of the Hungerford Massacre. *Journal of Medicine, Science and the Law.* 28: 291–295.

Argyle, M. (1976) Personality and Social Behaviour. In R. Harre (ed.) *Personality.* Oxford: Blackwell.

Argyle, M., Furnham, A. and Graham, J.A. (1981) *Social Situation.* Cambridge: Cambridge University Press.

Aron, R. (1977) *The Opium of the Intellectuals.* Westport: Greenwood Press.

Babuta, A.S. and Bragard, J. (1988) *Evil*. London: Weidenfeld and Nicolson.

Backer-Holst, T. (1994) A New Window of Opportunity. *Psychiatric Care*. 1 (1): 15–18.

Bailey, J. and MacCulloch, M.J. (1994) Judgements of Dangerousness and Release Decisions in Special Hospitals. *Issues in Criminological and Legal Psychiatry*. 21: 76–83.

Baudrillard, J. (1983) *Simulations*. New York: Semiotext(e), Inc.

Bauman, Z. (1989) *Modernity and the Holocaust*. Cambridge: Polity Press.

Bauman, Z. (1991) *Modernity and the Holocaust*. Cambridge: Polity Press.

Bavidge, M. (1989) *Mad or Bad?* Bristol: Bristol Classical Press.

Beardshaw, V. and Towell, D. (1990) Assessment and Case Management: Implications for the Implementation of 'Caring for People'. King's Fund Institute Briefing Paper 10. London: King's Fund.

Beattie, J. (1981) The Yorkshire Ripper Story. *Quartet/Daily Star*. London.

Becker, H.S. (1963) *Outsiders: Studies in the Sociology of Deviance*. New York: Free Press.

Bem, D.J. and Allen, A. (1974) On Predicting some of the People some of the Time: The Search for Cross-situational Consistency in Behaviour. *Psychological Review*. 81: 506–520.

Bentham, J. (1843) Panopticoan: *Or the Inspection House*. London: Payne.

Berger, P.L. and Luckman, T. (1966) *The Social Construction of Reality*. Garden City, NJ: Doubleday.

Berzon, P. and Lowenstein, B. (1984) A Flexible Model of Case Management. *New Directions for Mental Health Services*. 21: 49–57.

Bhugra, D. (1989) Attitudes Towards Mental Illness. *Acta Psychiatrica Scandinavica*. 80: 1–12.

Bingley, W. (1993) Can Good Practice Prevent Potential Future Disasters in High Security Hospitals? *Criminal Behaviour and Mental Health*. 3 (4): 465–471.

Birch, H. (1993) If Looks Could Kill: Myra Hindley and the Iconography of Evil. In H. Birch (ed.) *Moving Targets: Women, Murder and Representation*. London: Virago.

Blackburn, R. (1990) Psychopathy and Personality Disorder in Relation to Violence. In K. Howells and C. Hollin (eds) *Clinical Approaches to Violence*. Chichester: Wiley.

Blackburn, R. (1993) *The Psychology of Criminal Conduct: Theory, Research and Practice*. Chichester: John Wiley & Sons.

Blom-Cooper, L. (1992) *Report of the Inquiry into Allegations of Mistreatment at Ashworth Hospital*. London: HMSO.

Bluglass, R. (1980) *Psychiatry, the Law and the Offender: Present Dilemmas and Future Prospects.* Croydon: Institute for the Study and Treatment of Delinquency.

Bluglass, R. (1990) Prisons and the Prison Medical Service. In R. Bluglass and P. Bowden (eds) *Principles and Practice of Forensic Psychiatry.* London: Churchill Livingstone.

Bowden, P. (1983) Madness or Badness? *British Journal of Hospital Medicine.* 30: 388–394.

Box, S. (1981) *Deviance, Reality and Society,* 2nd edn. London: Rinehart and Winston.

Brunton, J. and Hawthorne, H. (1989) The Acute Non-hospital: A California Model. *The Psychiatric Hospital.* 20 (2): 95–99.

Buikhuisen, W. and Mednick, S.A. (1988) *Explaining Criminal Behaviour.* New York: E.J. Brill.

Bull, R. and Cullen, C. (1992) *Witnesses Who Have Mental Handicaps.* Edinburgh: The Crown Office.

Burrell, G. and Morgan, G. (1979) *Sociological Paradigms and Organisational Analysis.* Aldershot: Gower.

Burrow, S. (1991) The Special Hospital Nurse and the Dilemma of Therapeutic Custody. *Journal of Advances in Health and Nursing Care.* 1 (3): 21–38.

Burrow, S. (1993) The Role Conflict of the Forensic Nurse. *Senior Nurse.* 13 (5): 20–25.

Burrow, S. (1998) Therapy versus Security: Reconciling Security and Damnation. In T. Mason and D. Mercer (eds) *Critical Perspectives in Forensic Care: Inside Out.* London: Macmillan.

Cameron, D. and Frazer, E. (1987) *The Lust to Kill: A Feminist Investigation of Sexual Murder.* Cambridge: Polity Press.

Campbell, J. and Bonner, W. (1994) *Media, Mania and the Markets.* London: Fleet Street Publications Ltd.

Canter, D. (1989) Offender Profiling. *The Psychologist.* 2: 12–16.

Canter, D. (1994) *Criminal Shadows: Inside the Mind of the Serial Killer.* London: Harper Collins.

Caputi, J. (1988) *The Age of Sex Crime.* London: The Women's Press.

Central Council for Education and Training in Social Work (1995) *Forensic Social Work: Competence and Workforce Data.* London: CCETSW.

Clarke, R.V. and Cornish, D.B. (1985) Modelling Offenders Decisions: A Framework for Research and Policy. In M. Tonry and N. Morris (eds) *Crime and Justice, Vol. VI.* Chicago: University of Chicago Press.

Clothier, A. (1994) *The Allitt Inquiry: Independent Inquiry Relating to Deaths and Injuries on the Children's Ward at Grantham and Kesteven General Hospital During the Period February to April 1991.* London: HMSO.

Cloward, R.A. and Ohlin, L.E. (1960) *Delinquency and Opportunity.* New York: Free Press.

Coggan, G. and Walker, M. (1982) *Frightened For My Life.* London: Fontana.

Cohen, A.K. (1955) *Delinquent Boys.* Glencoe, Ill: Free Press.

Cohen, L.E. and Felson, M. (1979) Social Change and Crime Trends: A Routine Activity Approach. *American Sociological Review.* 44: 588–608.

Cohen, D. (1981) *Broadmoor.* London: Psychology News Press.

Cohen, L.E. and Land, K.C. (1987) Age Structure and Crime: Summetry versus Asymmetry and the Projection of Crime Through the 1990s. *American Sociological Review.* 94: 465–501.

Collins, J.J. (1989) Alcohol and Interpersonal Violence: Less than Meets the Eye. In N.A. Weiner and M.E. Wofgang (eds) *Pathways to Criminal Violence.* Newbury Park, CA: Sage.

Colombo, A. (1997) *Understanding Mentally Disordered Offenders: A Multi-agency Perspective.* Aldershot: Ashgate.

Colvin, M. and Pauly, J. (1983) A Critique of Criminology: Toward an Integrated Structural-Marxist Theory of Delinquency Production. *American Journal of Sociology.* 89: 513–551.

Conolly, J. (1856) *Treatment of the Insane Without Mechanical Restraints.* London: Dawsons of Pall Mall.

Conrad, P. and Schneider, J. (1980) *Deviance and Medicalisation: From Badness to Sickness.* London: CV Mosby.

Cooke, A., Ford, R., Thompson, T., Wharne, S. and Haines, P. (1994) 'Something to Lose': Case Management for Mentally Disordered Offenders. *Journal of Mental Health.* 3: 59–67.

Cooper, D. (1972) *Psychiatry and Anti-Psychiatry.* London: Paladin.

Cornish, D.B. and Clarke, R.V. (1986) *The Reasoning Criminal: Rational Choice Perspectives on Offending.* New York: Springer-Verlag.

Curt, B. (1994) *Textuality and Tectonics: Troubling Social and Psychological Science.* Buckingham: Open University Press.

Daily Star (1993) 25 November, p. 4.

Daily Star (1996a) Psycho II at Fun Park. 12 September, p. 1.

Daily Star (1996b) Porn Tests are Crazy. 26 September, p. 1.

Davis, K. (1938) Mental Hygiene and the Class Structure. *Psychiatry.* 1: 55–65.

DeFleur, M.C. and Quinner, R. (1966) A Reformulation of Sutherland's Differential Association Theory and a Strategy for Empirical Intervention. *Journal of Research in Crime and Delinquency.* 3: 1–22.

Del Quiaro, R. (1994) *The Marquis De Sade: A Biography and a Note of Hope.* London: Messidor.

Dell, S. (1980) Transfer of Special Hospital Patients to the NHS. *British Journal of Psychiatry.* 136: 222–234.

Dell, S. (1982) Transfer of Special Hospital Patients into National Health Service Hospitals. In J. Gunn and D.P. Farrington (eds) *Abnormal Offenders, Delinquency, and the Criminal Justice System.* Chichester: John Wiley & Sons Ltd.

Department of Health and Social Security (HOME OFFICE) (1987) Mental Health Act 1983, Supervision and After-care of Conditionally Discharged Restricted Patients, Notes for the Guidance of Social Supervisors. London: DHSS.

Department of Health (1989) Discharge of Patients from Hospital. Health Circular HC (89)5. London: HMSO.

Department of Health (HOME OFFICE) (1992) Review of Health and Social Services for Mentally Disordered Offenders and Others Requiring Similar Services: Final Summary Report. Cmmnd 2088. London: HMSO.

Department of Health (1990) Health and Social Services Development 'Caring for People' The Care Programme Approach for People with a Mental Illness Referred to the Specialist Psychiatric Services. Health Circular HC(90)23/LASSL(90)11. London: HMSO.

Dobash, R. and Dobash, R. (1992) *Women, Violence and Social Change.* London: Routledge.

Donnelly, M. (1983) *Managing the Mind: A Study of Medical Psychology in Early Nineteenth Century Britain.* London: Tavistock.

Duck, S. (1988) *Relating to Others.* Milton Keynes: Open University Press.

Dylan, B. (1967) A Hard Rain's Gonna Fall. *The Freeweelin Bob Dylan.* New York: CBS.

Eastman, N.L.G. (1993) Forensic Psychiatric Services in Britain: A Current Review. *International Journal of Law and Psychiatry.* 16: 1–26.

Elias, R. (1986) *The Politics of Victimization.* Oxford: Oxford University Press.

Ellis, B.E. (1991) *American Psycho.* London: Pan.

Epps, K. (1996) Sex Offenders. In C. Hollin (ed.) *Working with Offenders: Psychological Practice in Rehabilitation.* Chichester: John Wiley.

Epstein, S. (1979) The Stability of Behaviour: On Predicting Most of the People much of the Time. *Journal of Personality and Social Psychology.* 37: 1097–1127.

Fahy, T., Wessely, S. and Anthony, D. (1988) Werewolves, Vampires and Cannibals. *Journal of Medicine, Science and the Law.* 28 (2): 145–149.

Faith, K. (1994) Resistance: Lessons from Foucault and Feminism. In H. Radtke and H. Stam (eds) *Power/Gender: Social Relations in Theory and Practice.* London: Sage.

Farrington, D.P. (1986) Stepping Stones to Adult Criminal Careers. In D. Olweus, J. Block and M.R. Yarrow (eds) *Development of Antisocial and Prosocial Behaviour.* New York: Academic Press.

Farrington, D.P. (1992) Explaining the Beginning, Process and Ending of Antisocial Behaviour from Birth to Adulthood. In J. McCord (ed.) *Facts, Frameworks and Forecasts: Advances in Criminological Theory, volume III.* New Brunswick: Transactional Publishers.

Fattah, E.A. (1979) Some Recent Theoretical Developments in Victimology. *Victimology.* 4 (2): 198–213.

Fernando, S. (1992) Roots of Racism. *Open Mind.* 59: 10–11.

Fitzgerald, M. and Sim, J. (1982) *British Prisons*, 2nd edn. Oxford: Basil Blackwell.

Foucault, M. (1961) *Madness and Civilisation: A History of Insanity in the Age of Reason.* London: Tavistock.

Foucault, M. (1967) *Madness and Civilisation.* Cambridge: Tavistock.

Foucault, M. (1973) *The Birth of the Clinic: An Archaeology of Medical Perception.* London: Tavistock.

Foucault, M. (1977) *Discipline and Punish: The Birth of the Prison.* Harmondsworth: Penguin.

Foucault, M. (1978) About the Concept of the 'Dangerous Individual' in 19th-Century Legal Psychiatry. *International Journal of Law and Psychiatry.* 1: 1–18.

Foucault, M. (1988) The Dangerous Individual. In L.D. Kritzman (ed.) *Michel Foucault: Politics Philosophy Culture: Interviews and Other Writings 1977–1984.* London: Routledge.

Frank, L.K. (1948) *Society as the Patient: Essays on Culture and Personality.* New Brunswick, NJ: Rutgers University Press.

Friedson, E. (1970) *Profession of Medicine: A Study in the Sociology of Applied Knowledge.* New York: Dodd Mead.

Garfinkel, H. (1956) Conditions of Successful Degradation Ceremonies. *American Journal of Sociology.* 61: 420–424.

Garfinkel, H. (1964) Studies of the Routine Grounds of Everyday Activities. *Social Problems.* 11: 225–250.

Garfinkel, H. (1967) *Studies in Ethnomethodology.* London: Polity Press.

Garfinkel, H. (1986) *Ethnomethodological Studies of Work.* London: Routledge and Kegan Paul.

Garland, D. (1990) *Punishment and Modern Society: A Study in Social Theory.* Oxford: Clarendon Press.

Gelsthorpe, L. and Morris, A. (1988) *Feminist Perspective in Criminology.* Milton Keynes: Open University Press.

George, S. (1998) More Than a Pound of Flesh. In T. Mason and D. Mercer. *Critical Perspectives in Forensic Care: Inside Out.* London: Macmillan.

Gibson, B. and Cavadino, P. (1995) *Introduction to the Criminal Justice Process*. Winchester: Waterside Press.

Giddens, A. (1989) *Consequences of Modernity*. Cambridge: Cambridge University Press.

Glaser, D. (1956) Criminality Theories and Behavioural Images. *American Journal of Sociology*. 61: 433–444.

Glasgow University Media Group (1993) Mass Media Representation of Mental Health/Illness – Report for Health Education Board for Scotland. Glasgow University.

Goffman, E. (1952) On Cooling the Mark Out: Some Aspects of Adaptation to Failure. *Psychiatry: Journal for the Study of Interpersonal Relations*. 15 (4): 451–463.

Goffman, E. (1962) *Asylums: Essays on the Social Situation of Mental Patients and Other Inmates*. London: Penguin.

Goffman, E. (1963) *Stigma: Notes on the Management of Spoiled Identity*. London: Penguin.

Grob, G.N. (1966) *The State and the Mentally Ill: A History of Worcester State Hospital in Massachusetts 1830–1920*. Chapel Hill: University of North Carolina Press.

Gudjonsson, G.H. (1992) *The Psychology of Interrogarions, Confessions and Testimony*. Chichester: John Wiley and Sons.

Gudjonsson, G.H. (1994) Psychological Vulnerability: Suspects at Risk. In D. Morgan and G. Stephenson (eds) *Suspicion and Silence, the Right To Silence in Criminal Investigation*. London: Blackstone Press Ltd.

Gudjonsson, G.H. (1995) The Vulnerabilites of Mentally Disordered Witnesses. *The Journal of Medicine, Science and the Law*. 35 (2): 101–106.

Gunn, J. (1978) Criminal Behaviour and Mental Disorder. *British Journal of Psychiatry*. 130: 317–329.

Gunn, J., Maden, A. and Swinton, M. (1991) Treatment Need of Prisoners with Psychiatric Disorders. *British Medical Journal*. 303: 338–341.

Gunn, J., Robertson, G., Dell, S. and Way, C. (1978) *Psychiatric Aspects of Imprisonment*. London: Academic Press.

Guze, S.B. (1976) *Criminality and Psychiatric Disorders*. New York: Oxford University Press.

Hafner, H. and Boker, W. (1982) *Crimes of Violence by Mentally Abnormal Offenders*. Cambridge: Cambridge University Press.

Halfon, A., David, M. and Steadman, H. (1971) The Baxstrom Women: A Four Year Follow-up of Behavior Patterns. *Psychiatric Quarterly*. 45: 518–527.

Hall, R. (1985) *Ask Any Woman*. London: Falling Wall Press.

Hall, S. and Scraton, P. (1981) Law, Class and Control. In M. Fitzgerald, G. McLennan and J. Pawson (eds) *Crime and Society: Readings in History and Theory.* London: Routledge and Kegan Paul.

Hare, R.D. (1980) A Research Scale for the Assessment of Psychopathy in Criminal Populations. *Personality and Individual Differences.* 1: 111–119.

Harpending, H.C. and Sobus, J. (1987) Sociopathy as an Adaptation. *Ethology and Sociobiology.* 8 (3-supp): 63S–72S.

Harre, R. and Secord, P. (1972) *The Explanation of Social Behaviour.* Oxford: Blackwell.

Harrison, F. (1994) *Brady and Hindley: Genesis of the Moors Murders.* London: Harper Collins.

Heidensohn, F. (1995) Gender and Crime. In M. Maguire, R. Morgan and R. Reiner (eds) *The Oxford Handbook of Criminology.* Oxford: Clarendon Press.

Hersen, M. (1979) Modification of Skill Deficits in Psychiatric Patients. In A.S. Bellack and M. Hersen (eds) *Research and Practice in Social Skills Training.* New York: Plenum Press.

Hester, S. and Eglin, P. (1992) *A Sociology of Crime.* London: Routledge.

Hewitt, A. (1996) The Bad Seed: 'Auschwitz' and the Physiology of Evil. In J. Copjec (ed.) *Radical Evil.* London: Verso.

Hindelang, M. (1974) Public Opinion Regarding Crime, Criminal Justice and Related Topics. *Journal of Research in Crime and Delinquency.* 11: 101–116.

Hindelang, M.J., Gottfriedson, M.R. and Garofalo, J. (1978) *Victims of Personal Crime: An Empirical Foundation for a Theory of Personal Victimisation.* Cambridge, MA: Ballinger.

Hirschi, T. (1969) *Causes of Delinquency.* Berkeley: University of California Press.

HMSO (1774) *The Vagrancy Act.* Londonl: HMSO.

HMSO (1983) *The Mental Health Act.* London: HMSO.

HMSO (1991) *Criminal Justice Act.* London: HMSO.

HMSO (1992) *Report of the Committee of Inquiry into Complaints about Ashworth Hospital.* London: HMSO.

HMSO (1993) Sex Offenders with Mental Health Care Needs. In *Review of Health and Social Services for Mentally Disordered Offenders and Others Requiring Similar Services, Vol 5: Special Issues and Differing Needs.* London: HMSO.

Hobbes, T. (1968). *Leviathan.* London: Penguin (Original 1871).

Hogan, R. and Jones, W.H. (1983) A Role-theoretical Model of Criminal Conduct. In W.S. Laufer and J.M. Day (eds) *Personality Theory, Moral Development, and Criminal Behavior.* Lexington: Lexington Books.

Hodgins, S. (1993) *Mental Disorder and Crime.* London: Sage.

Hope, T. and Shaw, M. (1988) Community Approaches to Reducing Crime. In T. Hope and M. Shaw (eds) *Communities and Crime Reduction.* London: HMSO.

Howard, J. (1777) *The State of the Prisons in England and Wales with Preliminary Observations and an Account of some Foreign Prisons.*

Hunt, R.C. and Wiley, E.D. (1968) Operation Baxstrom After One Year. *American Journal of Psychiatry.* 124 (7): 134–138.

Hutter, B. and Williams, G. (eds) (1981) *Controlling Women: The Normal and the Deviant.* London: Croom Helm.

Ignatieff, M. (1978) *A Just Measure of Pain: The Penitentiary in the Industrial Revolution 1750–1850.* New York: Columbia University Press.

Ignatieff, M. (1981) The Ideological Origins of the Penitentiary. In M. Fitzgerald, G. McLennan and J. Pawson (eds) *Crime and Society: Readings in History and Theory.* London: Routledge and Kegan Paul.

Ignatieff, M. (1985) State, Civil Society and Total Institutons: A Critique of Recent Social Histories of Punishment. In S. Cohen and A. Scull (eds) *Social Control and the State: Historical and Comparative Essays.* Oxford: Basil Blackwell.

Illich, I. (1975) *Limits to Medicine: Medical Nemesis: The Expropriation of Health.* London: Marion Boyers.

Ingleby, D. (1985) Mental Health and Social Order. In S. Cohen and A. Scull (eds) *Social Control and the State: Historical and Comparative Essays.* Oxford: Basil Blackwell.

Jackson, D. (1995) *Destroying the Baby in Themselves.* Nottingham: Mushroom Publications.

Jackson, G. (1971) *Soledad Brother: The Prison Letters of George Jackson.* Harmondsworth. Penguin.

James, J. (1960) *Why Evil? A Biblical Approach.* Harmondsworth: Penguin.

Jayewardene, C. (1963) The English Precursors of Lombroso. *The British Journal of Criminology.* 4 (2): 164–170.

Jones, M. (1962) *Social Psychiatry: In the Community, in Hospitals, and in Prisons.* Springfield, Ill: Charles C. Thomas.

Jones, K. and Fowles, A.J. (1984) *Ideas on Institutions: Analysing the Literature on Long-term Care and Custody.* London: Routledge & Kegan Paul.

Karpman, B. (1954) *The Sexual Offender and his Offences.* New York: Julian Press. /

Kelley, H.H. (1972) Attributions in Social Interaction. In E.E. Jones (ed.) *Attribution: Perceiving the Causes of Behaviour.* Morristown, NJ: General Learning Press.

Kittrie, N. (1971) *The Right to be Different: Deviance and Enforced Therapy.* London: The John Hopkins Press.

Knight, B.J. and West, D.J. (1975) Temporary and Continuing Delinquency. *British Journal of Criminology*. 15: 43–50.

Kornhauser, R.R. (1978) *Social Sources of Delinquency: An Appraisal of Analytic Models*. Chicago: University of Chicago Press.

Kuhlman, T. (1988) Gallows Humor for a Scaffold Setting: Managing Aggressive Patients on a Maximum-Security Forensic Unit. *Hospital and Community Psychiatry*. 39 (10): 1085–1090.

Kurtines, W.M., Alvarez, M. and Azmitia, M. (1990) Science and Morality: The Role of Values in Science and the Scientific Study of Moral Phenomena. *Psychological Bulletin*. 107: 283–295.

Laing, R.D. (1960) *The Divided Self*. Harmondsworth: Penguin Books.

Laing, R.D. (1976) *The Facts of Life*. London: Allen Lane.

Laing, R.D. (1982) *The Voice of Experience*. London: Allen Lane.

Last, P. and Jackson, S. (1989) *The Bristol Fear and Risk of Crime Project (A Preliminary Report on Fear of Crime)*. Bristol: Avon and Somerset Constabulary.

Lehane, M. and Rees, C. (1996) What the Papers Say. *Nursing Standard*. 10 (28): 22–23.

Lemert, E.M. (1942) The Folkways and Social Control. *American Sociololgical Review*. 7: 394–399.

Lemert, E.M. (1951) *Social Pathology*. New York: McGraw-Hill.

Lemert, E.M. (1967) *Human Deviance, Social Problems and Social Control*. Englewood Cliffs, NJ: Prentice-Hall.

Levey, S., Howells, K. and Cowden, E. (1995) Dangerousness, Unpredictability and the Fear of People with Schizophrenia. *Journal of Forensic Psychiatry*. 6: 19–39.

Levi, M. (1995) Violent Crime. In M. Maguire, R. Morgan and R. Reiner (1995) *The Oxford Handbook of Criminology*. Oxford: Oxford University Press.

Lidberg, L. and Belfrage, H. (1991) Mentally Disordered Offenders in Sweden. *Bulletin of the American Academy of Psychiatry and Law*. 19 (4): 389–393.

Lilly, J.R., Cullen, F.T. and Ball, R.A. (1989) *Criminological Theory: Context and Consequences*. Newbury Park, Ca: Sage.

Lilley, P. (1993) *News of the World*. 7 March.

Linehan, T. (1996) Media Madness. *Nursing Times*. 92 (14): 30–31.

Lloyd, A. (1995) *Doubly Deviant, Doubly Damned: Society's Treatment of Violent Women*. Harmondsworth: Penguin.

Loeber, R. and Stouthamer-Loeber, M. (1986) Family Factors as Correlates and Predictors of Juvenile Conduct Problems and Delinquency. In M. Tonry and M. Norris (eds) *Crime and Justice, Vol. VII*. Chicago: University of Chicago Press.

Macfarlane, A. (1985) The Root of all Evil. In D. Parkin (ed.) *The Anthropology of Evil.* Oxford: Basil Blackwell.

Mannheim, K. (1960) *Ideology and Utopia.* London: Routledge and Kegan Paul.

Marsh, I. (1986) *Sociology in Focus: Crime.* London: Longman.

Mason, T. (1999) Long-term High Security Psychiatric Services: The Psychiatric 'Supermax' *International Journal of Law and Psychiatry.* In Press.

Mason, T. and Chandley, M. (1990) Nursing Models in a Special Hospital: A Critical Analysis of Efficacity. *Journal of Advanced Nursing.* 15: 667–673.

Mason, T. and Jennings, L. (1997) The Mental Health Act and Professional Hostage Taking. *The Journal of Medicine, Science and the Law.* 37 (1): 58–68.

Mason, T. and Mercer, D. (1998) Rehabilitation: The 'Ship of Fools'. In T. Mason and D. Mercer (eds) *Critical Perspectives in Forensic Care: Inside Out.* London: Macmillan.

Masson, J. (1985) *The Assault on Truth: Freud's Suppression of the Seduction Theory.* Harmondsworth: Penguin.

Masson, J. (1990) *Against Therapy.* London: Fontana.

Mednick, S.A., Schulsinger, F., Higgins, J. and Bell, B. (1974) *Genetics, Environment and Psychopathology.* New York: North-Holland.

Melossi, D. and Pavarini, M. (1981) *The Prison and Factory: Origins of the Penitentiary System.* London: Macmillan.

Menzies, R. (1987) Cycles of Control: The Transcarceral Careers of Forensic Patients. *International Journal of Law and Psychiatry.* 10 (3): 233–249.

Menzies, R., Webster, C.D. and Butler, B.T. (1981) Perceptions of Dangerousness among Forensic Psychiatrists. *Comprehensive Psychiatry.* 22: 387–396.

Menzies, R., Webster, C.D., McMain, S., Staley, S. and Scaglione, R. (1994) The Dimensions of Dangerousness Revisited: Assessing Forensic Predictions about Violence. *Law and Human Behaviour.* 18 (1): 1–28.

Mercer, D. (1998) Beyond Madness and Badness: Where Angels Fear to Tread? In T. Mason and D. Mercer (eds) *Critical Perspectives in Forensic Care: Inside Out.* London: Macmillan.

Mercer, D. and Mason, T. (1998) From Devilry to Diagnosis: The Painful Birth of Forensic Psychiatry. In T. Mason and D. Mercer (eds) *Critical Perspectives in Forensic Care: Inside Out.* London: Macmillan.

Merton, R.K. (1939) Social Structure and Anomie. *American Sociological Review.* 3: 672–682.

Merton, R.K. (1949) *Social Theory and Social Structure*. Glencoe, Ill: Free Press.

Merton, R.K. (1957) *Social Theory and Social Structure*. New York: Free Press.

Midgley, M. (1985) *Wickedness: A Philosophical Essay*. London: Routledge.

Miller, K. (1980) *Criminal Justice and Mental Health*. London: The Free Press.

Miller, H. (1994) *Unquiet Minds: The World of Forensic Psychiatry*. London: Headline.

Moffitt, T.E. (1990) The Neuropsychology of Juvenile Delinquency: A Critical Review. In M. Tonry and N. Morris (eds) *Crime and Justice, Vol. XII*. Chicago: University of Chicago Press.

Moffitt, T.E. and Silva, P.A. (1988) IQ and Delinquency: A Direct Test of the Differential Detection Hypothesis. *Journal of Abnormal Psychology*. 97: 330–333.

Monahan, J. (1984) The Prediction of Violent Behavior: Toward a Second Generation of Theory and Policy. *American Journal of Psychiatry*. 141: 1–15.

Monahan, J. (1988) Risk Assessment of Violence Among the Mentally Disordered: Generating Useful Knowledge. *International Journal of Law and Psychiatry*. 11: 249–257.

Moon, W. (1993) The Expanding Role of the Forensic Community Psychiatric Nurse. *The Journal for Nurses and other Professionals in Forensic Psychiatry*. 3: 12–13.

Moran, T. and Mason, T. (1996) Revisiting the Nursing Management of the Psychopath. *Journal of Psychiatric and Mental Health Nursing*. 3: 189–194.

Morgan, M., Calnan, M. and Manning, N. (1985) *Sociological Approaches to Health and Medicine*. London: Croom Helm.

Morrison, B. (1994) Children of Circumstance. *New Yorker*. 14 February.

Moscovici, S. (1984) The Phenomena of Social Representation. In R.M. Farr and S. Moscovici (eds) *Social Representations*. Cambridge: Cambridge University Press.

Mulvey, E.P. and Lidz, C.W. (1984) Clinical Considerations in the Prediction of Dangerousness in Mental Patients. *Clinical Psychology Review*. 4: 379–401.

NHS Management Executive (1994) Introduction of Supervision Registers for Mentally Ill People from 1st April 1994. Health Service Guidelines HSG(94)5. London: HMSO.

Norris, M. (1984) *Integration of Special Hospital Patients into the Community*. Aldershot: Gower.

Nunnally, J.C. (1961) *Popular Conceptions of Mental Health: Their Development and Change*. New York: Holt Rinehart and Winston.

Osborn, S.G. (1980) Moving Home, Leaving London and Delinquent Trends. *British Journal of Criminology.* 20: 54–61.

Owen, T. and Sim, J. (1984) Drugs, Discipline and Prison Medicine: The Case of George Wilkinson. In P. Scraton and P. Gordon (eds) *Causes for Concern.* Harmondsworth: Penguin.

Palmero, G., Smith, B. and Liska, F. (1991) Jails Versus Mental Hospitals: A Social Dilemma. *International Journal of Offender Therapy and Comparative Criminology.* 35 (2): 97–106.

Palmero, G.B., Gumz, E.J. and Liska, F.J. (1992) Mental Illness and Criminal Behaviour Revisited. *International Journal of Offender Therapy and Comparative Criminology.* 36 (1): 53–61.

Parker, I., Georgaca, E., Harper, D., McLaughlin, T. and Stowell-Smith, M. (1995) *Deconstructing Psychopathology.* London: Sage.

Parkin, D. (ed.) (1985) *The Anthropology of Evil.* Oxford: Basil Blackwell.

Parsons, T. (1951) *The Social System.* London: Routledge and Kegan Paul.

Partridge, R. (1953) *Broadmoor: A History of Criminal Lunacy and its Problems.* Westport Connecticut: Greenwood Press.

Peacock, J.L. (1986) *The Anthropological Lens: Harsh Light, Soft Focus.* Cambridge: Cambridge University Press.

Pederson, P. (1988) The Role of Community Psychiatric Nurses in Forensic Psychiatry. *Community Psychiatric Nursing Journal.* 8 (3): 12–17.

Penrose, L. (1939) Mental Disease and Crime: Outline of a Comparative Study of European Statistics. *British Journal of Medical Psychology.* 18: 1–15.

Philo, G. (1994) Media Images and Popular Belief. *Psychological Bulletin.* 18: 173–174.

Philo, G. (1996) *Media and Mental Distress.* London: Longman.

Pilgrim, D. and Eisenberg, N. (1985) Should Special Hospitals be Phased Out? *Bulletin of the British Psychological Society.* 38: 281–284.

Piliavin, I., Hardyck, A.J. and Vadum, A.C. (1968) Constraining Effects of Personal Costs on the Transgressions of Juveniles. *Journal of Personality and Social Psychology.* 10: 227–231.

Piliavin, I., Thornton, C., Gartner, R. and Matsueda, R.L. (1988) Crime, Deterrence, and Rational Choice. *American Sociological Review.* 51: 101–119.

PLATO (1990) *The Republic.* London: Guild Publishing. 375 B.C.

Plummer, K. (1995) *Telling Sexual Stories: Power, Change and Social Worlds.* London: Routledge.

Potier, M. (1993) Giving Evidence: Women's Lives in Ashworth Maximum Security Psychiatric Hospital. *Feminism and Psychology.* 3 (3): 335–347.

Prins, H. (1980) *Offenders, Deviants or Patients*. London: Routledge.

Prins, H. (1984) Vampirism: Legendary or Clinical Phenomenon? *Medicine, Science and the Law*. 24 (4): 283–293.

Prins, H. (1992) Beseiged by Devils: Thoughts on Possession and Possession States. *Journal of Medicine, Science and the Law*. 32 (3): 237–246.

Prins, H. (1994) Psychiatry and the Concept of Evil: Sick in Heart or Sick in Mind? *British Journal of Psychiatry*. 165: 297–302.

Prins, H. (1996) Risk Assessment and Management in Criminal Justice and Psychiatry. *Journal of Forensic Psychiatry*. 7 (1): 42–62.

Quen, J. (1994) Law and Psychiatry in America Over the Past 150 Years. *Hospital and Community Psychiatry*. 45 (10): 1005–1010.

Quinsey, V.I. and Maguire, A. (1986) Maximum Security Psychiatric Patients: Actuarial and Clinical Prediction of Dangerousness. *Journal of Interpersonal Violence*. 1 (2): 113–171.

Rabkin, J.G. (1979) Criminal Behavior of Discharged Mental Patients: A Critical Appraisal of the Literature. *Psychological Bulletin*. 86: 1–29.

Real Life Crimes. (1994) London: Chancellor Press.

Reckless, W.C. (1950) *The Crime Problem*. New York: Appleton-Century-Crofts.

Reed, J. (1979) Civil Disabilites, Attitudes and Re-Entry: Or How Can the Offender Re-Acquire a Conventional Status? *American Journal of Orthopsychiatry*. 40: 710–716.

Reed, J. (1992) *Review of Health and Social Services for Mentally Disordered Offenders and Others Requiring Similar Services*. London: HMSO.

Reed, J. (1994) *Report of the Department of Health and Home Office Working Group on Psychopathic Disorders*. London: DOH/HO.

Reeve, A. (1983) *Notes from a Waiting-Room: Anatomy of a Political Prisoner*. London: Heretic Books.

Reiss, A.J. (1986) Why are Communities Important in Understanding Crime? In A.J. Reiss and M. Tonry (eds) *Crime and Justice, Vol. VIII*. Chicago: University of Chicago Press.

Richman, J. and Mason, T. (1992) Quo Vadis the Special Hospitals? In S. Scott, G. Williams, S. Platt and H. Thomas (eds) *Private Risks and Public Dangers*. Aldershot: Avebury.

Richman, J., Mercer, D. and Mason, T. (1998) The Social Construct of Evil in a Forensic Setting. *The Journal of Forensic Psychiatry*. (in press).

Ritchie, J.H. (1994) *The Report on the Inquiry into the Care and Treatment of Christopher Clunis*. London: HMSO.

Rowett, C. and Vaughan, P. (1981) Women and Broadmoor: Treatment and Control in a Special Hospital. In B. Hutter and G. Williams (eds) *Controlling Women: The Normal and the Deviant*. London: Croom Helm.

Rutter, M., Maughan, B., Mortimore, P. and Ouston, J. (1979) *Fifteen Thousand Hours.* London: Open Books.

Sallah, D. (1994) Charting a New Route Through Policy: The Care Programme Approach and Supervised Discharge. *Psychiatric Care.* 1 (1): 8–9.

Salter, A. (1990) Foreword. In A. O'Connell, E. Leberg and C. Donaldson (eds) *Working with Sex Offenders: Guidelines for Therapist Selection.* London: Sage.

Sapsford, R. (1981) Individual Deviance: The Search for the Criminal Personality. In M. Fitzgerald, G. McLennan, and J. Pawson (eds) *Crime and Society: Readings in History and Theory.* London: Routledge and Kegan Paul.

Sarbin, T.R. (1967) On the Futility of the Proposition that some People be Labelled 'Mentally Ill'. *Journal of Consulting Psychology.* 31: 447–453.

Scheff, T.J. (1966) *Being Mentally Ill.* London: Weidenfeld and Nicolson.

Schwartz, R.B. and Skolnick, J.H. (1962) Two Studies of Legal Stigma. *Social Problems.* 10: 133–138.

Scull, A.T. (1985) Madness and Segregative Control: The Rise of the Insane Asylum. In P. Brown (ed.) *Mental Health Care and Social Policy.* London: Routledge and Kegan Paul.

Sellin, T. (1938) *Culture, Conflict, Crime:* New York: Social Science Research Council.

Shaw, C.R. and Mackay, H.D. (1942) *Juvenile Delinquency and Urban Areas.* Chicago: University of Chicago Press.

Sheppard, N. and Hardiman, E. (1986) Treatment of the Mentally Ill Offender in Ireland: An Examination of the Forensic Psychiatric Services. *Irish Journal of Psychiatry.* 7 (1): 13–19.

Shover, N. (1983) The Later Stages of Ordinary Property Offender Careers. *Social Problems.* 31: 208–218.

Showalter, E. (1987) *The Female Malady: Women, Madness and English Culture 1830 1980.* London: Virago.

Sim, J. (1990) *Medical Power in Prisons: The Prison Medical Service in England, 1774–1989.* Milton Keynes: Open University Press.

Simon, R. (1996) *Bad Men Do What Good Men Dream: A Forensic Psychiatrist Illuminates the Darker Side of Human Behavior.* London: American Psychiatric Press.

Skinner, L.J., Berry, K.K. and Grifith, S.E. (1995) Generalizability and Specificity of the Stigma Associated with the Mental Illness Label: A Reconsideration 25 Years Later. *Journal of Community Psychology.* 23: 3–17.

Smith, C. (1987) Prison Psychiatry and Professional Responsibility. *Journal of Forensic Sciences.* 32 (3): 717–724.

Smith, D.J. (1995) Race, Crime and Criminal Justice. In M. Maguire, R. Morgan and R. Reiner (eds) *The Oxford Handbook of Criminology.* Oxford: Clarendon Press.

Smith, D.J. (1994) *The Sleep of Reason: The James Bulger Case.* London: Century.

Smith, R. (1989) Expertise, Procedure and the Possibility of a Comparative History of Forensic Psychiatry in the Nineteenth Century. *Psychological Medicine.* 19 (2): 289–300.

Snowden, P.R. (1990) Regional Secure Units and Forensic Services in England and Wales. In R. Bluglass and P. Bowden (eds) *Principles and Practice of Forensic Psychiatry.* London: Churchill Livingstone.

Soothill, K. and Walby, S. (1991) *Sex Crime in the News.* London: Routledge.

Sounes, H. (1995) *Fred and Rose.* London: Warner Books.

South, N. (1995) Drugs: Control, Crime and Criminological Studies. In M. Maguire, R. Morgan and R. Reiner (eds) *The Oxford Handbook of Criminology.* Oxford: Clarendon Press.

Spry, W.B. (1984) Schizophrenia and Crime. In M. Craft and A. Craft (eds) *Mentally Abnormal Offenders.* London: Baillere Tindall.

Steadman, H.J. (1973) Follow-up on Baxstrom Patients Returned to Hospitals for the Criminally Insane. *American Journal of Psychiatry.* 130: 317–319.

Steadman, H.J. and Halfon, A. (1971) The Baxstrom Patients: Backgrounds and Outcomes. *Seminars in Psychiatry.* 3 (3): 376–385.

Steadman, H.J. and Cocozza, J. (1978) Selective Reporting and the Public's Misconceptions of the Criminally Insane. *Public Opinion Quarterly.* 41: 523–533.

Steadman, H.J., Cocozza, J.J. and Melick, M.E. (1978) Explaining the Increased Arrest Rate among Mental Patients: The Changing Clientele of State Hospitals. *American Journal of Psychiatry.* 135: 816–820.

Steadman, H.J., Monahan, J., Hartstone, E., Davis, S.K. and Robbins, D.C. (1982) Mentally Disordered Offenders: A National Survey of Patients and Facilities. *Law and Human Behavior.* 6: 31–38.

Sumner, C. (1990) *Censure, Politics and Criminal Justice.* Milton Keynes: Open University Press.

Sumner, C. (1994) *The Sociology of Deviance: An Obituary.* Buckingham: Open University Press.

Sun (1989) Monster in Shop Trip Horror. 22 Febraury. 1989, p. 1.

Sutherland, E.H. (1945) Is 'White Collar Crime', Crime? *American Sociological Review.* 10: 132–139.

Sutherland, E.H. and Cressey, D.R. (1974) *Criminology.* 9th edn. Philadelphia: Lippincott.

Suttles, G.D. (1972) *The Social Construction of Communities*. Chicago: University of Chicago Press.

Swarte, J.H. (1969) Stereotypes and Attitudes About the Mentally Ill. In H. Freeman (ed.) *Progress in Mental Health*. London: Churchill.

Sykes, G. and Matza, D. (1957) Techniques of Neutralisation: A Theory of Delinquency. *American Sociological Review*. 22: 664–673.

Szasz, T.S. (1960) The Myth of Mental Illness. *American Psychologist*. 15: 113–118.

Szasz, T.S. (1961) *The Myth of Mental Illness*. London: Harper and Row.

Szasz, T.S.(1963) *Law, Liberty and Psychiatry: An Inquiry into the Social Uses of Mental Health Practices*. New York: Macmillan.

Szasz, T. (1970) *The Manufacture of Madness: A Comparative Study of the Inquisition and the Mental Health Movement*. New York: Harper and Row.

Tannenbaum, F. (1973) The Dramatization of Evil. In E. Rubington and M. Weinberg (eds) *Deviance: The Interactionist Perspective. Text and Readings in the Sociology of Deviance*, 2nd edn. London: Collier-Macmillan.

Tannenbaum, F. (1938) *Crime and the Community*. New York: Columbia University Press.

Tarling, R. (1993) *Analysing Offending: Data, Models and Interpretations*. London: HMSO.

Taylor, I., Walton, P. and Young, J. (1973) *The New Criminology: For a Social Theory of Deviance*. New York: Harper and Row.

Thomas, W.I. and Thomas, D. (1929) *The Child in America*. New York: Harpers.

Thomas, M. (1994) *Every Mother's Nightmare: The Killing of James Bulger*. London: Pan Books Ltd.

Toch, H. and Adams, K. (1989) *The Disturbed Violent Offender*. New Haven: Yale University Press.

Topp, D. (1977) The Doctor in Prison. *Medicine, Science and the Law*. 17 (4): 261–264.

Trassler, G.B. (1962) *The Explanation of Criminality*. London: Routledge and Kegan Paul.

Tringo, J.L. (1970) The Hierarchy of Preference Towards Disability Groups. *Journal of Special Education*. 4: 295–306.

Trower, P. (1985) Social Fit and Misfit: An Interactional Account of Social Difficulty. In A. Furnham (ed.) *Social Behaviour in Context*. Boston: Allyn Bacon, Inc.

Turner, B.S. (1987) *Medical Power and Social Knowledge*. London: Sage.

Vaughan, P.J. and Badger, D. (1995) *Working with the Mentally Disordered Offender in the Community*. London: Chapman and Hall.

Von Hentig, H. (1948) *The Criminal and his Victim.* New Haven, Conn.: Yale University Press.

Walker, N. (1983a) Side-effects of Incarceration. *British Journal of Criminology.* 23: 61–71.

Walker, N. (1983b) Criminology. In D. Walsh and A. Poole (eds) *A Dictionary of Criminology.* London: Routledge, Kegan & Paul.

Walker, N. and Hough, M. (1988) *Public Attitudes to Sentencing: Surveys in Five Counties.* Aldershot: Gower.

Walklate, S. (1989) *Victimology: The Victim and the Criminal Justice Process.* London: Unwin Hyman.

Watts, A. and Courtois, C. (1981) Trends in the Treatment of Men who Commit Violence against Women. *The Personnel and Guidance Journal.* 60 (4): 245–249.

Westermeyer, J. and Kroll, J. (1978) Violence and Mental Illness in a Peasant Society: Characteristics of Violent Behaviours and 'Folk' Use of Restraints. *British Journal of Psychiatry.* 133: 529–541.

Wilson, R. (1986) *Devil's Disciples.* London: Express Newspapers PLC.

Winter, R. (1989) *Learning From Experience.* London: Falmer Press.

Wirth, L. (1931) Clinical Sociology. *American Journal of Sociology.* 37: 49–66.

Wolff, K. (1969) For a Sociology of Evil. *Journal of Social Issues.* 25 (1): 111–125.

Wolfgang, M.E. (1958) *Patterns in Criminal Homicide.* Philadelphia, PA: University of Pennsylvania Press.

World Health Organisation (1992) *The ICD-10 Classification of Mental and Behavioural Disorders: Clinical Descriptions and Diagnostic Guidelines.* Geneva: WHO.

Yarrow, M.R., Clausen, J.A. and Robbins, P.R. (1955) The Social Meaning of Mental Illness. *Journal of Social Issues.* 11: 40–41.

Yesavage, J.A., Benezech, M., Larrieu-Arguille, R., Bourgeois, M., Tanke, E., Rager, P. and Mills, M. (1986) Recidivism of the Criminally Insane in France: A 22 Year Follow-up. *Journal of Clinical Psychiatry.* 47: 465–466.

Young, J. (1981) Thinking Seriously about Crime: Some Models of Criminology. In M. Fitzgerald, G. McLennan and J. Pawson (eds) *Crime and Society: Readings in History and Theory.* London: Routledge and Kegan Paul.

Young, J. (1988) Risk of Crime and Fear of Crime: A Realist Critique of Survey-Based Assumptions. In M. Maguire and J. Pointing (eds) *Victims of Crime: A New Deal.* Milton Keynes: Open University Press.

Index